Disturbing Pleasures

Disturbing Pleasures

LEARNING POPULAR CULTURE

Henry A. Giroux

Routledge
New York London

Published by 1994 by

Routledge
29 West 35 Street
New York, NY 10001

Published in Great Britain by

Routledge
11 New Fetter Lane
London EC4P 4EE

Printed in the United States of America on acid free paper.

Library of Congress Cataloging-in-Publication Data

Giroux, Henry A.
Disturbing pleasures : learning popular culture / by Henry A. Giroux.
p. cm.
Includes bibliographical references and index.
ISBN 0-415-90900-7(hb)—ISBN 0-415-90901-5 (pbk)
1. Popular culture—United States. 2. Popular culture.
I. Title.
E169. 12.G56 1994
306.4′0973—dc20 93-36255
CIP

British Library Cataloguing-in-Publication Data also available.

To My Family

Contents

Preface

Growing up in a working-class neighborhood in Providence, Rhode Island, provided me with a particular orientation to the relationship between popular culture and schooling. Popular culture was where the action was—it marked out a territory where pleasure, knowledge, and desire circulated in close proximity to the life of the streets. There was always something forbidden about this culture, with its comics, pinball machines, restricted codes, visual excesses, and overly masculine orientation.

My friends and I collected and traded comic books, learned about desire through the rock and roll of Little Richard and Bill Haley and the Comets, and drank to the blues of Fats Domino. We hated Pat Boone and didn't know the suburbs even existed. We felt rather than knew what was really useful knowledge. And we talked, danced, and lost ourselves in a street culture that never stopped moving. Then we went to school.

Something stopped us in school. For me, it was like being sent to a strange planet. Teaching was exclusively centered on obscure books and the culture of print. Desire was mainly a male prerogative reserved for sports during recess time. The language we learned and had to speak was different, strange, and unusually verbose. Bodily and intellectual memories disappeared for working-class kids in this school. We were on a different train, one oriented toward a cheap imitation of the knowledge of high culture. Latin, Western civilization, math, spelling, social studies, and religion were given to us through the force-feeding methods that characterized public schools for kids who had little hope of leaving their neighborhood, even if they graduated. This is not to suggest that we didn't learn anything, but what we learned had little to do with where we came from, who we were, or where we thought, at least, we were going. Many of my friends dropped out of school early. Some endured it in order to get a decent job, and some, like myself, were lucky. I played basketball, won a college scholarship, and moved out of my working-class culture. It took me a long time after graduating from college to respect the culture I had left when I went to college. I never romanticized my background, it was much too contradictory and violent for that; but I lost my ability to deal with the memories it provided me with because I had gotten used to thinking that the only route out of my past was to escape into a middle-class world. I was dead wrong, and only in my thirties did I make the journey back to memories, histories, and old friends in order to understand the haunting and contradictory quality of my own sense of home and identity. It is that journey that has helped provide the structure of this book.

For years, I believed that pedagogy was a discipline developed around the narrow imperatives of public schooling. And yet, my identity has been largely fashioned outside of school. Films, books, journals, videos, and music in different and significant ways did more to shape my politics and life than did my formal education, which always seemed to be about somebody else's dreams. Of course, any discourse about identity is always one contingent upon an analysis of history and power.

I no longer believe that pedagogy is a discipline. On the contrary, I have argued for the last few years that pedagogy is about the creation of a public sphere, one that brings people together in a variety of sites to talk, exchange information, listen, feel their desires, and expand their capacities for joy, love, solidarity, and struggle. Though I do not wish to romanticize popular culture, it is precisely in its diverse spaces and spheres that most of the education that matters today is taking place on a global scale. Electronic media, the vastly proliferating network of images that inscribe themselves on us everyday, and the hybridized sounds of new technologies, cultures, and ways of life have drastically altered how identities are shaped, desires constructed, and dreams realized.

This book is not a theoretical exegesis of popular culture. Instead, it is a journey through some of the landscapes of popular culture. The map of the journey is drawn in an attempt to make clear how the pedagogical and the political come together in sites that are often ignored by the schools–in this case, sites where the struggle over knowledge, power, and authority translates itself into a broader battle over the meaning of pleasure, self-formation, and national identity. This is a book in which I begin with particular cultural texts and attempt to develop a theory of pedagogy out of their specific constructions. It is a book that I believe enlarges both the meaning of pedagogy and its relationship to the popular while simultaneously indicating how pedagogical interventions might be made on this terrain. It is not a book that speaks for a generic pedagogy, nor is it an attempt to speak for others. In simple terms, it is a book that arises out of my own experiences and attempts to locate those experiences in a language that gives them meaning without rendering them universal or dogmatic.

This book was written during a very difficult period of my life. I would like to thank Carol Becker, David Trend, Donaldo Macedo, Jim Fraser, Barry Kanpol, Peter McLaren, Ralph Page, Roger Simon, Stanley Aronowitz, Priscilla Ross, Susan Searls, Harvey Kaye, Ava Collins, Candy Mitchell, Larry Grossberg, and Lynda and Bob Haas for their generous friendship and intellectual support. I also want to thank my editor, Jayne Fargnoli, who has been throughout this project a source of constant support, inspiration, and friendship. She has played a major role in helping me both construct and bring to completion this book.

Earlier versions of the essays in this volume have appeared in *Cultural Studies*, *Cultural Critique*, *Afterimage*, *Transition*, *College Literature*, *The Review of Education*, and the *International Journal of Educational Reform*.

Disney, Benetton, and Beyond

1

Consuming Social Change: The United Colors of Benetton[1]

PROMOTIONAL CULTURE IN THE POSTMODERN AGE

> Diversity is good. . . . your culture (whoever you are) is as important as our culture (whoever we are).
>
> —*Colors,* Fall–Winter 1991

In spite of the alleged collapse of postmodernism as yet another theoretical fashion, the politics of representation that has occupied the center of its analysis has become indispensable for understanding how politics reaches into everyday life to mobilize particular lived experiences, desires, and forms of agency. While certain versions of postmodernism may have overestimated the degree to which the boundaries between images and reality have become blurred, the postmodernist approach does not underestimate the expanding power of representations, texts, and images in producing identities and shaping the relationship between the self and society in an increasingly commodified world.[2] If postmodern theory used concepts such as the decentered subject or plural identities to analyze the emergence of broader cultural and social changes, mass-market advertisers have seized upon the cultural logic of postmodernism to integrate politics and difference with the stylized world of aesthetics and consumption.[3] Situated in a vortex of globally produced images and representations, consumer postmodernism produces meanings mediated through claims to truth represented in images that circulate in an electronic, informational hyperspace which disassociates itself from history, context, and struggle. Images that shocked people in the past have become what David Bailey and Stuart Hall call "the most effective way of selling commodities today."[4]

There is a certain irony in the fact that while many social theorists claim that postmodernism is dead, mass advertisers have seized upon the postmodern condition with its celebration of images, its proliferation of differences, and its fragmented notion of the subject to create pedagogical practices that offer a sense of unity amid a world increasingly devoid of any substantive discourse of community and solidarity. It is through these concerted and often pernicious efforts to rearticulate the relationship among difference, human agency, and community that mass advertising increasingly succeeds in its promotional mission: to disguise the political nature of everyday life and appropriate the vulnerable new terrain of insurgent differences in the interests of a crass consumerism.

But there is more at stake here than advertising and commerce combining in the postmodern age to commodify through the ritualization of fashion that which has previously escaped its reach. More important, mass advertising has become the site of a representational politics that powerfully challenges our understanding of what constitutes pedagogy, the sites in which it functions, and who speaks under what conditions through its authorizing agency. With the emergence of advertising as a global enterprise, we are witnessing a new form of violence against the public. By this I do not mean simply the intrusion of violence into designated public spheres as much as I am suggesting what Andrew Payne and Tom Taylor have referred to as a "public whose essential predicate would be violence."[5] At the core of this violence are constituting principles which accentuate individualism and difference as central elements of the marketplace. Underlying this violence of the public is a notion of the social bereft of ethics, social justice, and any viable conception of democratic public cultures. Put another way, mass advertising and its underlying corporate interests represent a new stage in an effort to abstract the notion of the public from the language of ethics, history, and democratic community.[6]

The rearticulation and new intersection of advertising and commerce, on the one hand, and politics and representational pedagogy, on the other, can be seen in the emergence of Benetton as one of the leading manufacturers and retailers of contemporary clothing. Benetton is important not only because of its marketing success, but also because it has taken a bold stance in attempting to use advertising as a forum to address highly charged social and political issues. Through its public statements and advertising campaigns, Benetton has brought a dangerously new dimension to corporate appropriation as a staple of postmodern aesthetics. Inviting the penetration of aesthetics into everyday life, Benetton has utilized less deterministic and more flexible approaches to design, technology, and styling. Such postmodern approaches to marketing and layout privilege contingency, plurality, and the poetics of the photographic image in an attempt to rewrite the relationship among aesthetics, commerce, and politics. Instead of depoliticizing or erasing images that vividly, and in some cases shockingly, depict social and political events, Benetton has attempted to redefine the link between commerce and politics by emphasizing both the politics of representation and the representation of politics. In the first instance, Benetton has appropriated for its advertising campaign actual news photos of social events that portray various calamities of our time. These include pictures of a duck covered with thick oil, a bloodied mafia murder victim, depictions of child labor, and a terrorist car bombing. As part of a representation of politics, Benetton struggles to reposition itself less as a producer of commodities and market retailer than as a corporate voice for a particular definition of public morality, consensus, coherence, and community. This has been more recently revealed in an advertising campaign which depicts Senator Luciano Benetton posing nude with an accompanying text urging people of wealth to give away their "old" clothes to charity. Benetton justifies the ad by arguing that "business has to go on for everybody. Rich people should buy new stuff and be pleased that others can profit from [their old clothes]."[7] Justice in this case is appropriated in order both to regulate the production of consumerism and to legitimate it.

Within Benetton's worldview, the relationship among identity formation, commerce, pedagogy, and politics is being reworked. That is, such a relationship is now used to highlight how pedagogy can be conscripted into the service of relations of identity and difference that promote an apolitical egalitarianism veiled in an appeal to international harmony. The result is that Benetton offers itself as the promotional mediator of a version of the social that abstracts ethics from a history informed by diverse forms of resistance and collective struggle. Social consciousness and activism in this worldview are about purchasing merchandise, not changing oppressive relations of power.

In what follows, I want to provide a brief introduction to the history of Benetton's advertising campaign. Second, I want to analyze the structural relations and ideological rationale that inform the emergence of Benetton as a major distributor of clothing in the post-Fordist age and as a corporate advocate for a particular approach to multiculturalism and diversity. Third, I will examine in some detail what I will call Benetton's pedagogy of representation, focusing on its claim to realism and its politics of (de)contextualism. In addition, I will attempt to deconstruct three of its more politically charged photojournalistic advertisements. In conclusion, I will attempt to analyze briefly how cultural workers might challenge the implications of Benetton's pedagogy and cultural politics.

SMALL BEGINNINGS AND GLOBAL CONTROVERSIES

> All over the world Benetton stands for colorful sportswear, multiculturalism, world peace, racial harmony, and now, a progressive approach toward serious social issues.
>
> —Benetton[8]

In 1965, Luciano Benetton and three siblings established a small business, Fratelli Benetton, near Treviso, Italy. Originally designed to produce colorful sweaters, the business expanded into a full range of personal apparel and eventually developed into a two billion dollar fashion empire producing eighty million pieces of clothing a year for seven thousand franchise stores in over one hundred countries.

Benetton's advertising campaign over the last decade has been instrumental in its success in the fashion world. The advertising campaign is important not merely as a means of assessing Benetton commercial success in extending its name recognition, it is crucial for understanding how the philosophy of the company has attempted to reinscribe its image within a broader set of political and cultural concerns. In 1984, Benetton hired Oliviero Toscani, an award-winning photographer, to head its advertising campaign. Given a free hand with the advertising budget, Toscani focused initially on culturally diverse young people dressed in Benetton attire and engaged in a variety of seemingly aimless and playful acts. Linking the colors of Benetton clothes to the diverse "colors" of their customers from all over the world, Toscani attempted to use the themes of racial harmony and world peace to register such differences within a wider unifying articulation. In 1985, Toscani adopted The United Colors of Benetton as a recurring trademark of the Benetton ideology. In 1991, Toscani initiated a publicity campaign that removed Benetton merchandise from the firm's advertising, and started using its eighty million dollar global ad budget to publish controversial and disturbing photographs in magazines and on billboards. Taking full control of the ad blitz, Toscani personally photographed many of the shots that dominated the 1991 Benetton campaign. These included a number of compelling images that created a provocative effect: variously colored, blown-up condoms floating in the air, a nun kissing a priest on the lips, a row of test tubes filled with blood, and a newborn baby girl covered in blood and still attached to her umbilical cord. In 1992 Toscani embarked on his most dramatic effort to combine high fashion and politics in the service of promoting the Benetton name. He selected a series of highly charged, photojournalistic images referencing, among other things, the AIDS crisis, environmental disaster, political violence, war, exile, and natural catastrophe. These appeared in various journals and magazines as well as on billboards without written text except for the conspicuous insertion of the green and white United Colors of Benetton logo located in the margins of the photograph.

Benetton's shift in advertising strategy between 1984 and 1991 needs to be considered as part of a wider politics and pedagogy of representation. The earlier photographs representing children of diverse races and colors dressed in Benetton clothing have what Michael Stevens calls a "netherworld quality that gives the viewers the impression they're glimpsing some fashionable heaven."[9] Depicted in these photographs of children hugging and holding hands is a portrayal of racial harmony and difference that appears both banal and sterile. The exaggerated precision of the models and the primary colors used in the advertisements render racial unity as a purely aesthetic category while eliminating racial conflict completely in this two-dimensional world of make-believe. Within these ad campaigns, race and ethnicity are both accentuated and fixed. According to Les Back and Vibeke Quaade, "Throughout the campaigns, human difference is reduced to a set of simplified caricatures which are presented as archetypes. In fact, what we find in Benetton advertising is a parade of racial essences. Thus, the 'whites' have blue eyes and blond hair, the 'blacks' are 'Negroid,' and the 'Orientals' are likewise locked in a crass image of 'racial' traits."[10] In addition, the "colorful" images in the early phase of the United Colors campaign appear almost too comfortable, and seem at odds with a world marked by political, economic, and cultural conflict. In the early ads racial differences are accentuated, but are linked primarily to the dynamics of consumption and largely subordinated to the logic of the marketplace and commerce. But at the same time, the harmony and consensus implied in these ads often mock concrete racial, social, and cultural differences as they are constituted amid hierarchical relations of struggle, power, and authority. Benetton's corporate image in this case seems strangely at odds with its own market research, which

United Colors of Benetton 1991 Spring/Summer advertising campaign.
PHOTO: O. TOSCANI

indicated that its "target customers—18–34 year old women—are more socially active and aware than any generation that precedes them."[11]

The switch in the ad campaign to controversial photojournalistic images reflects an attempt on the part of Benetton to redefine its corporate image. In order to define itself as a company concerned with social change, Benetton suspended its use of upscale representations in its mass advertising campaign, especially in a world where, as Carol Squires writes, "denial in the service of upbeat consumerism is no longer a workable strategy as we are continually overwhelmed by disturbing and even cataclysmic events."[12] In a postmodern world caught in the disruptive forces of nationalism, famine, violence, and war, such representations linked Benetton's image less to the imperatives of racial harmony than to the forces of cultural uniformity and yuppie colonization. Moreover, Benetton's move away from an appeal to utility to one of social responsibility provides an object lesson in how promotional culture increasingly uses pedagogical practices to shift its emphasis from selling a product to selling an image of corporate responsibility.[13] Given the increase in sales, profits, and the widespread publicity Benetton has received, the campaign appears to have worked wonders.

The response to the campaign inaugurated in 1991 was immediate. Benetton was both condemned for its appropriation of serious issues to sell goods and praised for incorporating urgent social concerns into its advertising. In many cases, the Benetton ads were either banned from particular countries or refused by specific magazines. One of the most controversial ads portrayed AIDS patient David Kirby surrounded by his family shortly before he died. The Kirby ad became the subject of heated debate among various groups in several countries. In spite of the criticism and perhaps in part owing to it, the company's profits rose 24 percent, to $132 million worldwide, in 1991. The Benetton name has even infiltrated popular literary culture, with Douglas Coupland coining the phrase "Benetton Youth" in his novel *Shampoo Planet* to refer to global kids whose histories, memories, and experiences began in the Reagan era of greed and conspicuous consumption. *Adweek* reports that because of the success of the Benetton campaign, Toscani has become something of a commercial "star," and has been asked by American Express to develop marketing concepts for them. Benetton's stock is up because of the visibility of the company, and David Roberts, an analyst with Nomura International-London, claims that Benetton's "name recognition is approaching that of Coca-Cola."[14]

Benetton's practical response to the controversy has been threefold. First, Benetton and its spokespersons have reacted aggressively within a number of public forums and debates in order to defend the firm's advertising policies by either condemning the criticism as a form of censorship or criticizing other ad companies for producing advertising that merely engages in the most reductionistic forms of pragmatism. Second, it has used the debate to reorder its identity as a corporate force for social responsibility. Third, it has seized upon the controversy itself as a pretext for further marketing of its ideology in the form of books, magazines, talks, interviews, articles, and the use of stars such as Spike Lee to endorse its position in the debate.[15]

Benetton has attempted to articulate and defend its position through material found in campaign copy sent to its various stores around the world, particularly the Fall-Winter and Spring-Summer 1992 versions. Moreover, it has attempted to deflect criticism of its ads by allowing selected executives to speak in interviews, the press, and various popular magazines. The three major spokespersons for Benetton have been Luciano Benetton, founder and managing director, Oliviero Toscani, creative director, and Peter Fressola, Benetton's director of communications in North America. All three provide different versions of a similar theme: Benetton is not about selling sweaters but social responsibility, and it is a company that represents less a product than a lifestyle and worldview.

Recently elected as a senator to the Italian Parliament, Luciano Benetton is the principal ideologue in the Benetton apparatus. He is chiefly responsible for defining the structuring principles that guide Benetton as both a corporate entity and an ideological force. His own political beliefs are deeply rooted in the neoliberal language of the free market, privatization, the removal of government from the marketplace, and the advocacy of business principles as the basis for a new social imaginary. Hence, it is not surprising that, in addition to defending the ads for their role in generating public awareness of controversial issues, Luciano Benetton readily admits that the advertising campaign "has a traditional function, . . . to make Benetton known around the world and to introduce the product to consumers."[16] More than any other spokesperson, Luciano Benetton articulates the company's position concerning the relationship between commerce and art and acts as a constant reminder that the bottom line for the company is profit and not social justice.

Peter Fressola, on the other hand, promotes Benetton's ideological position, and claims that the ad campaign does not reflect the company's desire to sell sweaters. He argues, "We're not that stupid. We're doing corporate communication. We're sponsoring these images in order to change people's minds and create compassion around social issues. We think of it as art with a social message."[17] Of course, the question here is, Whose minds does Benetton want to shape? In part, the answer lies in its own advertising material, which states that "various studies have shown that in 1992 consumers are as concerned by what a company stands for as they are about the price/value relationship of that company's product."[18] There is nothing in Fressola's message that challenges the legacy of the corporate use of communications to advance, if only tacitly, "some kind of self-advantaging exchange."[19]

On one level logos permeate our everyday world to such a degree that they have become commonplace symbols that blur the line between art, politics, and commodification. As a new form of cultural capital, they distinguish upscale or trendy corporations from less prominent corporate players. But more important, they constitute the borders within which cultural objects and practices are constituted as a form of capital. Logos in this sense do not simply signify goods, they serve as a marker to remind us that there are no public spheres, desires, practices, and needs that can escape being commodified. Logos have become central to a politics of identity in which they provide people with forms of representation in which they can identify themselves and their relationship to others. The political and cultural implications of the use of logos to connect identities to the dictates of corporate ideologies is captured by Susan Willis in her analysis of the Disney logo.

> In late twentieth-century America, the cultural capital of corporations has replaced many of the human forms of cultural capital. As we buy, wear, and eat logos, we become the henchmen and admen of the corporations, defining ourselves with respect to the social standing of the various corporations. Some would say that this is a new form of tribalism, that in sporting corporate logos we ritualize and humanize them, we redefine the cultural capital of the corporations in human social terms. I would say that a state where culture is indistinguishable from logo and where the practice of culture risks infringement of private property is a state that values the corporate over the human.[20]

Benetton's response to such criticisms is either to occupy the moral high ground or to displace the wider political and ideological significance of the logo by making a pragmatic appeal to the results of extensive market research. For example, when questioned about the use of the Benetton logo imprinted on all ad copy and photographs, Fressola, Toscani, and other spokespeople generally reply by evading the question and pointing to the use of such photographs as part of their support for art, controversy, and public dialogue around social issues. But the presence of the logo is no small matter. In light of their market research, which stresses what Raymond Loewy called the need for designer corporate symbols to index visual memory retention, the presence of the Benetton logo partakes of a powerful advertising legacy. It asserts that, regardless of the form it takes, the purpose of advertising is to subordinate all values to the imperatives of profit and commercialization. Loewy's argument, "We want anyone who has seen the logotype, even fleetingly, to never forget it, or at least to forget it slowly," provides a powerful indictment of Benetton's rationale and the claim that Benetton is engaging in a *new* form of corporate communication.[21] By refusing to disrupt or challenge this haunting and revealing legacy of designer logos, communication in these terms appears to do nothing more than link the commodification of human tragedy with the imperatives of brand recognition while simultaneously asserting the discourse of aesthetic freedom and the moral responsibility of commerce. This is captured in part in a statement that appeared in Benetton's Fall-Winter 1992 advertising campaign literature: "Among the various means available to achieve the brand recognition that every company must have, we at Benetton believe our strategy for communication to be more effective for the company and more useful to society than would be yet another series of ads showing pretty girls wearing pretty clothes."[22]

Toscani goes so far as to separate his economic role as the director of advertising from what he calls the process of communication by claiming rather blithely, "I am responsible for the company's communications; I am not really responsible for its economics."[23] Toscani appeals in this case to the moral high ground, one that he suggests is untarnished by the commercial context that informs the deep structure of his job. Should we assume that Benetton's market research in identifying target audiences has nothing to do with Toscani's creative endeavors? Or perhaps that Toscani has found a way to avoid linking his own corporate success to the rise of Benetton's name recognition in a global marketplace? Toscani is well aware of the relationship between representation and power, as he most certainly is of his own role in giving a new twist to the advertising of commodities as cultural signs in order to promote a particular system of exchange.

POST-FORDISM AND THE POLITICS OF DIFFERENCE

> Capital has fallen in love with difference; advertising thrives on selling us things that will enhance our uniqueness and individuality. . . . From World Music to exotic holidays in Third-World locations, ethnic TV dinners to Peruvian knitted hats, cultural difference sells.
>
> —Martin Davidson, *The Consumerist Manifesto*

In the world of international capital, difference is a contentious and paradoxical concept. On the one hand, as individuals increasingly position themselves within and across a variety of identities, needs, and lifestyles, capital seizes upon such differences in order to create new markets and products. Ideas that hold the promise of producing social criticism are insinuated into products in a attempt to subordinate the dynamics of social struggle to the production of new lifestyles. On the other hand, difference is also a dangerous marker of those historical, political, social, and cultural borderlands where people who are considered the "Other" are often policed, excluded, and oppressed. Between the dynamics of commodification and those of resistance, difference becomes a site of conflict and struggle over bodies, desires, land, labor, and the distribution of resources. It is within the space between conflict and commercial appeal that difference carries with it the legacy of possible disruption and political struggle as well as the possibility for colonizing diverse markets. Within the logic of restructured global capital markets, cultural differences have to be both acknowledged and depoliticized in order to be contained. In a world riddled with conflicts over cultural, ethnic, and racial differences, Benetton defines difference in categorical rather than relational terms and in doing so accentuates a warmed-up diet of liberal pluralism and harmonious consensus.

Central to Benetton's celebration of cultural differences are the dynamics of economic restructuring and the company's own rise from a local business venture to a global marketing conglomerate. Benetton's commercial success and the ideological legitimation upon which it constructs its United Colors of Benetton worldview derive, in part, from its aggressive adaptation to the shifting economic and cultural circumstances of what has been called post-Fordism.

Although post-Fordism is not an unproblematic term for designating the changes that have taken place in manufacturing and retailing in advanced industrial countries since 1950, it does focus attention on a number of economic and ideological tendencies that alert us to the need for new descriptions and analyses of what Stuart Hall calls the "shifting social and technical landscapes of modern industrial production regimes,"[24] which are refiguring the relationship between capital and everyday life. Hall has succinctly described some of the most salient characteristics of post-Fordism:

> "Post-Fordism" is a [broad] term, suggesting a whole new epoch distinct from the era of mass production. . . . it covers at least some of the following characteristics: a shift to the new information "technologies"; more flexible, decentralized forms of labor process and work organization; decline of the old manufacturing base and the growth of the "sunrise," computer-based industries; the hiving off or contracting out of functions and services; a greater emphasis on choice and product differentiation, on marketing, packaging, and design, on the "targeting" of consumers by lifestyle, taste, and culture rather than by the categories of social class; a decline in the proportion of the skilled, male, manual working class, the rise of the service and white-collar classes and the "feminization" of the work force; an economy dominated by the multinationals, with their new international division of labor and their greater autonomy from nation-state control; and the "globalization" of the new financial markets, linked by the communications revolution.[25]

Capitalizing on global shifts in the order of economic and cultural life, Benetton has seized upon post-Fordist production techniques and methods of retailing that integrate various aspects of production, design, distribution, and a flexible labor force into a single coordinated system. With great skill and ingenuity, Benetton uses its computerized planning systems, flexible production technology, and marketing resources to both forecast and respond immediately to consumer demands from all over the world. Once consumer orders from various Benetton retailers are tallied at the end of the day, they are sent to a centralized computer system that allows the orders to be filled within days. Benetton's concern with difference is in part rooted in the hard realities of a global market and its need to serve various consumer needs. But difference is more than just a feature of commerce, it is also about social movements, collective memories of resistance, and the struggle on the part of subordinate groups to reclaim their histories and collective voices. In response to the latter, Benetton has developed a representational politics in the service of a corporate narrative whose purpose is to harness difference as part of an ideology of promotion and political containment.

In this case, Benetton's post-Fordist economic policies are underwritten by a neoconservative political philosophy that supports minimum state intervention in the world of commerce, accentuates privatization in the form of subcontracting, wages a full-fledged assault on unionized labor, and dramatically expands the service sector. While preaching the gospel of social responsibility, Benetton has become a "corporate model" for new post-Fordist production techniques in which workers are increasingly forced to take jobs with less security, fewer benefits, and lower wages. In the new world of subcontracting, as Clare Ansberry writes, more and more "office and factory employees are getting transplanted overnight to a temporary or subcontracting nether world [in order] to save the mother company paperwork and cost."[26]

This assault on workers is coupled with a call for less state regulation of business. As a senator in the Italian Parliament, Luciano Benetton has made it clear that he would promote a "lesser State presence in the economy,"[27] and apply the logic of business to the larger world of politics. Within this scenario, Benetton's discourse of social justice appears transparently cynical next to its conglomerate-building management practices, increasing use of temporary workers at the expense of a full-time, unionized workforce, and aggressive attempts to subordinate all aspects of political and cultural discourse to the logic of capital and commerce.[28]

The economic mandates of Benetton's post-Fordism are informed by an underlying ideological imperative: the need to contain potentially antagonistic cultural differences and an insurgent multiculturalism through a representational politics that combines pluralism with a depoliticized appeal to world harmony and peace. This becomes more clear by recognizing that the politics of difference à la Benetton intersects diverse vectors of representation. Economically, the company's post-Fordist organizational structure acknowledges cultural difference as a vehicle for expanding its range of markets and goods; diversity in the commercial sense entails a move away from standardized markets and the intrusion of business into the postmodern world of plural identities. The representation of difference becomes a crucial component in a market-driven attempt to expand production of a variety of apparel for vastly different individuals, groups, and markets. Benetton's corporate ideology, therefore, bespeaks the need to construct representations which affirm differences at the same time they deny their radical possibilities within a corporate ideology that speaks to global concerns. Difference in this sense poses the postmodern problem of maintaining the particularity of diverse groups while simultaneously unifying such differences within Benetton's concept of a "world without borders."

Benetton addresses this problem in both pedagogical and political terms. Pedagogically, it takes up the issue of difference through representations based in the conventions of fashion, style, and spectacle. Adapting its widely circulated magazine *Colors* to an MTV format, it uses the journal to focus on transnational topics such as music, sex, birth control, and a wide range of issues that incorporate popular culture while simultaneously depoliticizing it. Popular culture, in this case, becomes the pedagogical vehicle through which Benetton addresses the everyday concerns of youth while at the same time blurring the lines between popular cultures of resistance and the culture of commerce and commercialization. Interspersed amid commentaries on music, pizza, national styles, condoms, rock stars, and the biographies of various Benetton executives, *Colors* parades young people from various racial and ethnic groups wearing Benetton apparel. In this context, difference is stripped of all social and political antagonisms and becomes a commercial symbol for what is youthfully chic, hip, and fashionable. At the same time, *Colors* appears to take its cue from the many concerns that inform the daily lives of teenagers all over the industrialized world.

But *Colors* does more than signify the commodification of popular culture, it also signifies Benetton's attempt to both rewrite the content of ads *and* blur the boundaries and cultural codes that structure their very forms. Within this context, the distinction between "the news," advertising, mass communication, public events, editorials, and feature stories breaks down. Subordinated to the logic of the spectacle, the selling of fantasies, and the pleasures of buying, the distinctions between these genres disappear. Back and Quaade's analysis of *Colors* is worth quoting at length:

> The paper constantly crosses the line between forms of mass communication, provides commodity information (adverts) and news information ("the news"), but takes on the usual form of a newspaper, with editorial and feature stories. Its format is that of the non-tabloid morning paper, divided into eight sections dealing with familiar and newsworthy global problems, including waste disposal, North-South inequality, and the plight of refugees and immigrants. It also includes

> more style-oriented issues like music, hairstyles and sub-cultures. Benetton turn [*sic*] the usual relationship between advertising and news media inside out. Unlike conventional newspapers, where advertising is carried as an income-generated appendix to the news, *Colors* uses its news as Benetton's advertising. The news stories are edited with the philosophy of the paper, which is, in turn, associated with the brand quality of its products.[29]

Politically, Benetton develops a strategy of containment through advertising practices using journalistic photos that address consumers through stylized representations whose structuring principles are shock, sensationalism, and voyeurism. In these images, Benetton's motives have less to do with selling particular products than with offering the company's publicity mechanisms to diverse cultures as a unifying discourse for solving the great number of social problems that threaten to uproot difference from the discourses of harmony, consensus, and fashion. In substituting the "manufactured" studio shot for the hyperrealism of photodocumentary images, Benetton collapses the boundaries between the lurid fantasies that promote consumption and those visions that compel social responsibility.

REPRESENTATIONS OF HOPELESSNESS

> Many people have asked why we didn't include a text that would explain the image. But we preferred not to because we think the image is understandable by itself.
>
> —Luciano Benetton

> I think to die is to die. This is a human situation, a human condition. . . . But we know this death happened. This is the real thing, and the more real the thing is, the less people want to see it. It's always intrigued me why fake has been accepted and reality has been rejected. At Benetton, we are trying to create an awareness of issues. AIDS is one of today's major modern problems in the world, so I think we have to show something about it.
>
> —Oliviero Toscani[30]

In defense of the commercial use of sensational, journalistic photographs which include the aforementioned dying AIDS patient, a terrorist car bombing, and a black soldier with a gun strapped over his shoulder holding part of the skeletal remains of another human being, Benetton's spokespeople combine an assertion of universal values and experiences with the politics of realism. Arguing that such images serve as a vehicle for social change by calling attention to the real world, Benetton suggests that its advertising campaign is informed by a representational politics in which the "truth" of such images is guaranteed by their purchase on reality. From this perspective, "shocking" photos register rather than engage an allegedly unmediated notion of the truth. This appeal to the unmediated "truth-effects" of photographic imagery is coupled with a claim to universal truths ("to die is to die") that serve to deny the historical, social, and political specificity of particular events. Ideologically, this suggests that the value of Benetton's photos resides in their self-referentiality, that is, their ability to reflect both the unique vision of the sponsor and their validation of a certain construction of reality. Suppressed in this discourse is an acknowledgment that the meaning of such photos resides in their functions within particular contexts.

Before discussing specific examples from Benetton's advertising campaign, I want to comment briefly on some of the structuring devices at work in the company's use of photojournalistic images. All of Benetton's ads depend upon a double movement of decontextualization and recontextualization. To accomplish the former move, the photos militate against a reading in which their context and content are historically and culturally situated. Overdetermined by the immediacy of the logic of the spectacle, Benetton's photos become suspended in what Stewart Ewen has called "memories of style."[31] That is, by dehistoricizing and decontextualizing the photos, Benetton attempts to render ideology innocent by blurring the conditions of production, circulation, and commodification that present such photos as unproblematically real and true. By denying specificity, Benetton suppresses the history of these images and, in doing so, limits the range of meanings that might be brought into play. At issue here is a denial of how shifting contexts give an image different meanings. Of course, the depoliticization that is at work here is not innocent. By failing to rupture the dominant ideological codes (i.e., racism, colonialism, sexism) that structure what I call Benetton's use of hyperventilating realism (a realism of sensationalism, shock, and spectacle), the ads simply register rather than challenge the dominant social relations reproduced in the photographs.

The viewer is afforded no sense of how the aesthetic of realism works to mask what Abigail Solomon-Godeau calls "the codes and structures which give photographs meaning as well as the historical contingencies (e.g., patriarchal structures which normalize notions of looking) which give such codes salience."[32] There is no sense of how the operations of power inform the construction of social problems depicted in the Benetton ads, nor is there any recognition of the diverse struggles of resistance which attempt to engage with such problems. Within this aestheticization of politics, spectacle foregrounds our fascination with the hyperreal and positions the viewer so as to simply see horror and shock without critically responding to it. Roland Barthes has referred to this form of representation as one that positions the viewer within the "immediacy of translation."[33] According to Barthes, this is a form of representational politics that functions as myth, because "it abolishes the complexity of human acts, it gives them the simplicity of essences, it does away with all dialectics, with any going back beyond what is immediately visible, it organizes a world which is without contradictions because it is without depth, a world wide open and wallowing in the evident, it establishes a blissful clarity: things appear to mean something by themselves."[34] Isolated from historical and social contexts, Benetton's images are stripped of their political possibilities and reduced to a spectacle of fascination and terror that appears primarily to privatize one's response to social events. That is, the form of address both reproduces dominant renderings of the image and translates the possibility of agency to the privatized act of buying goods rather than engaging in forms of self- and social determination. This process and its effects become clear in analyzing one of Benetton's more controversial ads, in which AIDS patient David Kirby is portrayed on his deathbed surrounded by members of his grieving family.

As I noted above, this image involves a double movement. On the one hand, it suppresses the diverse lifestyles, struggles, and realities of individuals in various stages of living with AIDS. In doing so, it reinforces dominant representations of people with AIDS, reproducing what Douglas Crimp, in another context, refers to as "what we have already been told or shown about people with AIDS: that they are ravaged, disfigured, and debilitated by the syndrome [and that] they are generally . . . desperate, but resigned to their inevitable deaths."[35] The appeal to an aesthetic of realism does little to disturb the social and ideological force of such inherited dominant representations. On the other hand, by not providing an analysis of representations of AIDS as a de facto death sentence, relying instead on the cliches enforced through dominant images and their social effects, the Benetton ad reproduces rather than challenges conventional representations that portray people with AIDS as helpless victims.

The politics at work in the Benetton photographs is also strikingly revealed in the use of photojournalistic images that are decontextualized from any meaningful historical and social setting and then recontextualized through the addition of the United Colors of Benetton logo. In the latter movement, the logo produces a representational "zone of comfort" confirming a playfulness which allows the viewer to displace any ethical or political understanding of the images contained in the Benetton ads.

The logo serves largely to position the audience within a combination of realism and amusement. Public truths revealed in Benetton's images, regardless of how horrifying or threatening, are offered, according to Dick Hebdige, "as a kind of joke in which the reader is invited to participate (the 'joke' is how low can we go?), but its potential dangers are also pretty clear: today aliens from Mars kidnap joggers, yesterday Auschwitz didn't happen, tomorrow who cares what happens?"[36] Of course, the "joke" here is that anything is for sale and social commitment is just another gimmick for selling goods. In this type of representational politics, critical engagement is rendered ineffective by turning the photo and its political referent into an advertisement. If the possibility of social criticism is suggested by the ad, it is quickly dispelled by the insertion of the logo, which suggests that any complicity between the viewer and the event it depicts is merely ironic. The image ultimately references nothing more than a safe space where the logic of the commodity and the marketplace mobilize consumers' desires rather than struggle over social injustices and conflicts. In the case of the AIDS ad, the use of the Benetton logo juxtaposes human suffering and promotional culture so as to invite the viewer to position him- or herself between the playfulness of commodification and an image of apocalypse rendering social change either ironic or unimaginable. This serves less to situate a critical viewer who can mediate social reality and its attendant problems than to subordinate the viewer to the demands and aesthetic of commerce. One consequence of such a position has been captured by Stuart Ewen: "By reducing all social issues to matters of perception, it is on the perceptual level that social issues are addressed. Instead of social change, there is image change. Brief shows of flexibility at the surface mask intransigence at the core."[37]

In the second instance, recontextualization appeals to an indeterminacy which suggests that the images diffused by Benetton can be negotiated by different individuals in multiple and varied ways. Hence, Benetton's claim that such photos generate diverse interpretations. While such an assumption rightly suggests that viewers always mediate and rewrite images in ways that differ from particular ideologies and histories, when unqualified, it also overlooks how specific contexts privilege some readings over others. In other words, while individuals produce rather than merely receive meanings, the choices they make and the meanings they produce are not free-floating. Such meanings and mediations are, in part, formed within wider social and cultural determinations that propose a range of reading practices that are privileged within power relations of dominance and subordination. The reading of any text cannot be understood independently of the historical and social experiences which construct how audiences interpret other texts. It is this notion of reading formation that is totally missing from Benetton's defense of its endless images of death, pain, danger, and shock. Tony Bennett is helpful on this issue: "The concept of reading formation . . . is an attempt to think context as a set of discursive and inter-textual determinations, operating on material and institutional supports, which bear in upon a text not just externally, from the outside in, but internally, shaping it—in the historically concrete forms in which it is available as a text-to-be-read from the inside out."[38]

Bennett's point can be illustrated by examining two of Benetton's racially marked ads. The first depicts a black woman and a white baby. The second portrays two hands, one black, one white, handcuffed together. In the former ad, the viewer is presented with the torso of a robust black woman suckling a white baby. A crimson cable-knit cardigan is pulled down over her shoulders to reveal her breasts. Her hands reveal traces of scar tissue, and her nails are trimmed short. This is not a traditional Benetton model. How might one decipher this potent, overdetermined set of signifiers? I say overdetermined in the double sense; first, the racial coding of the image is so overdetermined that it is difficult to imagine that this black woman nursing a long, pale pink baby is the child's mother. Given the legacy of colonialism and racism that informs this image, I

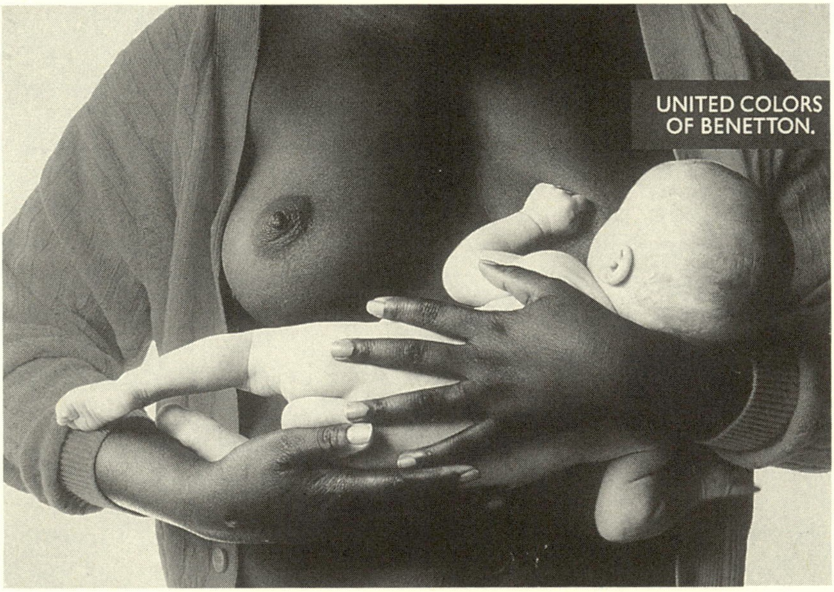

United Colors of Benetton 1989 Fall/Winter advertising campaign.
PHOTO: O. TOSCANI

believe that the photo privileges a range of dominant readings which suggest the ingrained racial stereotype of the black-slave wet nurse or mammy.[39] Other than the logo, there are no signifiers in this photo which would threaten or rupture such an imperialist coding. It is precisely the absence of referents related to resistance, rupture, and critique that allows the reader to be perfectly comfortable with such a configuration of race and class while at the same time accepting the image as nothing more than a "playful" ad.

In the second ad, there is a calculated and false equality at work in the image of a black hand and a white hand handcuffed together. Is the viewer in the United States, England, France, or South Africa to believe that the black hand is the signifier of law, order, and justice? Or, given the legacy of white racism in all of these countries, is it more probable that the image, at least at the level of the unconscious, reproduces the racist assumption that crime, turmoil, and lawlessness are essentially a black problem?[40] Restaging race relations in these terms exploits the racially charged tensions that underlie current racial formations in the Western industrial countries while simultaneously reducing the historical legacy of white supremacy to a representation of mere equality or symmetry. The emotionally charged landscape of race relations, in this instance, becomes

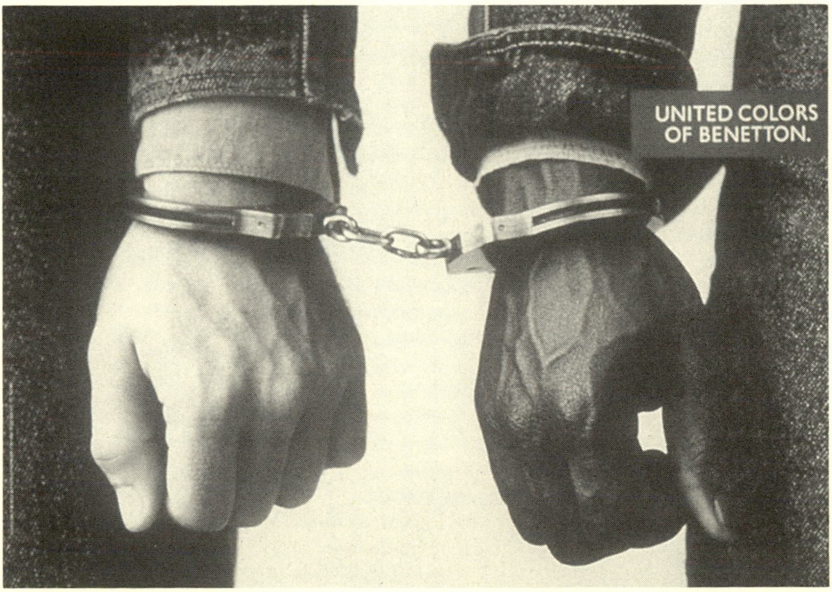

United Colors of Benetton 1989 Fall/Winter advertising campaign.
PHOTO: O. TOSCANI

another example of how social problems become "packaged" in order, as Hal Foster has written, to "reinject the real into our lives as spectacle."[41]

CONCLUSION: PEDAGOGY AND THE NEED FOR CRITICAL PUBLIC CULTURES

The new postmodern pedagogy of mass advertising poses a central challenge to the role cultural workers might play in deepening their politics through a broader understanding of how knowledge is produced, identities shaped, and values articulated as a pedagogical practice that takes place in multiple sites outside the traditional institution of schooling. The struggle over meaning is no longer one that can be confined to programs in educational institutions and their curricula. Moreover, the struggle over identity can no longer be seriously considered outside the politics of representation and the new formations of consumption. Culture is increasingly constituted by commerce, and the penetration of commodity culture into every facet of daily life has become the major axis of relations of exchange through which corporations actively produce new, increasingly effective forms of address.

This is not to suggest that the politics of consumption in its various circuits of power constitutes an unadulterated form of domination. Such a view is often more monolithically defensive than dialectical and less interested in understanding the complex process by which people desire, choose, and act in everyday life than in shielding the guardians of high modernism, who have always despised popular culture for its vulgarity and association with the "masses."[42] What is at stake in the new intersection of commerce, advertising, and consumption is the very definition and survival of critical public cultures. I am referring here to those spheres of daily life where people can debate the meaning and consequences of public truths, inject a notion of moral responsibility into representational practices, and collectively struggle to change dominating relations of power. Central to my argument has been the assumption that these new forms of advertising and consumption do not deny politics, they simply reappropriate it. They enact a politics, according to Hebdige, that "actively creates one version of the social,"[43] one that exists in harmony with market ideologies and initiatives. Such a politics offers no resistance to a version of the social as largely, in Bill Moyers's words, a "democracy of images," a public media extravaganza in which politics is defined largely through the "consuming of images."[44]

Cultural workers need to reformulate the concept of resistance usually associated with these forms of colonization. Such a reformulation has to begin with an analysis of how a postmodern pedagogy works by problematizing the intersection of power and representation in an ever-expanding democratization of images and culture. Representations in the postmodern world reach deeply into daily life, contributing to the increasing fragmentation and decentering of individual and collective subjects. Not only are the old categories of race, gender, sexuality, age, and class increasingly rewritten in highly differentiating and often divisive terms, but the space of the social is further destabilized through niche marketing which constructs identities around lifestyles, ethnicity, fashion, and a host of other commodified subject positions. Central here is the issue of how power has become an important cultural and ideological form, particularly within the discourse of difference and popular culture. Cultural workers need a new map for registering and understanding how power works to inscribe desires and identities and create multiple points of antagonism and struggle. Also in serious need of consideration is the creation of a new kind of pedagogical politics and pedagogy organized through guiding narratives that link global and local social contexts, provide new articulations for engaging popular culture within rather than outside new technologies and regimes of representation, and offer a moral language for expanding the struggle over democracy and citizenship to ever-widening spheres of daily life.

Clearly, more is at issue here than understanding how representations work to construct their own systems of meaning, their own social organizations, their own cultural identifications. In part, cultural workers must investigate the new politics of commerce not merely as an economic issue, that is, as symptomatic of the new configurations of a post-Fordist world, but as a reaction to the emergence and, in the words of David Bennet and Terry Collits, the "assertion of new ethnicities, problems of racism, problems of nationality, of law, of discrimination, and the assertion of particular communities."[45] Furthermore, this type of analysis suggests reformulation of a politics and pedagogy of difference around an ethical discourse that both challenges the ideological grounds and representations of commerce and limits those public spheres it attempts to appropriate. If a politics of difference is to be linked not merely to registering "otherness" but to identifying the conditions through which others become critical agents, the ethic of consumerism must be challenged by exposing its limits. As cultural workers we need to take up the challenge of teaching ourselves, our students, and others to acknowledge our and their complicity in the discourse and practice of consumerism while at the same time bringing the hope mobilized by such practices to a principled and persistent crisis. This is not to invoke a vulgar critique of the real pleasures of buying, or to underestimate the diverse ways in which people negotiate the terrain of the market or reappropriate goods through resisting and oppositional practices. Rather these practices require recognition of the political and pedagogical limits of consumerism, its often active involvement in creating new identities, and its ongoing assault on the notion of insurgent differences in a multicultural and multiracial democracy. Individual and collective agency is about more than buying goods, and social life in its most principled forms points beyond the logic of the market as a guiding principle. It is up to cultural workers and other progressive educators to address these issues directly as part of a postmodern political and pedagogical challenge.

2

Politics and Innocence in the Wonderful World of Disney

An alarming defensiveness has crept into America's official image of itself, especially in its representations of the national past. Every society and official tradition defends itself against interferences with its sanctioned narratives; over time these acquire an almost theological status, with founding heros, cherished ideas and values, national allegories having an inestimable effect in cultural and political life.

—Edward Said, *Culture and Imperialism*

Ideas, texts, even people can be made sacred . . . but even though such entities, once their sacredness is established, seek to proclaim and to preserve their own absoluteness, their inviolability, the act of making sacred is in truth an event of history. . . . And events in history must always be subject to questioning, deconstruction, even to declarations of their obsolescence. To respect the sacred is to be paralysed by it.

—Salman Rushdie, *Imaginary Homelands*

POPULAR CULTURE AND THE STRUGGLE FOR MEMORY

In different ways, Edward Said, in *Culture and Imperialism,* and Salman Rushdie, in *Imaginary Homelands,* are addressing the complex relationship between memory and history on the one hand and culture and power on the other. By historicizing culture, and problematizing knowledge, both authors point to the necessity for a cultural politics that engages the relationship between knowledge and authority, how the latter are established, and what relationship they have to dominant regimes of representation. By far the most visible debates are being played out in the university, in public schools, and in the popular press over the issue of curriculum reform and the struggle to define what constitutes the canon of great literature. While discussion of this issue has performed an invaluable theoretical service in addressing questions of culture, sexuality, race, and agency, it has failed to apply its more trenchant critiques to the sphere of popular culture and to expand the meaning of cultural texts outside of the dominant disciplinary emphases on high culture and the book as the primary sources of knowledge. More specifically, the dominant debates regarding knowledge and authority have failed to include the full range of symbolic modes of production, whether they be electronically produced images, written texts, talk, or actions, as influential public texts that construct meanings amid diverse social struggles and modes of contestation.

The ideological contours of this debate, sometimes referred to as the culture wars, are largely organized around liberal and conservative arguments, each making claims on the way the "past is remembered, understood, and linked to the present," as Roger Simon writes.[1] On one side conservatives invoke claims to national unity and world responsibility through an appeal to a nostalgic past written as an unchanging narrative the loss of which marks a crisis of leadership and innocence. On the other side various nationalists and progressives embrace collective memory as something to be merely recovered, an essentialized force that must be granted its place in the public arenas that define the parameters of cultural authority.

The many casualties produced by this debate over culture, authority, and the canon include important theoretical insights regarding the relationship between culture and power which have developed during the 1980s and 1990s from the emerging discourses of cultural studies, postcolonialism, feminism, and postmodernism. Diverse theorists in these fields have been generally united in their attempts to demonstrate, as David Bailey and Stuart Hall state, that "the question of power has important cultural and ideological aspects."[2] For example, by focusing on cultural resistance as a form of political resistance, they have given theoretical impetus to a new politics of culture that has redefined the range of cultural texts available for critical inquiry while simultaneously making popular culture a serious object of social criticism and analysis.[3]

This "voicing of the margins" has resulted in a cultural politics that has generated critical attention to issues dealing with the production of plural identities, struggles around difference, and what Hall calls the "appearance of new subjects on the political and cultural stage."[4] Moreover, the shift in the political toward popular practices has made clear that the hybridized space of popular culture is where the conflicts over the related issues of memory, identity, and representation are being most intensely fought over as part of a broader attempt by dominant groups to secure cultural hegemony. To translate the theoretical insights of the new cultural politics into a viable strategy for political activism progressive cultural workers will need to understand more critically how the dynamics of culture and politics have changed given the emergence of electronic media and their global capacity to create "new images of centrality." As Edward Said points out, it would be irresponsible politically for cultural workers to underestimate the profound effects the new media are having on the shaping of everyday life and global agendas. Unlike traditional cultural forms, the emergence of the new media marks a unique moment in the expansion of cultural imperialism into the sphere of everyday life. As Said writes, "The difference here is that the epic scale of the United States' global power and the corresponding power of the national domestic consensus created by the electronic media have no precedents. Never has there been a consensus so difficult to oppose nor so easy and logical to capitulate to unconsciously."[5]

The new shift toward culture as a terrain of struggle accentuates not only the emerging role of the media in securing cultural authority, it also requires that cultural workers become more attentive to the various intellectual sites in which the politics of remembering and forgetting produce different narratives of a national past, present, and future. There is no escape from the politics of representation; moreover, issues of textuality, meaning, and identity cannot be limited to the academy or subordinated to the allegedly more "serious" single issues related to low pay, poverty, child care, and other material concerns.[6] At the very least, any viable notion of political activism must reject the traditional binarism and strategies of reversal that abstract cultural considerations from so-called concrete material issues. The challenge is to theorize how a cultural politics can transform dominant social forms by expanding the sites of contestation and the range of social capacities necessary for individuals, as Kobena Mercer writes, "to become subjects and agents, rather than the alienated objects, of representation."[7] Cultural practices are produced and regenerated in a variety of social sites and the weight of their "social gravity" is manifested in how they are inscribed on the body, move people to social action, and set limits to the range of possibilities through which individuals negotiate their identities and sense of social agency. Needless to say, there is a reality outside of texts and cultural politics, but it is not one that can be understood outside of a politics of representation.

I want to argue that the theoretical and political move toward culture must be simultaneously engaged, in postcolonial terms, as an inquiry into the formation of national identity, or in this case a conjuring of what might be called the "character" of the United States. This suggests on one level that activists in a variety of sites must focus on the politics of culture. That is, cultural workers need to be more critically attentive to how power is organized through the enormous number of cultural apparatuses that range from libraries, movie theaters, and schools to high-tech media conglomerates that circulate signs and meanings through newspapers, magazines, advertisements, electronic programming, machines, films, and television programs. In this instance, the sphere of politics vastly broadens its potential for both cultural hegemony and political resistance.

But the new cultural politics cannot be limited to expanding the range of sites where politics, pedagogy, and power are manifest as spaces of contestation. A new cultural politics must also critically address those discourses outside of traditional domains of knowledge in order to extend the historical and relational definition of cultural texts while simultaneously redefining how, as Toni Morrison writes, "knowledge, however mundane and utilitarian, plays about in linguistic images and forms cultural practices."[8] The need for such analyses is exemplified in the powerful role the media is increasingly assuming in producing images and texts that intrude into ever-expanding areas of daily life. Under the rubric of fun, entertainment, and escape, massive public spheres are being produced which appear too "innocent" to be worthy of political analyses. Such is the case with the Disney Company. The Disney logo and characters have become almost synonymous with the very notion of American popular culture. In what follows, I want to address the relationship between Disney's representation of itself and the politics of innocence through which it attempts to secure its moral and pedagogical legitimacy.

DISNEY AND THE POLITICS OF INNOCENCE

There are few cultural icons in the United States which can match the signifying power of the Disney Company. Relentless in its efforts to promote a happy, kindly, paternal image of its founder, Walt Disney, and an endless regime of representations and commodities that conjure up a nostalgic view of the United States as the "magic kingdom," the Disney Company has become synonymous with a notion of innocence which aggressively rewrites the historical and collective identity of the American past. Given their prominence in the construction of popular memory, Disney productions play an important but often overlooked role in the cultural battles over the present and future. Behind the ideological appeal to nostalgia, wholesome times, and the land that is "the happiest place on earth," there is the institutional and ideological power of a multinational conglomerate that wields enormous social and political influence. Writing about the power of the Disney Company, Jon Weiner illuminates the scope and power of the $4.7 billion company:

> The Walt Disney company not only makes movies and runs the world's various Disneylands, it owns the Disney Channel and a TV station, it records music and publishes books, it buys books to make into movies that are shown on its cable channel and it licenses and produces songs and stories to publishers. Half a dozen other multinational media conglomerates do more or less the same thing: Time Warner, Times Mirror, Rupert Murdoch's News Corporation, Hearst, Bertelsmann. Their growing power to control the written word is bad news for readers, and for writers.[9]

When politics is cloaked in the image of innocence, there is more at stake than simple deception. There is the issue of cultural power and how it influences public understandings of the past, national coherence, and popular memory as a site of injustice, criticism, and renewal.[10] Innocence in Disney's world becomes the ideological vehicle through which history is both rewritten and purged of its seamy side. In this case, innocence becomes important as an ideological construct less through its appeal to nostalgia, stylized consumption, or a unified notion of national identity than it does as a marker for recognizing the past as a terrain of pedagogical and ideological struggle. The Disney Company is not ignorant of history; it reinvents it as a pedagogical and political tool to secure its own interests, authority, and power.

Innocence is not only a face of discursive domination, it is also a pedagogical device that locates people in particular historical narratives, representations, and cultural practices. But before I discuss this "pedagogy of innocence," I want to define more specifically the central theoretical dimensions of pedagogy as a cultural politics and social practice. Needless to say, since the very meaning and purpose of pedagogy is constantly struggled over as a signifier, it is important to stress that the concept of pedagogy must be used with considerable discretion. There is no absolute sign under which pedagogy can be defined. Instead, pedagogy refers to the production of and complex relationships among knowledge, texts, desire, and identity; it signals how questions of audience, voice, power, and evaluation actively work to construct particular relations between teachers and students, institutions and society, and classrooms and communities.

In both conservative and progressive discourses pedagogy is often treated simply as a set of strategies and skills to use to teach prespecified subject matter. In this context, pedagogy becomes synonymous with teaching as a technique or the practice of a craft—like a skill. Any viable notion of critical pedagogy must reject this definition and its endless slavish imitations even when they are claimed as part of a radical discourse or project. Pedagogy in the more critical sense illuminates the relationship among knowledge, authority, and power. It draws attention to questions concerning who has control over the conditions for the production of knowledge. Moreover, it delineates the ways in which the circuit of power works through the various processes through which knowledge, identities, and authority are constructed within particular sets of social relations. In this case, critical pedagogy as a form of political activism refers to a deliberate attempt by cultural workers to influence how knowledge and subjectivities are produced within particular social relations. It draws attention to the ways in which knowledge, power, desire, and experience are produced under specific basic conditions of learning. This approach to critical pedagogy does not reduce educational practice to the mastery of methodologies; it stresses instead the importance of understanding what actually happens in classrooms and other educational settings by raising questions regarding, in Roger Simon's words, "what knowledge is of most worth, in what direction should one desire, and what it means to know something."[11] Of course, the language of critical pedagogy does something more. Pedagogy is simultaneously about the knowledge and practices that teachers, cultural workers, and students might engage in together and the cultural politics and visions such practices legitimate. It is in this sense that cultural workers need to be attentive to pedagogy as a political practice and the cultural practices of pedagogy.

As a pedagogical construct that promotes a particular view of history in Disney's diverse public cultures, innocence, when coupled with a mythic rendering of the past and present, offers people the opportunity to envision themselves as agents of history, as part of a community longing for security and redemption in a world that often seems hostile to such desires.

Capitalizing on its inroads into popular culture, Disney generates representations that secure images, desires, and identifications through which audiences come to produce themselves and their relationships to others. By ordering and structuring such representations, Disney mobilizes a notion of popular memory that parades under the longing for childlike innocence, wholesome adventure, and frontier courage. Organized through affective and ideological forms of address, such representations make particular claims upon the present and serve to define how, as Stuart Hall has written, we "come to know how we are constituted and who we are."[12] What is so important about the "wonderful world of Disney," as what James Clifford calls an "historical-cultural theater of memory,"[13] is that it powerfully represents the degree to which, in Hall's words,

> popular culture has historically become the dominant form of global culture . . . the scene, par excellence, of commodification, of the industries where culture enters directly into the circuits of . . . power and capital. It is the space of homogenization where stereotyping and the formulaic mercilessly process the material and experiences it draws into its web, where control over narratives and representations passes into the hands of established cultural bureaucracies, sometimes without a murmur.[14]

The Wonderful World of Disney is more than a logo; it signifies how the terrain of popular culture has become central to commodifying memory and rewriting narratives of national identity and global expansion. Disney's power and its reach into popular culture combine an insouciant playfulness and the fantastic possibility of making childhood dreams come true—yet only through the reproduction of strict gender roles, an unexamined nationalism, and a notion of choice that is attached to the proliferation of commodities.

The strategies of entertaining escapism, historical forgetting, and repressive pedagogy in Disney's books, records, theme parks, movies, and TV programs produce a series of identifications that relentlessly define the United States as white, middle-class, and heterosexual. Pedagogy in Disney's texts functions as a history lesson that excludes the subversive elements of memory. Reduced to vignettes of childhood innocence, adventure, and chivalry, memory is removed from the historical, social, and political context which defines it as a process of cultural production that opens up rather than closes down history. It is precisely this pedagogical policing that undercuts memory as a form of critical remembrance that positions human agency between the possibilities of freedom and cultural largess, on the one hand, and the restrictions and boundaries set by the historical past, on the other. For Disney, memory has nothing to do with remembering differently, nor is it a compelling force for arousing what Walter Adamson calls "dormant emancipatory energies . . . [and] intellectually satisfying and emotionally compelling political images."[15] On the contrary, narrating the past becomes a vehicle for rationalizing the authoritarian, normalizing tendencies of the dominant culture that carry through to the present. Hence, Disney's pretense to innocence is shattered under the weight of a promotional culture predicated on the virtues of fun, family values, and, most important, consumption. The claim to high-spirited adventure and childlike innocence, albeit mischievous, in this case obscures a cultural universe that is largely conservative in its values, colonial in its production of racial differences, and middle-class in its portrayal of family values.

For example, both Jane Kuenz and Susan Willis have analyzed how in Disney's theme parks, intimacy, imagination, and spontaneity are replaced by the expertise of the well-placed park attendants, the picture-perfect photo sites, and the endless spectacles in which fun becomes consumption and memory is reduced to the purchase of souvenirs.[16] Similarly, theorists such as A. Dorfman and A. Matellart have indicated how Disney's comics serve to reproduce sexist, racist, and colonial ideologies.[17] Moreover, the mythology of an unproblematic innocence and clean virtue that has been carefully constructed by the Disney Company has been further demystified by a number of revelations indicating that Walt Disney, the founder of the Disney empire, served, according to Herbert Mitgang, "from 1940 until his death in 1966 . . . as a secret informer for the Los Angeles office of the Federal Bureau of Investigation."[18] It seems that Walt Disney was not only a special agent (code name: S.A.C. Contact) dedicated to rooting out communist agitators in the film industry, but he also allowed the FBI access to the Disneyland facilities for "use in connection with official matters and for recreational purposes."[19] Most disturbingly, Disney allowed J. Edgar Hoover, the director of the FBI, to censor and modify the scripts of such Disney films as *Moon Pilot* (1962) and *That Darn Cat* (1965) so as to portray bureau agents in a favorable light.

Behind the pretense to innocence and its appeal to a childlike state in which forgetting the past becomes more important than engaging it, the policing of memory erases its emancipatory possibilities. This is illuminated, in part, through recent public revelations indicating that the Disney Company has, on occasion, exceeded the moral boundaries of its promotional enthusiasm by preventing the publication of books critical of Walt Disney and the Disney Company's image.[20] It appears that beneath the promotion of the magical name of Disney and the public spaces it represents as "the happiest place on earth" lurks the power of a multinational conglomerate that has little regard for free speech and public criticism.

As an ideological construct that mobilizes particular cultural practices in diverse regimes of representation, whether it be a question of theme parks, comics, or movies, Disney's appeal to pristine innocence and high adventure is profoundly pedagogical in its attempt to produce specific knowledge, values, and desires. It is precisely this intersection of the political and the pedagogical as a hegemonic practice that necessitates making Disney's world of representations the object of critical analysis. Moreover, such an analysis is not warranted simply through its claim to wielding deconstructive skills, it is also important because it offers possibilities for educators and other cultural workers to understand more clearly how politics and pedagogy intersect in the production, circulation, and reception of popular culture and the formation of national identity.

As part of a broader attempt to make the political more pedagogical, I will analyze how Disney films inscribe the link between the related issues of memory, politics, and identity. More specifically, I want to show how the Disney Corporation through its Touchstone Films[21] subsidiary uses the discourse of innocence to police and constrain the potentially subversive notions of memory and popular culture. In what follows, I will analyze the films, *Good Morning, Vietnam* (1987) and *Pretty Woman* (1990) as exemplary texts for exploring the terrain of popular culture as it is constructed within the discourse of innocence and "fun" that lies at the heart of the Disney Company's worldview. Both films are products of Disney's Touchstone Films division, an enterprise developed during the 1980s to permit Disney to make films for older audiences. Yet, as will become evident in this discussion, although not produced for children, both *Good Morning, Vietnam* and *Pretty Woman* project the same insidious ethos of childhood innocence the Disney Company rigidly enforces in all of its past and present products. In different ways both films demonstrate how the discourse of patriarchy, class, and sexism is couched in the language and representations of innocence, and how such representations mobilize popular memory to incorporate not only a particular view of what Renato Rosaldo calls "imperialist nostalgia" but also a politics of forgetting in producing a specific vision of class relations, consumerism, patriarchy, and family values. I will focus primarily on the film *Good Morning, Vietnam* because I believe it contains the most overtly political theme that Disney has addressed through its Touchstone Films division in the last decade.

It is also important to note that while Disney's ideology has been largely analyzed through critiques of his theme parks and comics, such analyses have had very little to say about Disney films (Touchstone and Hollywood) or the relevance of pedagogical criticism for analyzing Disney's texts as ideological narratives. Pedagogical critiques are warranted on two counts. First, Disney's films construct and reach a much wider public audience than Disney's other cultural enterprises. Second, Disney films have enormous value as popular texts that are readily available for pedagogical and cultural criticism.

THE WAR OF LAUGHTER AND FORGETTING

> All across America, moviegoers want mature entertainment. But they don't want violence. They don't want exploitation. They don't want tasteless themes. They want quality. They want standards. And that is what we want at Disney's Touchstone Films.
>
> —Disney Promotional Text

It has become a commonplace that the Vietnam War represents a watershed in United States history. Marked by widespread popular protest against American colonialism, the war demythologized the role of the United States as a world leader; it mobilized diverse movements of resistance and revealed a deep-seated racism that structured policies toward both minorities at home and people of color outside of our national boundaries. Moreover, this was a postmodern war, a media event that signaled the limits of conventional warfare and the power of American militarism and imperialism while simultaneously transforming war's horror and violence into a television spectacle. The postmodern spectacle of the Vietnam conflict signaled not simply the death of "truth" but also what Theodor Adorno has called in another context "the withering of experience" and hence the displacement of the imperatives of moral responsibility and human agency.

> The total obliteration of the war by information, propaganda, commentaries, with cameramen in their first tanks and war reporters dying heroic deaths, the mishmash of an enlightened manipulation of public opinion and oblivious activity: all this is another expression for the withering of experience, the vacuum between men and their fate, in which their real fate lies. It is as if the reified, hardened plaster-cast of events takes the place of events themselves. Men are reduced to walk-on parts in a monster documentary film.[22]

In the 1970s and 1980s, the rewriting of the United States intervention in Vietnam became the focus of celluloid history. Vietnam as a spectacle provided the impetus for a series of Hollywood films engaged in the process of organized forgetting, a process that substituted myths for reality, redemption for truth, and collective self-pity for social justice.

With few exceptions, Hollywood's rendition of the Vietnam War paralleled and legitimated the nation's imperialist strategy in Southeast Asia. It shifted the focus of the war away from those who were the victims of long-standing Western and, specifically, North American imperialism to the personal and social struggles of Americans involved in the war.

The legacy of historical amnesia during the 1980s and the construction of popular memory in Hollywood Vietnam films is well known and need not be repeated in depth.[23] After all, this was the decade in which the United States needed to reassert itself as the leader of the new world order by exorcising the critical legacy of the 1960s and reversing the public humiliation it suffered during the Iran hostage crisis. At the same time, the United States was actively obscuring and erasing its own legacy of military intervention and terrorism in world affairs by constructing Third World peoples as either terrorists or religious fundamentalists.

It is impossible to separate the critical acclaim and popular success of *Good Morning, Vietnam* from the context and content of Vietnam films that preceded it. Directed by Barry Levinson, written by Mitch Markowitz, and produced by Walt Disney's Touchstone Films, *Good Morning, Vietnam* appealed to a generation of youth whose knowledge of the Vietnam War comes from the electronic media. This is a generation twice removed from the exacting moral and political issues that surrounded the Vietnam conflict. In fact, David Butler, author of *The Fall of Saigon*, revealed in a *New York Times* article that one of the key elements in making the film was "the coming [of age] of a younger audience for whom the war is less controversial." According to Butler, "Vietnam intrigues the yuppie generation but it doesn't torture them."[24] Barry Levinson, director of the film, supports this position through his own experience of the Vietnam conflict. While working at a television station in the late 1960s, Levinson claims he learned about Vietnam by watching daily footage come in over the CBS feed. Although, it is hard to discern what he learned since he claims that he didn't understand what the war was about.[25]

In addition to the emergence of a new generation of movie watchers, and a director who had no political or personal commitment to the Vietnam War, the third major factor structuring the context of this film was the role it provided for Robin Williams to demonstrate the breadth of his comic, manic improvisations. This is borne out not simply by the endless reviews of the film which focus almost exclusively on Williams's comic wit in the film, but by Jeffrey Katzenberg, chairman of Walt Disney Studios, who claimed that *Good Morning, Vietnam* appealed to him because it gave Williams a chance to enact the full range of his improvisations.[26]

What separates *Good Morning, Vietnam* from other Vietnam films is its unabashed refusal to engage the Vietnam conflict through the traditionally dominant tropes of homelessness, revenge, and patriotism. Instead *Good Morning, Vietnam* willfully expunges the discourses of history, politics, and ethics from its narrative to appeal to a generation of youth raised on the affective energies of high-tech rock, 1980s yuppie buffoonery, and a narcissistic assertion of whiteness as the singular referent for intelligence, manhood, and sensuality. In this instance, a Reagan-era inspired slapstick conception of the world functions to license a reactionary view of the war that substitutes spectacle for critical engagement. But there is more at work in this film than the specter of United States military aggression hiding behind the legacy of happy times that informed the propaganda machine of the Reagan and Bush administrations. It is precisely because of its facile dismissal of politics and history that *Good Morning, Vietnam* unwittingly lays bare, through its omissions and self-righteous moralism, the ideological components at work in its representational politics and its wider articulation of the broader discourse of Western colonialism.

Good Morning, Vietnam takes place in Saigon in 1965. The film is a partly fictionalized comedy drama about an army disc jockey, Adrian Cronauer, played by Robin Williams, who is sent to Vietnam to beef up the morale of the troops at a point when the military conflict is beginning its steep escalation. Cronauer arrives with two weapons in his personal arsenal. Deeply iconoclastic in style and wit, he combines his sense of irreverence with a manic wit that immediately breathes new life into the American Armed Forces radio station. Cronauer's short-lived sojourn in Saigon constitutes the heart of the film and parallels that period of the Vietnam conflict marked by increased protest against the war at home and the escalation of military aggression against the Vietnamese people.

Cronauer first appears in Saigon as an irrepressible motormouth who combines the style of the 1960s counterculture with the comic humor of an irreverent Bob Hope. Waiting to meet Cronauer at the Saigon military airport is Edward Garlick, an African-American soldier played by Forest Whitaker. Garlick is one of the few blacks to appear in the film, and is immediately cast as a shuffling, clumsy grunt whose only mission in life appears to be to laugh indiscriminately at all of Cronauer's jokes and to be his dutiful servant. Within the first minute of the film, Cronauer rattles off five jokes and insults Garlick by telling him to get a new name and learn how to drive a jeep. Removing any doubt about his role as the colonial master, Cronauer allows Garlick to serve as his "domestic" tour guide, and orders him to follow various Vietnamese women about whom he makes sexist remarks while being driven to the military base. In many ways, Cronauer's arrival and his drive to the base set up one of the primary structuring principles of the film. Not only does humor serve to position the identity of Vietnamese women as merely Western sexual commodities, it also links the objectification of the Vietnamese to the internal colonialism that Cronauer reproduces in his relationship with Garlick. But Cronauer's racism, sexism, and unquestioned belief in the moral righteousness of the war are neither framed nor tempered in the scorching realism of earlier Vietnam films. Instead they are couched in daily routines and actions that appear to simply provide fodder for the incessant delivery of one-liner jokes. Grounded in comic routines, Cronauer's reference to the Vietnamese as "little people" and his claim that the Vietnamese women have "behinds designed by a Jewish scientist in Switzerland" position the audience to indulge their own complicity with such racism and sexism without having to be morally responsible for it.

But because his actions are grounded in comedy, Cronauer still personifies all of the "sweetness and goodness" typical of Disney characters. Besieged on all fronts, he moves between the irreverence of Donald Duck and the gritty humanism of Dick Tracy. The first display of Cronauer's resistance appears early in the film over the choice of music to be aired on the army radio station. Confronted by his immediate army superiors, whose musical taste was shaped in the 1940s and is totally out of touch with the musical interests of the troops, Cronauer ditches the Mantovani/Percy Faith-style programming and unleashes a barrage of rock and roll music, filling space with his satirical skits. To the dismay of his commanding officers, Cronauer's radio show becomes a big hit among the troops and Cronauer himself begins to emerge as a popular, controversial figure in Saigon. By stressing the subversive qualities of rock and roll and popular culture, the film constructs one of the three major conflicts that will serve to define the Disney/Levinson view of the war.

In the first instance, the struggle over popular music suggests that the war was primarily a generational conflict between teenage soldiers reared on the rock and roll of James Brown, Martha and the Vandellas, and Wayne Fontana and the antiquated, middlebrow taste of an insensitive, out-of-touch military leadership. But the use of rock and roll music in this film also serves to transform the politics of the war into a stylized aesthetics that renders the presence of the American troops in terms fashioned out of a tourist magazine. With few exceptions, the voice-over music is played against images of American soldiers playing volleyball, lounging casually on boats, and walking in the streets of Saigon. One gets the impression that the soldiers in Vietnam are holiday visitors flooding the local economy with their good will and buying power or that they mostly hang around when on duty listening to the radio. As the champion of popular culture, Cronauer combines a touch of MTV hipness with a traditional dose of upbeat patriotism. Iconoclasm links in this case a depoliticized form of resistance with the highly political task of attempting to boost the morale of army soldiers intent on "exterminating the enemy."

The second major conflict that Cronauer faces concerns the military censorship of news. After a terrorist bombing of Jimmy Wha's, a popular Saigon nightclub, Cronauer defies his commanding officer and reports the incident in his radio news broadcast. What in fact might have emerged as an illuminating insight into the role of the media, government, and army in distorting the information given to the public about the war emerges instead as a narrative of personal anguish and self-pitying disillusionment. Suspended from his job, Cronauer offers neither critical insight into the broader reasons behind his dismissal nor any resistance to his fate. Instead, he soothes his wounded ego by hanging out in Saigon bars, fraternizing with Vietnamese nationals, and telling jokes to anyone who will listen. By privatizing the issue of media censorship, Disney/Levinson erase any reference to the historical conditions that necessitated such censorship in the first place and shift the terrain of anguish and suffering away from the massive devastation being wreaked on the Vietnamese people. In the end the audience is positioned to sympathize with the problems of a disgruntled middle-class white man who also happens to be actively complicitous with a military machine, according to John Pilger, "that dropped the greatest tonnage of bombs in the history of warfare [on Vietnam]—half a ton of explosives for every man, woman, and child" in that country.[27]

The third major conflict that structures the film concerns Cronauer's relationship with "otherness," that is, those Vietnamese men and women who inhabit the landscape outside of Cronauer's radio station. Soon after Cronauer arrives in Vietnam, he accosts and then follows a Vietnamese woman to an English class for Vietnamese civilians. He bribes the army officer teaching the class and takes it over in order to make contact with the woman he has followed. Using the class as the vehicle for a comedy routine, Cronauer attempts to teach English by focusing on the nuances of street-corner American slang. This is a significant movement in the film not merely because of its unabashed celebration of portraying Vietnamese women as simply objects of a white, American male's sexual desire, but also because it further denies the cultural specificity of the linguistic and historical setting that Cronauer inhabits. After all, why should Vietnamese nationals be learning English? And why should they be learning American slang taught by a white man talking as if he were a working-class black? But more important is the refusal to recognize that the Vietnamese have a rich culture and history that is at the heart of this scene. English has a long tradition of being the linguistic face of colonialism and that tradition is reinforced rather than disrupted in this film.

At the end of the class, Cronauer is confronted by the Vietnamese woman's brother, Tran, who tells him to keep away from his sister. Tran is quite clear about Cronauer's motives and describes him as simply another colonialist trying to buy his way into the culture. Cronauer ignores the comment and attempts to befriend him by taking him to a local nightclub. While at Jimmy Wha's club, Tran is confronted by some racist GIs who insult him and try to throw him out of the bar. Cronauer, once again, occupies center stage and in attempting to defend Tran initiates a full-fledged brawl. Amazingly, Tran then becomes his Vietnamese friend and sidekick. Functioning as a devoted guide, Tran saves Cronauer from Jimmy Wha's nightclub minutes before it is blown up by the Vietcong. He arranges for Cronauer to visit his village, and he eventually saves Cronauer's life by rescuing him from a Vietcong patrol that has blown up his jeep and is searching for him in the jungles outside of Saigon. What is startling about Tran's character is that near the end of *Good Morning, Vietnam* it is revealed that he is a Vietcong terrorist!

Tran's character is significant because it combines a dual reading and interpretation, one that is both racist and colonial. In the first instance, Tran embodies the racial stereotypes that have long permeated dominant forms of popular culture in the United States.[28] More specifically, Tran's character and his relationship to Cronauer exemplify the use of racial representations to designate "otherness" as the embodiment of infantilism, as a signifier for excluding those who do not belong to the national community. In this representation, Tran is denied any significant human presence. Instead he is presented through a dominant fantasy which reduces the Other to an object of pleasure and servility. Like Garlick, Tran is the Vietnamese version of Tonto serving his colonial master obediently and generously. Within such representations, Tran is denied any sense of agency that would problematize the American military presence in Vietnam. Within what Judith Butler calls this "racially saturated field of visibility,"[29] Tran becomes simply another "gook" who is both marginal and irrelevant to the viewer's understanding of the political and historical nature of the Vietnam War. Commenting on the use of such representations in American literature, Toni Morrison puts it well. "Cooperative or sullen," she writes, "they are Tontos all, whose role is to do everything possible to serve the Lone Ranger without disturbing his indulgent delusion that he is indeed alone."[30]

But Tran is doubly represented in this film. Not only is he presented as the Hollywood version of Tonto, he is also portrayed at the end of the film as a Vietcong terrorist. Shocked by the revelation that his trusted friend is in real life a member of the Vietnamese resistance, Cronauer searches Tran out and castigates him for betraying their friendship and trust. Embodying both the myth of the solitary hero and the righteous, puritanical American, Cronauer employs the language of humanism to highlight his own angst and to position Tran (and all Vietnamese resistance fighters) as a criminal and terrorist. Mobilizing all of the courtroom drama that was recently played out in the public press over the Los Angeles uprising, *Good Morning, Vietnam* presents criminality and lawlessness as a racial category. In this instance, Tran symbolizes all those "Others" who jeopardize American national unity and threaten Western culture and civility.

If Tran is the colonial Other, Tran's sister is nearly invisible except as an object of lust and desire. Though she refuses to date Cronauer, her identity is completely constructed within his patriarchal gaze. Her refusal is not expressed as a form of resistance to American imperialism or to the relentless assaults of Cronauer's sexism, but to the Vietnamese custom of civility. Tuan refuses to become romantically involved with Cronauer because her family and community frown on such behavior by Vietnamese women. When Cronauer is about to leave Saigon he meets with her and his class of students one last time. As a parting gesture, he engages in a game of American baseball with the students and appears forlorn that he could not consummate his romantic fantasies. Tuan also smiles, indicating that if it weren't for the war, they would be able to indulge their repressed passions. In this instance, Tuan is portrayed as a tragic character who has to repress her desires because of the inconvenience of the war. Tuan becomes nothing more than a stick figure, a Barbie doll who merely testifies to the frustration, heterosexuality, and virility of the lonely American hero. At the conclusion of the film, an extraordinary display of Disney sentimentality is made when Cronauer's English class thanks him for teaching them English and Tuan in turn thanks him for being so kind!

There are two related but important scenes that frame the conclusion of *Good Morning, Vietnam*. As Cronauer is being driven to the airfield, the camera focuses on the new recruits entering Saigon. On one level, this is an obvious comment on the increasing escalation of the war that took place in 1965. On another, less obvious level, it expresses the deeply racist nature of this film. Almost all of the recruits are white and middle-class. This is an amazing representation given that a disproportionate number of soldiers who fought in Vietnam were poor, high school drop-outs, African-American, and Latino. As Cronauer is about to catch his plane, he says to Garlick, his black aide, "Carry on, Montesquieu." True to the colonial character of the film, Garlick replies, "I like that, it makes me feel British."

Good Morning, Vietnam does more than produce a series of racial and colonial representations. It erases any sense of collective agency or responsibility and builds its narrative structure around the emotional and "heart-rending" experiences of the isolated, alienated American resister. Moreover, it redefines resistance in terms that are apolitical and ahistorical. Completely missing from this film is any indication that there was a massive antiwar movement or an enormous number of soldiers who opposed the war, as well as any indication of the nature of the colonial and racist policies that produced such resistance in the first place.

WORKING-CLASS WOMEN AND THE FAMILY IN DISNEY'S WORLD

Popular memory and the discourse of innocence in Disney's Touchstone films do not limit themselves to reasserting dominant versions of national identity, nor do they attempt to fashion such a discourse in isolation from other ideological considerations. Cultural identities are also produced and consumed through Disney's aggressive attempts, as David Morley and Kevin Robins put it, to "articulate the private and public spheres: to connect the family and the nation."[31] The pervasive symbol of ideological unification through which Disney defines its view of capitalism, gender, and national identity is the family. In this case, the white, nuclear, middle-class family becomes the ethical referent for linking consumerism, gender roles, motherhood, and class chivalry. It is around the family as the primary unit of stability, culture, ethics, and agency that Disney circulates in many of its films the articulating principle that links, say Morley and Robins, "individuals and their families to the centers of national life, offering the audience an image of itself and of the nation as a knowable community, a wider public world beyond the routines of a narrow existence."[32] Disney's attempt to structure issues of gender and class around family values is especially evident in one of its most financially lucrative films, *Pretty Woman* (1990).

Directed by Gary Marshall, *Pretty Woman*, on the one hand, is a contemporary rewrite of the Pygmalion and Cinderella classics. Innocence triumphs over adversity when the down-and-out, though not unvirtuous, working-class prostitute Vivian (played by Julia Roberts) steps into a dream world by meeting, seducing, saving, and then marrying the rich corporate raider Edward Lewis, played by Richard Gere. On another level, *Pretty Woman* signifies Disney's attempt to renegotiate the relationship between the new patriarchy (i.e., the sensitive man) and the modern "single woman" of the 1980s and 1990s with respect to the logic of the marketplace and traditional family values. In this attempt to renegotiate the relationship between patriarchal control and power and the agency of the "new" woman, Touchstone Films reveals its political strategy and ideological imperatives. That is, the company demonstrates its willingness to struggle over the terrain of popular culture. It does so by adjusting its ideological weapons to the shifting assumptions and practices that characterize the changing conceptions of work, consumption, and identity that men and women are experiencing in what might be termed a post-Fordist society.[33]

In general terms, the story evolves around the unprobable courtship of Edward and Vivian. Edward is a charming corporate thug, who buys companies, breaks them up, and then sells off the various parts for enormous profits. Vivian is a Disney version of the child-woman, who has left her family to find herself lost and desperate in the big city, reduced to selling her sexual knowledge on the street to keep herself alive. Both characters have fallen from grace in this Disney narrative, and both are given the status of the tragic hero and heroine. Edward's masculinity is embodied in a rapacious capitalist desire to control property, companies, and women. But it is not patriarchal desire that is subject to criticism in *Pretty Woman*. On the contrary, Edward's need to position Vivian as his "beck-and-call girl," ready to fulfill his every desire, is used as a cinematic device to give Vivian the opportunity to become an agent of her own sexual and consumer desires. Disney's version of patriarchy is used to expand the agency of women into the public sphere of the marketplace.

Edward's patriarchal obsessions are not the focus of criticism in *Pretty Woman*; it is the ruthlessness he employs in the buying and selling of companies. But in the innocent world of Disney such ruthlessness is presented not as a systematic feature of capitalism, but as a psychological problem resulting from the breakdown of traditional values in Edward's own family. In a revealing conversation with Vivian, Edward tells her that his father left his music-teacher mother for another woman. Along with his infidelity, Edward's father also made off with all of the family wealth. His mother died soon afterward, leaving Edward angry and unsettled over his father's destruction of the family.

Adding a theoretical twist to the idea that the marketplace can provide effective therapy, Edward exhibits a new Oedipal turn by destroying his father's company through a corporate buyout that he personally oversees. In this instance, Edward combines corporate greed and personal vengeance, adding a therapeutic advantage to the practice of corporate sleaze.

The cultural and material capital at work in *Pretty Woman*, which was written as a narrative of investment and return, celebrates Edward's willingness to invest in a woman who is also bereft of the regulating laws of the traditional family. Edward's "generosity" and business acumen gain for him the benefits of Vivian's sexual expertise, while simultaneously creating the conditions for Vivian's own sense of agency. In Disney's terms, the agency of women outside of the traditional family is reduced to the freedom to buy expensive clothing and to reinvent their identities within the logic and terms of white, middle-class cultural capital. As Hilary Radner has noted, Vivian's "transformation from prostitute to woman of privilege is effected solely through her ability to purchase and wear fashionable garments—to 'look good' in fashionable clothing. This is her most obvious skill, the necessary complement to her willing expertise in the bedroom."[34] Patriarchy in this instance becomes the vehicle through which Edward becomes a born-again capitalist, and Vivian redeems her identity through her consumer practices.[35] In the end, both Vivian and Edward throw off the psychological baggage incurred as the result of either the loss or the abandonment of the family and come together to reestablish the promise and viability of marriage and the middle-class, heterosexual family as a vehicle for upward mobility on the one hand and the moral redemption of the humanist, capitalist subject on the other. Of course, beneath the play of innocence redeemed in *Pretty Woman* lies the violent erasure of avarice and sexism that links capitalism, consumerism, and patriarchy in Disney's world.

In the final scene of *Pretty Woman*, Edward has his black chauffeur drive him to Vivian's apartment where he rescues her from an impending life of destitution and poverty. In one of the final cuts, the camera pans back to the street from Vivian's apartment and frames the black chauffeur standing next to a white stretch Cadillac. Like Garlick and so many other black characters in Disney films, he appears ecstatic to share in the emotional joy surrounding the merger of Edward's capital and Vivian's body. It is precisely this colonial signifier of whiteness, power, and degradation that reveals the racist ideology underlying *Pretty Woman*. This is a film for men whose desire for wealth can now be mediated by the "new woman," who, in Hilary Radner's words, will "bring [them] back to the fold of a capitalism regulated by the law of the family and patriarchal responsibility."[36] In this film, white men constitute the source of all authority; women provide sexual pleasures and the potential for new markets; and people of color and working-class people "dream" about the possibilities of upward mobility.

PEDAGOGIES OF POWER AND THE IMPERATIVE OF PEDAGOGY

Good Morning, Vietnam and *Pretty Woman* are exemplary cultural texts because they offer the potential for a critical reading of how the politics of innocence works to conceal the ideological principles used to legitimate a racist conception of global imperialism, a nostalgic sense of history, and a dominant assertion of family values. As popular culture texts, these films function through a series of discursive and ideological practices that are both pedagogical and political. As part of a larger cultural apparatus, they signify the importance of film as a central medium of popular culture, which must be addressed not simply as a pedagogical apparatus actively involved in diverse identity formations, but also for the crucial role it plays in the construction of national identities in the service of global expansion and colonialism. I am suggesting the need for social movements and cultural workers to redefine the parameters of the relationship between the political and the pedagogical and to recognize the need to produce alternative approaches to mass culture which would disrupt dominant attempts to mobilize popular memory that, according to Abigail Solomon-Godeau, enable "cultural institutions and cultural arbiters to present their histories as seamless, disinterested, and authoritative, and their hierarchies of value as universally valid, ecumenical, and effectively consensual."[37]

In recognizing that cultural texts such as *Good Morning, Vietnam* and *Pretty Woman* mobilize social and popular memories to legitimate particular versions of the past, it becomes imperative for progressive activists to expand their understanding of the sites where a pedagogy of power is used to produce particular narratives, representations, and stories about who is authorized to speak, under what conditions, and in whose interest. If we live in an age which borders on a crisis of forgetting, it is all the more imperative to expand the boundaries of the political to encompass not merely formerly marginalized cultural practices, but also a new politics of representation.[38] At the very least such a politics would require, as Roger Simon has pointed out,[39] a consideration of all those various pedagogical sites in which the past is being constructed as crucial locations of struggle. This suggests extending the meaning and practice of pedagogy far beyond the boundaries of schools. Furthermore, it suggests redefining how cultural politics can be understood beyond the often highly guarded boundaries of single-issue considerations and identity politics. This is both a call for a hybridized politics and the recognition that questions concerning the relationship between authority and power must address who has control over the conditions necessary for the production of knowledge. At stake here are questions of access, political economy, and a representational politics that lays bare its own practices in relation to the dominant relations of cultural, material, and social production.[40]

By erasing the political and ethical considerations that make history a site of struggle, Disney has produced a filmic version of popular culture through a pedagogy that rewrites history as inheritance and human agency as a condition for adapting to existing sites of injustice. Electronically mediated images, especially television and film, will represent one of the most potent arms of cultural hegemony in the twenty-first century. Constituted as a public sphere with an enormous global reach, the electronic media have a power that reinforces Stuart Hall's claim that there is no politics outside of representation. But if progressive cultural workers are to take such a politics seriously, they must use pedagogy as an articulating category to unravel how they might actively share in developing alternative conditions for giving people ownership over the control and production of knowledge and authority in the service of a radical democratic politics. The influential pedagogues of the twentieth century are not simply the hard-working teachers of the public school system; they are the hegemonic cultural agents who mediate the public cultures of advertising, radio talk shows, the malls, and the cinema complexes. It is in these representational domains, fashioned through powerful forms of address, that the intersection of unmet needs and the mundane desires of daily life are made concrete. Within these public cultures people both identify with and lose themselves differently in representations that bring them the promise of hope or, more likely, the swindle of fulfillment.

The challenge of a new cultural politics, one that takes popular and media culture seriously, is as much a pedagogical challenge as it is a political one. The issue for cultural workers is not merely to recognize the importance of cultural texts such as *Good Morning, Vietnam* and *Pretty Woman* in shaping social identities, but to address how representations are constructed and taken up through social memories that are taught, learned, mediated, and appropriated within particular institutional and discursive formations of power. Any social movement, regardless of how theoretically enlightened it may be, which ignores this issue runs the risk of reproducing a politics that is silent about its own pedagogical formation and thus unresponsive to how it silences or terrorizes in the name of a self-serving appeal to social justice. Central to the formation of a new cultural politics are both the need for a renewed interest in the relationship between material determinations and the arousal of dormant emancipatory memories and the construction of social movements that are as deeply pedagogical as they are political in their attempts to revitalize the institutional and ideological conditions necessary for diverse forms of political activism aimed at sustaining democratic public life.

3

Schools for Scandal: Whittling Away at Public Education

INTRODUCTION

It is no secret that in the Reagan/Bush era greed and selfishness became quite respectable. The last decade can be credited with the dubious honor of distinguishing itself by turning its back on the poor, on the rights of women, and on the civil rights gains of the three preceding decades. The United States has now moved into a time in which it is fashionable not only to blame the victims, but to actually scorn them. This is a time when to be a liberal appears as disreputable as it was to be a communist in the 1950s. Of course, ideologies don't stand still, nor do they simply dominate. They also arouse anger, challenges, and forms of resistance. But social antagonisms, even when organized around the most blatant violations of civil rights and human dignity, do not guarantee the emergence of social movements dedicated to democratic struggles. Nowhere is this more evident than around the issue of race and the politics of cultural difference.

In spite of the widening gap between the rich and the poor, the massive unemployment levels among white and, especially, black youths, and the increasing number of homeless on our nation's streets, there is little reason to believe that the growing tide of racial injustice will be stemmed at any time in the immediate future. Nor is there any indication that the issue of racism will be addressed by the Clinton administration as a central problem in American education. In fact, as the white working class sees its dream of moving up the social and economic ladder imperiled, it is increasingly coming to view affirmative action, school integration policies, and the changing nature of our national and cultural identity as threats to its own sense of security and possibility. Instead of embracing African Americans and other ethnic groups as allies in the struggle to dismantle the master narratives of Eurocentrism with the discourse of a multiracial and multicultural democracy, working-class whites have embraced a legacy of institutional and ideological racism that appears to have reached a dangerous threshold. One of the most ominous expressions of this new racism can be found in the collaborative efforts of business and government to commercialize the classrooms of the public schools, further reducing such schools to channeling colonies for the children of poor and minority parents. Moreover, there is a corresponding attempt by government officials and corporate interests to develop a schools-for-profit movement that would appeal to the legacy of nativism and racism that propels white flight away from public schools toward tracked, elite private schools. With this in mind, I want to examine the class and racist underpinnings of the ideology that has structured the school-business intersection, focusing more specifically on the recent endeavors of Whittle Communications and their promotion of Channel One and the Edison Project.

BUSINESS AND THE COMMERCIALIZATION OF THE CURRICULUM

Since the early 1980s, big business has attempted to play a vital role in redefining the purpose and meaning of public schooling. Rejecting a concern with issues of equity, racial justice, sexual equality, and cultural democracy, conservatives have reasserted the debate over making schools relevant to students' lives by reducing the curriculum to little more than job preparation. In part, this has meant educating the vast majority of students for a type of functional literacy in which they would be educated to read, write, and possess skills for specialized employment, while simultaneously being provided with a curriculum in which they would learn how to be efficient consumers. Within this educational scenario, schools would produce workers who could willingly perform the specialized tasks required by an economy facing a high level of increased competition from abroad.

The dual emphasis of training and consumption that characterized the early stage of the conservative reform movement is worth elaborating. In the first instance, conservatives and corporate executives redefined the meaning of "excellence," by which they usually meant that schools should offer a more rigorous science and math curriculum—a notion in keeping with the conservative idea that the mastery of techniques was equivalent to progress. In this discourse, terms such as "achievement," "excellence," "discipline," "values," and "performance" in practice meant a return to the authoritarian classroom where transmission, standardization, and control are the defining principles of the curriculum.

For the conservatives of the Reagan era, the education debate had little to do with fulfilling the American dream of social equality. Justice was beside the point for the new conservative reformers. Their major concern was in changing the modern international division of labor and developing the New World Order. Schools became important as producers of human capital. Supply-side economics ascribed the failure of the United States to maintain its lead in capital accumulation and world competition to a waning competitive environment produced in part by the failure of schools to promote competition and industrial training.

In the absence of secure markets at home and abroad, industry in the 1980s once again rediscovered education. Supply-side economics argued that government should get out of the way of entrepreneurial innovation by reducing taxes, thereby increasing business incentives to reinvest capital in modernizing production and expanding the output of consumer goods. On the ideological side, conservatives fully embraced the discourse of an older Taylorism and argued that schools could upgrade themselves by changing curricula and instituting new management systems that reflected corporate values, dominant social practices, and individualist goals. This approach spawned a growing connection between schools and the business community, which can be measured in the levels of capital investment in the public schools made over the last decade by the corporate sector. For example, business leaders in major cities organized "compacts" with school districts, in which the corporate sector provided money and expertise for the schools while simultaneously influencing curricula and school administration. In addition, corporations such as General Electric, Exxon, Kodak, IBM, and Adolph Coors donated large sums to upgrade the public schools. Their reasons for doing so were far from altruistic. The costs to American business for training entry-level employees exceeded $30 billion in 1990. Companies like American Express made it clear that their involvement in public education was based on what they termed enlightened self-interest, which translated into reducing the cost of training employees by shifting the financial costs to the public schools.

If the first emphasis of the corporate-inspired reform movement was on training, the second was on consumption. This has been clearly documented in Sheila Harty's *Hucksters in the Classroom*. Harty illustrates how big business attempted to influence school curricula through the free distribution and use of materials designed to fulfill its own corporate needs. For example, the McDonald's Corporation promoted its Nutrition Action Pack, in which each "Action Pack" provided a mimeo stencil for teachers to run off student handouts. On the bottom of each mimeo stencil was the McDonald's Golden Arches logo. Harty notes that Standard Brands published and distributed to thousands of schools its "Mr. Peanut's Guide to Ecology," in which the last page of the guide was illustrated with Planters Peanut products. In "Mr. Peanut's Guide to Physical Fitness," under the heading "To Teachers and Parents," we find: "Boys need to be physically fit so that they can compete in sports—and later can compete in society. Girls need to be physically fit because it makes them more attractive."[1] Clearly, more is being sold in this guidebook than the desire to consume; at issue here are also the construction of social identities, specific worldviews, and particular visions of how differences are constituted across gender, racial, and class lines. In recent years, the penetration of schools by corporate marketers has escalated rapidly. Motivated by the potential of a $250 billion youth market, corporations such as Sears, Roebuck and Co., Nike, and Pepsi-Cola are stepping up their efforts to commercialize the classroom. For example, Cover Concepts Marketing Services, Inc., distributed free over one million textbook covers to high school students in 1990. The textbook covers promoted such products as Nike shoes, Milky Way candy bars, and Fine apple juice. It has been reported that "ad space on these book cover billboards [ranged] from $25,000 for an inside flap to $49,000 for a front cover."[2]

SCHOOLS AS SITES OF CAPITAL ACCUMULATION

In light of the massive corporate intervention in schools, I want to argue that the relationship between business and schooling has dramatically changed in the last four years. During the first half of the 1980s, neoconservative and corporate interests were primarily concerned with reforming the curricula and pedagogies of public schools. A new spirit of entrepreneurship emerged during the Bush era that is not concerned simply with either training workers or producing a new generation of consumers. On the contrary, the new spirit of reform has expanded its sights and is increasingly intent on creating schools for profit. Schools have become a site of contestation and struggle not only over the construction of a new type of worker/consumer but also over the accumulation of capital itself. In one sense, this new entrepreneurial spirit has been largely taken up by the right wing of the Republican party, and has the financial backing of both conservative foundations and major corporate players such as Time-Warner, Philips Electronics, and others.[3] Of course, national advertisers are quick to recognize that since many public schools are strapped for resources, they are easy targets for commercial exploitation. An example of this type of disreputable venture can be found in attempts by a Minnesota broadcasting company to entice schools to accept free programming and $5000.00 worth of video equipment in exchange for the right to broadcast music and advertisements for 45 minutes before and after school, and during lunch. The radiocasts will not air in classrooms but in the schools' hallways, cafeterias, and lounges. In exchange for the equipment and programming, the participating schools receive up to 60 percent of the advertising revenue raised through local programming. Students would be asked to solicit and sell the local advertising. In this instance, the school gets free equipment, runs 130 minutes of radio programming, and solicits revenue by selling advertising time to local businesses. Scott Plum, the director of sales and marketing for Star Broadcasting, defends such a policy by claiming that, "with all their budget cuts, schools are obtaining resources more independently. . . . An average school with about 1,500 students could expect about $20,000 [in revenue] over the year. Schools really need the money."[4] Schools certainly need the money, but the fact of the matter is that corporate interests are, in part, responsible for their deficits. Corporations play a double role here. On the one hand, they aggressively support tax-cutting measures such as Proposition 13 in California and Proposition 2 1/2 in Massachusetts. On the other hand, they then offer the financially strapped schools "crumbs" that allow private business interests to turn the schools into market niches. Of course, if public schools were adequately funded in the first place such bribes wouldn't be necessary. At risk is both the traditionally civic, democratic function of public schooling and the very nature of how we define democratic community, critical citizenship, and the most basic premises of teaching and learning.

It is worth noting that during the Reagan and Bush administrations federal programs for funding social services and education were drastically cut. A downsizing of the manufacturing sector in urban areas and a tax revolt by middle-class whites resulted in a drop in property values and a massive reduction of revenue from the tax base. One consequence has been a funding crisis in many of the urban school districts serving poor and minority children. In light of this crisis, corporate money in the last few years has been pouring into public schools along with corporate perceptions about how schools should be organized, what should be taught, how teachers should teach, and how students should learn. Janice

Shamon points to this new level of corporate spending and its implication for public schools.

> In 1991, IBM and Exxon led with contributions of $24 million each. Not far behind was Ford with $22 million; General Electric kick[ed] in $17 million. In a *Fortune* poll of their industrial 500 and service 500 companies, 24 percent of the 301 respondents had donated more than $1 million; the average contribution was $344,000. . . . Corporate priorities and attitudes are changing how schools operate. With these changes come a very real alteration in the political culture of schools; changes in attitudes and perceptions among students and staff, changes which may well result in a redefinition of the mission of public education and of who merits membership in a school community. Public education is being privatized.[5]

This new intersection of business and schools can be seen in the rising levels of corporate philanthropy, in attempts by major corporations to escalate the commercialization of the classroom, and in the aggressive bids by big business to take over public school services. For example, Dunkin' Donuts, Pizza Hut, Dairy Queen, McDonald's, Taco Bell, and other fast-food chains are attempting to get a direct share of the school cafeteria market, peddling junk food to students at enormous profits. What has happened in this case is that the corporations have discovered that in addition to being "trained" as future consumers, students also offer big business a captive and lucrative market. The crudeness of the ideology that sometimes accompanies these efforts was recently echoed by Joseph Fenton, director of cooperative advertising at Donelley Marketing. He refers to the students his marketing efforts are targeting as consumers that must be reached "at their most formative point."[6]

Needless to say, the school cafeteria is not the only place where a new market can be etched for big business. The most daring campaign to turn schools into direct profit-making institutions has been waged by Chris Whittle, founder and chairman of Whittle Communications. Whittle's ideology represents the most advanced stage of the neoconservative assault on schools and is closely aligned ideologically with the reform efforts of the ideologues who served in the Bush administration. In fact, the interlocking economic and ideological interests shared by Whittle, Chester Finn, Jr., former Secretary of Education Lamar Alexander, and other White House advisors "[symbolize] the new alliances between business and government to exploit the educational system."[7] Since I believe that Whittle represents the most glaring and pernicious threat to public schooling, I will spend some time analyzing the ideology and implications of his reform efforts.

COMMODIFICATION AND RACISM IN WHITTLE'S VIEW OF SCHOOLING

Chris Whittle is the driving force behind two schools-for-profit ventures, Channel One and the more recent Edison Project. Capitalizing on federal cuts to the states and large reductions in city budgets, Whittle has moved quickly to take advantage of the increased reliance on private money by urban public schools. Underwritten by financial giants such as Time-Warner and the British publisher Associated Newspapers, Whittle has created Channel One in order to integrate the allure and dazzle of electronic information technology with the profit-making incentive of selling products to captive student audiences. Appealing to cash-hungry schools, Whittle provides each school with $50,000 in "free" electronic equipment, including VCRs, televisions, and satellite dishes, on the condition that the schools agree to broadcast a ten-minute program of current events and news material along with two minutes of commercials. In addition, each participating school must show Channel One on at least 90 to 95 percent of the days when the school is in session; schools are required to broadcast the program in its entirety to all students at a single time on television sets provided exclusively by Whittle; and each participating school is required to maintain records that Whittle Communications has the right to monitor in order to determine compliance with the contract.

The primary impetus for establishing Channel One is far from generous. While Benno C. Schmidt, Jr., Chester Finn, Jr., and others may push the boundaries of newspeak with their claim that Whittle's approach to educational reform will revolutionize teaching, usher in a new era in schooling, or "bring schools out of their cottage-industry resistance to new technology,"[8] the bottom line in this rhetoric appears to be about profits. According to *U.S. News & World Report*, commercial advertisers pay $157,000 per thirty-second "spot" on Channel One. By running four ads each day, and reaching a daily market estimated at over six million students, Whittle, claims *Marketing News*,[9] earns about $630,000 a day and a gross annual revenue of more than $100 million. Companies that have signed up to advertise on Channel One include Nike, Mars, Gillette, Proctor and Gamble, Pepsico, Quaker Oats, and Burger King. As of August 1992, Whittle has signed up over 8,000 schools for Channel One. The profits do not simply end up in Whittle's pocket. Whittle has hired such archconservatives as Chester Finn, Jr., to the tune of a million dollars spread over a three-year period.[10] He has hired the former president of Yale University Benno C. Schmidt, Jr., employed voucher and school-choice advocate John Chubb, and engaged in lucrative financial deals with former Secretary of Education, Lamar Alexander.[11] Outside of amassing huge salaries for the executive leadership at the helm of Whittle Communications, the most pressing pedagogical problem in this reform effort appears to be how to package the hard sell rather than how to promote the type of education that would inspire all students to learn how to think critically, make discriminating ethical judgments, and take seriously their responsibilities as critical citizens.

Whittle's entry into the public school market does more than simply trivialize learning by subordinating it to the dictates of commercial interests. In hard economic times, Channel One sells a watered down, if not dangerous, view of the student as primarily a "mind to meet a corporate demand,"[12] as one school principal remarks. Moreover, it opens up the curriculum to a set of standards that ignores fundamental questions of cultural difference, student experience, and history. That is, it presents a prepackaged set of materials to teachers, whose only option then is to work with the content of the shows. Central here is the issue of a politics of representation, particularly around issues of who speaks, for whom, and under what conditions.

While it is true that teachers and students can mediate the Channel One material in a variety of ways, the issue of what students learn is related not only to the content, form, and context of the shows, but also to what is missing from such programs. Two important issues intersect here with respect to the relationship between power and knowledge. First, given Whittle's monopoly on classroom television broadcasts, what opportunities will students have to view programs that raise serious social questions about the ethics of business (i.e., questions related to pollution, corruption, militarism for profit, etc.) or that adopt controversial positions at odds with the highly politicized stand of Whittle and his right-wing associates? A University of Michigan study, while failing to address these issues, did point out that the design and news format of the Whittle shows failed to keep the interest of most students. Moreover, the study indicated that students who watched Channel One scored on average 3.3 percent higher on a thirty-question test of current events than those students in schools without Channel One. The report called this gain so small as to be educationally unimportant.[13]

The results of the study may have less to do with the students' indifference to current events, as some commentators have claimed, than with an MTV format that trivializes important issues.[14] As David Norlin argues, "At its deepest, Whittle news is shallow. Typical episodes devote only 125 seconds to 7 news stories—18 seconds per story—while 4 ads rate 120 seconds. The MTV pace is meant to drive home a lot of message in a little time. Dialogue is fast-forwarded to 140 words per minute, twice as fast as normal. Whittle's clear purpose is to sell, not shed light."[15] A certain skepticism may be in order regarding whether Whittle's pedagogical goals include teaching students media literacy in order to give them the knowledge and tools necessary to understand and critically address how commercials and other programs reproduce certain values and views of the world.

The second serious issue concerns how knowledge and power come together in Whittle's pedagogical practice to promote a particular politics of representation. Given Whittle's emphasis on standardized, preselected programs, it appears that the Channel One approach weakens or undermines the possibilities for teachers to develop curriculum material that relates to the histories, voices, and experiences of the students they actually work with. Standardized news formats do not by any means address how to develop pedagogical practices that are context-specific and attempt to link what is learned in schools to the actual lives of the students themselves. In this case, those events that might allow students to locate themselves in history, become subjects rather than the objects of media literacy, and produce their own news programs are sacrificed to the dictates of a news format whose major purpose is to sell youth-oriented products and a materialistic way of life. Whittle and his associates seem well aware that financial insecurity on the part of schools provides the perfect opportunity to subordinate critical teaching and learning to the imperatives of boutique consumerism and brand-name loyalty.

Whittle Communications has not limited its reach to restructuring the context and content of public school curricula. Through an ambitious new program known as the Edison Project, Whittle plans to create as many as 1,000 for-profit schools in the coming years. According to the *Wall Street Journal*, "Initially, the plans call for 65 school 'campuses,' each with classes and services ranging from preschool through high school, enrolling an estimated 65,000 students by 1996. Edison's goal is to enroll one million students nationwide by 2003."[16] These schools will showcase Whittle's high-tech learning systems and serve as an additional outlet for advertisements. They will charge a tuition of $5,500 and cut costs through an increasing pedagogical use of automated learning, student performance of custodial chores, and a heavy reliance on school volunteers. Of course, such schools will not have to bear the "burden" of teacher unions, school boards, PTAs, or any other group that would inject the possibility for democratic governance into the school organization. If John Dewey envisioned laboratory schools as experiments in democracy, Whittle and his associates envision schools more like laboratories for reprivatizing public schools and educating students to uphold the virtues of individual competitiveness, free enterprise, and corporate loyalty. Within this discourse, the distinction between the business of schooling and schooling for business disappears.

At first, it appears that Whittle has simply utilized the most opportune approach in redefining both the terrain of public schooling and the private school sector. But if one takes a closer look, what Whittle is doing amounts to more than simply making profits in a variety of schooling sites. First, he is building up a sizable amount of capital by targeting those schools most strapped for financial aid. These are schools that are generally urban, segregated, and filled with the children of the working class, immigrants, and people of color. In the years ahead, these schools will grow more and more dependent on the support and priorities of the business community. The intrusion of business into such schools calls their very identity as public institutions into question; but it is precisely this blurring of boundaries between the public and the private that benefits Whittle's corporate ideology. Whittle's pedagogy and ideology of commercialization will not impact seriously on middle- and upper-class schools. But it will impede the possibilities for creative teaching, organizing, and learning for the poor and the marginalized. In fact, if the Edison Project gets off the ground, Whittle will further impoverish these schools by arguing for a voucher plan that would cream off the best students while reinforcing white flight to private schools that cater to a middle-class constituency. Whittle will further contribute to the class-based and racist tracking that so violently undermines a decent education for children of value who occupy the economic and racial margins of this society.

Second, Whittle's scheme of developing a pedagogy of commercialization for the poor, on the one hand, and high-tech, abundantly financed private schools for the middle class, on the other, will reinforce a central goal of the Reagan and Bush administrations. That is, it will tailor the organization of public and private schooling to the shifting demographics of race, class, and age and in doing so will pander to interests of mostly white, suburban, middle-class, older Americans while simultaneously reproducing a highly segregated, two-tier system of schooling. This is not to suggest that for-profit schools willfully promote the legacy of white supremacy, racism, and nativism that has always dislodged the call for privatization from the language of equity. But it is precisely because of this legacy that serious questions have to be raised regarding why Chris Whittle, Chester Finn, Jr., and John Chubb say so little about the deeply rooted connections between the dilemmas of American schooling and the broader issues of race, cultural difference, urban decay, and poverty facing American society.

After all, if educational reformers are serious about dealing with the interrelated issues of providing jobs, health care, food, and housing for

America's children, 25 percent of whom live in poverty, it appears that more capital will be required for financing state and local governments. But this suggests, in part, providing tax increments to finance education and other public services, something that corporations have lobbied against for years[17]. Similarly, any viable educational reform movement would also have to address the gross disparities between the rich and the poor, which have grown even wider in the last decade, with the "richest one percent of Americans . . . owning more assets than 90 percent of the American people combined."[18] In addition, the glaring disparities of class and racial inequality are etched into the very fabric of schooling and cannot be ignored either by facile appeals to choice or by a crass celebration of profit as the primary motive for school reform. Educational reform warrants more than appeals to glitzy technology and the commercialization of curricula; it needs a public discourse that makes an ethical, financial, and political investment in creating schools that educate all students to govern rather than be governed.

TOWARD A POLITICS OF IDENTITY AND DEMOCRATIC SOLIDARITY

In order to more fully understand the ideological battle being waged against schools by conservatives such as Chris Whittle and others, it is important to connect such work to the broader conservative attack on multiculturalism, the arts, civil rights legislation, and the democratization of the academic canon.[19] In effect, the Right has attempted to respond to new social divisions, movements, and the mobilizing potential of a radical multiculturalism by either obliterating or reincorporating those worldviews that challenge its most fundamental hegemonic assumptions.

With the rise of new ethnicities, the proliferation of global and cultural identities, and the rewriting of the academic canon within the discourses of hybridity and heterogeneity, conservatives feel besieged.[20] Lacking the courage to rework dominant traditions in light of a changing present and future, conservatives continue to develop "imaginary unities" ("common culture," "national identity," etc.) aimed at creating rigid cultural boundaries that serve to seize upon fear and cultural racism. Theorists such as Stuart Hall, Paul Gilroy, and others expand this theme and argue that conservatives utilize a two-pronged attack against difference. In the first instance, the Right promises what Jonathan Rutherford calls "strong defenses and well-policed frontiers against the transgressive threat and displacements of difference. Even as it claims the universal nature of its constituent identities, its struggle to maintain the cultural, sexual and racial dichotomies of Self and Other make and reproduce social formations of domination and inequality."[21] Rutherford adds an insightful twist to the second strategy used by conservatives to control and displace cultural differences. In this case, difference is translated into a commodity relation and "otherness is sought after for its exchange value, its exoticism and the pleasures, thrills and adventures it can offer. The power relation is closer to tourism than imperialism, an expropriation of meaning rather than materials."[22] In both cases, conservatives attempt to depoliticize difference by inserting it in a power-neutral discourse. Whether the appeal is to an imaginary unity allegedly free of ideological interests or to a commodity designed to promote pleasure and consumption, difference is delegitimated as a terrain of political struggle and contestation. The deadly paradox in the conservative offensive is constructed around a politics of difference that attempts to depoliticize politics while simultaneously politicizing culture. Difference in the first instance is assigned to either the realm of the aesthetic or to a harmonizing discourse of cultural diversity that, as Homi Bhabha points out, serves to "locate cultures in a universal time-frame that acknowledges their various historical and social contexts only eventually to transcend them and render them transparent."[23] Critics such as Paul Gilroy and Chandra Mohanty have deepened and extended this critique by arguing that cultural diversity, as opposed to the more power-sensitive discourse of cultural difference, serves to contain issues of identity, culture, and agency within the harmonizing discourse of consensus, common culture, and national unity.[24]

DIFFERENCE, ETHICS, AND REPRESENTATION

Within the last decade, the new politics of cultural difference has presented an argument for recognizing that the issue of cultural and political identity needs to be rethought rather than abandoned; it also makes the related issues of difference and identity central to the discourse of democracy, politics, and agency. In doing so, it offers educators a new language for retheorizing how cultural identities are constantly being reworked and transformed within differences negotiated through the play of history, memory, language, and power. It also points to how the discourse of difference can be used to rewrite the social contract between groups in ways that deepen and extend the potential for a democratic community. Central to the new politics of cultural difference is the need for cultural workers and educators to develop a new vocabulary that makes the relationship between unity and difference a political project, one that promotes contemporary alliances among oppositional groups. In more general terms, the central question at stake here is, how can the politics of identity and difference be expanded so as to promote, as Kobena Mercer puts it, forms of "democratic representation and participation that would be responsive to the diversity of social identities active in the contemporary polity"?[25]

Theorists such as Hazel Carby, Chantal Mouffe, and Jeffrey Weeks argue that the answer rests, in part, in the creation of a set of principles based on the acceptance of and necessity for a political community that makes diversity central to the meaning of democracy. According to Carby, this means that theories of difference must be concerned not only with the representation of identities, but must also address crucial issues regarding relations of power. It is not enough merely to read the texts of the "Other." In fact, as Carby argues, the desire for knowing the Other "cannot replace the desire to challenge existing frameworks of segregation." Put more bluntly, she asks, "Have we, as a society, successfully eliminated the need for achieving integration through political agitation for civil rights and opted instead for knowing each other through cultural texts?"[26] This suggests that educators and other cultural workers need to develop a concept of critical citizenship informed by a set of values that embraces the pluralization of democratic rights, entitlements, and obligations as part of the wider discourse of struggle, agency, and ethics. Without imitating an all-embracing humanism, progressives need to acknowledge the shifting nature of identity, while not eliminating the issue of human agency; at the same time, cultural workers and other educators need to expand the basis for dialogue and community without erasing a politics of difference. As Jeffrey Weeks has written, "We may not be able to find, indeed we should not seek, a single way of life that would satisfy us all. That does not mean we cannot agree on common political ends: the construction of what can best be described as a 'community of communities,' to achieve a maximum political unity without denying difference."[27]

The intersection of difference and identity is a marker not only for one's sense of location, a shifting narrative of identifications that provides a conception of individuality, but also a dialogic process in which the issue of self-representation is constituted in our relationship with others. Hence, as Stuart Hall points out, "The critical thing about identity is that it is partly the relationship between you and the Other. Only when there is an Other can you know who you are. . . . And there is no identity . . . without the dialogic relationship to the Other. The Other is not outside, but also inside the Self, the identity. So identity is a process, identity is split. Identity is not a fixed point but an ambivalent point. Identity is also the relationship of the Other to oneself."[28]

Homi Bhabha rightfully argues that the issues of hybridity and cultural translation open up a "third space" where it becomes possible to challenge the modernist construction of history, progress, the myth of the unified nation, and ethnocentrism which lies at the heart of Western civil societies. Hybridity does not merely suggest that all forms of culture are related, it also challenges the great structuring principles of modernism by accentuating the emergence of new global subjects, diasporic communities, and border identities. Bhabha's third space provides a new theoretical marker which "enables other positions to emerge. This third space displaces the histories that constitute it, and sets up new structures of authority, new political initiatives, which are inadequately understood through received wisdom. . . . This process of cultural hybridity gives rise to something different, something new and unrecognizable, a new area of negotiation of meaning and representation."[29] Bhabha's notions of hybridity and cultural translation do more than authenticate different histories; they offer the promise of exposing and interrogating the colonial face of modernity. At the same time they call forth new sites of political mediation, sites which displace dominant terms of negotiation and, in doing so, rewrite the possibility for creating critical public spheres, such as schools and other social arenas where politics and pedagogy unite to "open up an interaction or a dialogism of the powerful and the powerless, and it is this site which enables another distribution of meaning, a change in the ratio of powers, because neither of the two settled moments prior to this hybrid site are imported into it in their previous form."[30]

CONCLUSION

One important challenge facing critical educators is to address the politics of identity in pedagogical terms that rewrite the discourses of commercialism and separatism. This means rethinking the relationship among identity, culture, and difference so as to address how, for example, race, class, and gender can be analyzed in their historical context and specific interrelationships. Identity politics offers a cautionary note against the pitfalls of essentialism by addressing the historical and social conditions that produce and disrupt a variety of cultural identities. At issue here is both the pedagogical process of cultural memory and a politics of cultural resistance that refuses essentialism. In the first instance, cultural workers must break with the institutional and internalized racism of the current conjuncture by focusing on the real victories that have emerged from what Stuart Hall has called the "voicing of the margins."[31] Such victories include the production of new identities, the appearance of new subjects, and the pluralization of critical public spaces in the arts, schools, media, and various other cultural sites. These new subjects, spaces, and movements, with their hybridized languages and cultural practices need to be addressed in order to, as Mercer has written, "extend the conversation about power and ideology in particular regimes of representation."[32] The forms of cultural criticism that have emerged from these spaces must be employed to aggressively fight what Hall calls "the current resistance to cultural difference, the attempt to restore the canon of Western civilization, the assault, direct and indirect, on multiculturalism, the return of the grand narratives of history, language, and literature (the three great supporting pillars of national identity and national culture), the defense of ethnic absolutism, and the cultural racism"[33] that continue to surface as standard policy in the Clinton era.

Secondly, if issues of difference and identity are not to fall prey to the language of fashion and essentialism, it is crucial for cultural workers to grasp the dialogical relations and hybridized forms in which identities are represented and represent themselves. Identities are not simply one more hot commodity of the post-Fordist 90's. Essentialism as it is expressed in the current fascination with "otherness" is purchased at the price of repressing those complex representations, doubts, transgressions, and ambiguities that, for example, challenge identities and experiences as singularly "black," "gay," "working-class," "feminist," and "other." The rejection of essentialism in identity politics, in part, suggests not simply a more critical discourse about representing identities in shifting, hybridized terms, but also a recognition that identities of difference, in Homi Bhabha's words, are both "conceptual categories for understanding the workings of the hierarchy of power" and "sites of political discrimination, cultural contestation, social disjunction, and 'subaltern' solidarity that have been crucial in forming the historic memories and psychic identities of minority communities."[34] Identities, in this context, must be seen as the effect of social struggles between different communities over issues of representation, the distribution of material resources, and the practice of social justice.

Identity politics suggests that educators need to be attentive to the necessity of developing a pedagogy of place and struggle. In part, such a pedagogy refuses the pre-packaged curricula of Whittle and company, teaching that denies the cultural resources of different students, and the cynicism that emerges when teachers are asked to deskill themselves. A pedagogy of place is not only oppositional to the Whittle emphasis on standardization and the elimination of difference, but is always attentive to what Lemuel Johnson calls the "density of specification,"[35] that is, those particular histories, experiences, languages, and cultural memories which offer the conditions for an insurgent subjectivity. Similarly, a pedagogy of place points to the need for cultural workers to reinvent and reconstruct new spaces for engaging critical pedagogy as an ever-becoming relation of theory and practice. In this instance, the relationship between theory and practice must focus not simply on the pedagogy of identity formation, but also on addressing how structures of inequality and injustice can be understood and transformed. Central to such a position is creating a discourse of agency, one which recognizes that the problem is not the geography of multiple subject positions that students and others inhabit, but how they actually negotiate them within a geography of desire, affect, and rationality.

In addition, a radical notion of identity politics points to the necessity for educators to become more self-conscious and reflective about their own cultural and political locations. That is, teachers and cultural workers must make clear the power, limits, partiality, and indeterminacy of the sites which inscribe and enable their sense of place, identity, and the possibilities for action. What is called for, in this case, is a pedagogy that prompts educators to turn the tools of dialogue and self-criticism upon their own work. Such a pedagogy suggests that critical educators take a stand without standing still. That is, such intellectuals need to challenge both educational practices and social relations that promote certain forms of material and symbolic knowledge, and they must also be deeply attentive to how their own authority can be made problematic in the service of a radical cultural politics. Pedagogically, this means that the authority they legitimate in the classroom must become both an object of autocritique and, as R. Radhakrishnan suggests, a critical referent for expressing a more "fundamental dispute with authority itself."[36] In addition, critical intellectuals must move beyond recognizing the partiality of their own narratives so as to address more concretely the ethical and political consequences of the social relations and cultural practices generated by the forms of authority used in the classroom. In this way, educators can take a stand while simultaneously refusing either a cynical relativism or doctrinaire politics.

The pedagogy advocated here suggests that educators and cultural workers must move within multiple discourses. Critical educators have to become border crossers, allowing the focus of their analysis to shift, move, circle back on itself, and push against its own language so as to extend and deepen its implications for critical pedagogy while tracing out a recognizable image of the complexity that informs its underlying project. In part, this is a pedagogy that rejects all essentialist renderings of identity for one that is more fluid, contingent, and open to chance.

It is important for educators to unlearn, within different degrees of power and oppression, the multiple forms of domination with which they might be complicit, it is also crucial to make questions of a substantive democracy central to the emancipatory project that informs their struggles. This means developing a politics that reasserts the primacy of the social, incorporates multiple struggles, builds alliances, and recaptures the concept of solidarity as a central element of a pedagogy and politics of hope and possibility. More specifically, this suggests a number of practices. First, cultural workers need to examine the issue of cultural production and its relationship to texts, economies, institutions, audiences, and communities and how these social forms and the practices that inform them can be understood within and across the different circuits of power that characterize the wider society. In part, this can be done by focusing on pedagogy as an articulatory concept that provides a discourse of unity, one in which differences are not erased but linked within a set of unifying principles. Second, critical educators need to develop a new understanding of how teachers and other cultural workers can produce new cultural zones and public spheres, engage in new forms of cultural production, and address the challenges provided by multiple audiences. Once again, such a task suggests the need for critical educators to offer a new vision and space for rewriting not only the relationship between culture and power, identity and pedagogy, but also between cultural work and the project of democratic renewal. In what follows, I want to spell out these issues in more detail.

Central to the notion of critical pedagogy is the need to rewrite the dynamics of cultural and pedagogical production as part of a broader vision that extends the principles and practices of human dignity, liberty, and social justice. In this view, the task of pedagogy is to deepen diverse democratic struggles which extend the ideological and material possibilities for self and collective determination across a broad range of economic, social, and political spheres. In part, this means taking up pedagogy as a form of cultural politics that addresses how different identities and experience get produced, and how they come to function in the broader community. At its best, critical pedagogy would establish the conditions to refigure a variety of human experiences within a discourse where diverse political views, sexual orientations, races, ethnicities, and cultural differences can mutually coexist amid social relations that support free expression and uninhibited debate. In this case, critical pedagogy is inseparable from cultural democracy. On one level, this means deepening the political aspects of the pedagogical by providing equal access for cultural workers to the educational and cultural institutions that organize daily life; on another level, it means making the pedagogical more political by reconstructing the very concept of pedagogy as a social practice that generates new knowledge, opens up contradictions, and challenges all hierarchical structures of power that demand reverence at the expense of dialogue and debate.

The concept of cultural worker expands the meaning of pedagogy without romanticizing either the risk taking nature of such work or the marginal locations from which such work is often attempted. At the same time the practical orientation of such work refuses to be defined outside of a historical and theoretical context.

The concept of cultural worker in its more narrow definition has generally been understood to refer to artists, writers, and media producers. Critical educators need to further develop the theoretical groundwork for extending the range of people associated with this term to those working in professions including law, social work, architecture, medicine, theology, education, and literature.[37] By expanding the concept of cultural work and practice to include issues related to public philanthropy, media reception, town meetings, and popular education, critical educators can make a vital contribution to rewriting the cartography of innovation and struggle that such work involves. And in doing so teachers and cultural workers can extend those spaces/locations and potential alliances from which the production of knowledge can be interrogated and reconstructed within the primacy of political and pedagogical considerations.

The pedagogical dimension of cultural work refers to the process of creating symbolic representations and the practices within which they are engaged. This includes a particular concern with the analysis of textual, aural, and visual representations, and how such representations are organized and regulated within particular institutional arrangements. It also addresses how various people engage such representations in the practice of comprehension and signification. As a cultural practice, pedagogy both contests and refigures the construction, presentation, and engagement of various forms of images, text, talk, and action which result in the production of meaning, through which students construct their individual and collective futures. Pedagogy in this sense combines the language of self and social criticism with the need for a project of possibility.[38]

Crucial to critical pedagogy is the recognition that the political dimension of cultural work reveals that the symbolic presentations which take place in various spheres of cultural production in society manifest contested and unequal power relations rooted in discursive and nondiscursive social forms. As a form of cultural production, pedagogy is implicated in the construction and organization of knowledge, desires, values, and social practices. It also serves to contest dominant forms of symbolic production. Cultural work, in this sense, informs a project whose intent is to mobilize knowledge and desires that may lead to significantly minimizing the degree of oppression in people's lives. What is at stake is a political imaginary which extends the possibilities for creating new public spheres and alliances in which the principles of equality, liberty, and justice become the primary organizing principles not only for structuring relationships between the self and others, but also for creating new social movements.

As I've mentioned previously, critical educators also need to develop a conception of pedagogical voice whose aim is not merely to uncover identities of otherness, as if they were self-contained, packaged, and ready to be unwrapped and named; on the contrary, a critical pedagogy demands naming and asserting differences that matter within rather than outside relations of power. Differences in this instance can be analyzed through the complex traces of identity that mark dominant and subordinate groups by providing students with the opportunities to examine critically how the relationship between the self and Other is written and reworked within the shifting narratives of the past, present, and future. By making difference and identity central to the spirit and experience of democratic learning, critical educators could take the offensive in the current debates on multicultural education by pointing to intolerance and bigotry, not cultural differences, as the enemy of democracy.

Educators and other cultural workers need to offer new theoretical elements for rethinking how to create multiple public cultures; such cultures need to be seen as critical spaces that offer the opportunity for diverse groups to engage in dialogue and exchange as part of a broader effort to make and remake their identities through an attempt to identify with the suffering, actions, thoughts, and feelings of others. But there is more at stake here than simply developing an empathy for difference or an appreciation of the pleasure that can be produced in the discourse and relations of difference; there is also the need "to reveal the structure of power relations at work in the racialization of our social order."[39] In order to challenge and transform the institutional basis of inequality and exploitation.

To return to my analysis of Whittle, I want to reiterate that a radical, as opposed to a commercialized, educational reform movement would be grounded in a vision of schooling that strongly endorses the imperatives of reconstructing a multiracial and multicultural democracy rather than filling the heads of students with the ephemeral desires of consumerism and the overly individualized language of the marketplace. As Jonathan Kozol has clearly demonstrated in *Savage Inequalities*, educational reformers need to challenge the deep divisions of race and class that are tearing this society apart and destroying its system of schooling, one which is increasingly segregated and unequal. These problems are not going to be solved by reprivatizing public schools, injecting commercials into school curricula, or turning schools into sites for capital accumulation. Whittle and his cronies don't have a reform agenda for addressing the ills of America's schools, they have a slick MTV advertisement for elevating greed to the status of a pedagogical virtue.

4

White Utopias and Nightmare Realities: Film and the New Cultural Racism

> For, if the global postmodern represents an ambiguous opening to difference and to the margins and makes a certain kind of decentering of the Western narrative a likely possibility, it is matched, from the very heartland of cultural politics, by the backlash: the aggressive resistance to difference; the attempt to restore the canon of Western civilization; the assault, direct and indirect, on multiculturalism; the return to grand narratives of history, language, and literature (the three great supporting pillars of national identity and national culture); the defense of ethnic absolutism, of a cultural racism that has marked the Thatcher and the Reagan/[Bush] eras; and the new xenophobias that are about to overwhelm fortress Europe.
>
> —Stuart Hall, "What Is This 'Black' in Black Popular Culture?"

UNSETTLING DIFFERENCES

As old borders and zones of cultural difference become more porous or eventually collapse, questions of culture increasingly become interlaced with the issues of power, representation, and identity. Dominant cultural traditions once self-confidently secure in the modernist discourse of progress, universalism, and objectivism are now interrogated as ideological beachheads used to police and contain subordinate groups, oppositional discourses, and dissenting social movements. Struggles over the academic canon, the conflict over multiculturalism, and the battle for either extending or containing the rights of new social groups dominate the current political and ideological landscape.[1] What is at stake in these struggles far exceeds the particular interests that structure any one of them or the specific terrains on which they are subject to debate, whether they be the academy, the arts, schools, or other spheres of public life. Underlying the proliferation of these diverse and various battles is a deeper conflict over the relationship between democracy and culture, on the one hand, and identity and the politics of representation, on the other.

Central to this debate is an attempt to articulate the relationship among identity, culture, and democracy in a new way. For the Left, this has generally meant launching an assault on monumentalist views of Western culture, a one-dimensional Eurocentric academic canon, the autonomous subject as the sovereign source of truth, and forms of high culture which maintain sexist, racist, homophobic, and class-specific relations of domination. More specifically, the challenges raised by feminism, postmodernism, and postcolonialism have contributed to a redefinition of cultural politics that addresses representational practices in terms that analyze not only their discursive power to construct common sense, textual authority, and particular social and racial formations, but also what Tony Bennett calls the "institutional conditions which regulate different fields of culture."[2] While many of the implications of such a cultural politics are still unclear, it has at the very least rendered visible, as Rita Felski points out, a number of important political/cultural projects. These include:

> the proliferation of information technologies and the gradual shift towards a postindustrial (although not postcapitalist) society, the declining authority of liberalism and Marxism as symptomatic of an increasing skepticism towards metanarratives, the reemergence of feminism and other social movements which have foregrounded difference and exposed the patriarchal, heterosexist, and ethnocentric nature of dominant Western ideals, an expanding aestheticization of everyday life through the mass dissemination of signs and images and a simultaneous questioning of the art/life opposition inherent in high modernism, a shift in philosophical and social theory towards linguistic paradigms accompanied by a sustained critique of foundationalist thought.[3]

The central challenge for educators and other cultural workers attempting to address these problems is to redefine the relationship between culture and politics in order to deepen and extend the basis for transformative and emancipatory practice. As part of such a challenge, the political side of culture must be given primacy as an act of resistance and transformation by addressing issues of difference, identity, and textuality within rather than outside of the problematics of power, agency, and history. The urgent issue here is to link the politics of culture to the practice of a substantive democracy.[4] Stuart Hall and David Held foreground the importance of this task by arguing that any radical politics of representation and struggle must be situated within what they call "a contemporary politics of citizenship."[5]

The value of such a politics is that it makes the complicated issue of difference fundamental to addressing the discourse of substantive citizenship; moreover, it favors looking at the conflict over relations of power, identity, and culture as central to a broader effort to advance the critical imperatives of a democratic society. Essential to such a struggle is rethinking and rewriting difference in relation to wider questions of membership, community, and social responsibility.

> A contemporary "politics of citizenship" must take into account the role which the social movements have played in expanding the claims to rights and entitlements to new areas. [This means addressing] questions of membership posed by feminism, the black and ethnic movements, ecology and vulnerable minorities like children. But it must also come to terms with the problems posed by "difference" in a deeper sense: for example, the diverse communities to which we belong, the complex interplay of identity and identification in modern society, and the differentiated ways in which people now participate in social life. The diversity of arenas in which citizenship is being claimed and contested today is essential to any modern conception of it because it is inscribed in the very logic of modern society itself.[6]

Identity politics since the 1960s has played a significant role in refiguring a variety of human experiences within a discourse in which diverse political views, sexual orientations, races, ethnicities, and cultural differences are taken up in the struggle to construct counternarratives and create new critical spaces and social practices. Yet the history of identity politics is not one that has moved unproblematically from resistance to a broader politics of democratic struggle. While identity politics was central to challenging the cultural homogeneity of the 1950s and providing spaces for marginal groups to assert the legacy and importance of their diverse voices and experiences, it often failed to move beyond a notion of difference structured in polarizing binarisms and an uncritical appeal to a discourse of authenticity. Identity politics enabled many formerly silenced and displaced groups to emerge from the margins of power and dominant culture to reassert and reclaim suppressed identities and experiences; but in doing so, these groups often substituted one master narrative for another, invoked a politics of separatism, and suppressed differences within their own "liberatory" narratives. Ellen Willis provides a severe but insightful critique of the theoretical and political dead end in which identity politics found itself in the 1970s and 1980s, and of the legacy she believes must be challenged in the 1990s.

> The appeal of "identity politics" is that it arises from a radical insight—that domination is systematically structured into the relations between social groups. The problem is that [identity politics] gives rise to a logic that chokes off radicalism and ends up by supporting domination. If the present obsession with group identity as the basis of politics is hard to imagine, much less build, a broad-based radical collectivity, it has even more tellingly stood in the way of a principled commitment to the freedom and happiness of individuals, without which no genuine radicalism is possible.[7]

Despite the moralism, anti-intellectualism, and suspect romanticization of authentic experience associated with issues of identity politics, these issues have begun to occupy the center of academic and popular debates around concerns regarding culture, difference, and democratic renewal. Moreover, identity politics is no longer simply a one-dimensional, discursive feature of left-wing theory and practice. At the same time, the radical possibilities associated with the link between democracy and the politics of cultural difference have not been lost on the New Right in the United States. In what has turned into a cultural blitz, the New Right of the Reagan/Bush era has continuously chipped away at the legal, institutional, and ideological spheres necessary to the existence of a democratic society. During the last decade, conservatives have rolled back civil rights legislation, waged antipornography campaigns against the arts in order to eliminate public funding for "politically offensive" groups, and attempted to replace state provision and public service with privatization programs designed to expand the power of capital, individual competitiveness, and corporate freedom.[8] One result has been the savaging of funds for public schools, health care programs, and an overall assault on the most basic presumptions of democratic life.[9]

Central to the new conservative offensive has been a renewed interest in addressing the radical politics that informs recent developments in the emerging discourses on culture and democracy. In particular, the New Right has focused on postmodernist, feminist, postcolonialist, and other minority discourses that have raised serious questions regarding how particular forms of authority are secured through the organization of the curriculum at all levels of schooling. The radical call to reclaim the legacy of substantive democracy by reappropriating the language of equality, justice, and cultural difference has not been lost on conservative ideologues and public intellectuals. For example, Samuel Lipman, writing in the *New Criterion*, argues that "culture and democracy cannot co-exist, for democracy by its nature represents the many, and culture, by its nature is created by the few. What the many cannot immediately comprehend, they destroy. . . . What is necessary are definitions of culture and democracy based . . . less on inclusions and more on exclusions, less on finding similarities between conflicting realities, concepts, and goals and more on recognizing the differences between them."[10]

Lipman is not alone in viewing the extension of democratic ideology and political representation as a serious threat to dominant configurations of power and control. Conservative columnist Patrick Buchanan openly embraces an authoritarian populism which views cultural democracy as a threat to the "American way of life." What is interesting for our purposes is the way in which Buchanan embraces the language of difference. For Buchanan, the reality of cultural difference, with its plurality of languages, experiences, and histories, poses a serious threat to both national unity and what he defends as Judeo-Christian values. According to Buchanan, calls for expanding the existing limits of political representation and self-determination are fine as long as they allow Americans to "take back" their country. In this conservative discourse, difference becomes a signifier for racial exclusivity, segregation, or, in Buchanan's language, "self-determination." For Buchanan, public life in the United States has deteriorated since 1965 because "a flood tide of immigration has rolled in from the Third World, legal and illegal, as our institutions of assimilation . . . disintegrated." Rewriting the discourse of nativism, Buchanan asks, "Who speaks for the Euro-Americans? Is it not time to take America back?"[11]

Similarly, right-wing whites in America now echo a view of difference not as a marker for racial superiority but as a signifier for cultural containment, homogeneity, and social and structural inequality. The appeal is no longer to racial supremacy but to cultural uniformity parading under the politics of nationalism and patriotism. In this case, difference is removed from the language of biologism and firmly established as a cultural construct only to be reworked within a hegemonic project that connects race and nation against the elimination of structural and cultural inequality. In the same spirit of displaying difference in order to displace it within a hegemonic project of national unity, Frank Kermode, writing in the *New York Times*, dismisses some of the more articulate advocates of a progressive politics of difference as "a noisy crowd of antihomophobes, antiracists and antiwhites."[12] This is a remarkable statement that conjures up the specter of race as an ideological signpost for an assault on whites. Race in this context is invoked not to eliminate differences but to preserve them within self-contained cultural and social borders that cannot be crossed and preclude forging new identities within new spaces or spheres of cultural difference. Of course, the Los Angeles uprising at the end of April 1992 not only ruptures the legitimacy of the new racial politics of containment, it also reveals how liberal and conservative discourses become complicitous with the underlying conditions that created the uprising by refusing to link race and class, by refusing to recognize that racism in the United States is deeply embedded in a politics of social, economic, and class divisions.

Renato Rosaldo focuses on the issue in arguing that "questions of culture seem to touch a nerve because they quickly become anguished questions of identity."[13] The struggles emerging over "anguished questions of identity" have taken a new turn in the last decade. The "culture wars" that have beset American politics since the advent of the Reagan/Bush reign have become increasingly dominated by a politics of representation rooted in an authoritarian populist discourse that is powerfully refiguring the relationship between identity and culture, particularly as it is addressed in the discourse of racial difference.

There is a certain irony in the fact that at this current historical conjuncture, when many left critics appear to be fed up with identity politics, conservatives have seized upon it with a vengeance.[14] Writing in *Tikkun* magazine, left social critic Ilene Philipson reduces identity politics to the discourse of anxiety, alienation, and inadequacy. In this view, attempts on the part of various social groups to combat racism, homophobia, or sexism are overly determined by psychological concerns with self-identity, self-esteem, and anomie. Philipson makes the point succinctly:

> Identity politics provides a way of avoiding self-blame for feelings of powerlessness and anomie that are, at their root, politically and socially constructed. But as such, the politics of identity inevitably misdirects our attention away from the fact that, apart from a tiny group at the top of the class hierarchy (to use a forgotten term), alienation, a sense of not being recognized for who one is, and feelings of impotence and failure affect us all—certainly to different degrees and with different repercussions. . . . identity politics is not sufficiently radical to speak to this distress, to get at the root sources of our alienation and individually experienced lack of social recognition.[15]

Philipson's reductionism is disturbing. Identity politics covers a complex and diverse terrain of theoretical positions and discourses concerned with questions of subjectivity, culture, difference, and struggle. In its hard and soft versions, this terrain extends from the cultural politics of black nationalists like Louis Farrakhan to the more radically progressive discourses of ethnicity and cultural difference in the works of Stuart Hall and Homi K. Bhabha. But there is more at stake here than a species of theoretical carelessness on the part of left critics who simply dismiss identity politics as separatist, elitist, and reactionary, there is also the politically shortsighted willingness to abandon identity politics at a time when right-wing conservatives are reappropriating progressive critiques of race, ethnicity, and identity and using them to promote rather than dispel a politics of cultural racism. This is a serious mistake. While the end of identity politics is something that left critics and cultural workers seem to be endlessly debating, they do not appear to have fully come to grips with its political and racial consequences. As Stuart Clarke points out, the issue of identity politics will not go away in the 1990s. Identity politics has become one of the more powerful commonsense constructions developed by the right wing in its attempt to "blunt progressive political possibilities . . . [by privileging] race as a sign of social disorder and civic decay."[16]

Rather than merely dismissing identity politics, left cultural workers need to engage the issue more dialectically. In this case, a critical perspective on identity politics should be seen as fundamental to any discourse or social movement that believes in the radical renewal of democratic society. With this qualification in mind, the relationship between identity and politics can be reformulated within a politics of representation which is open to contingency, difference, and self-reflexivity but still able to engage in a hegemonic project that reconstructs public life through a politics of democratic solidarity. Not to do so is to place left social movements and cultural workers outside rather than inside the public debate about identity, difference, and culture. Stuart Clarke puts it well: "The point of this is to indicate that the complex, even contradictory, character of identity politics must be accounted for in efforts to develop a politically effective critical perspective. Identity politics will remain a persistent feature of our political landscape in part because it produces limited but real empowerment for its participants."[17]

In part, Clarke's concern is legitimated by the ideological shift that has taken place among cultural conservatives in the last few years. With the advent of the assault by a wide range of conservative groups on "political correctness," multiculturalism, and radical intellectuals in the academy, identity politics has replaced the Cold War signifier of "communism" as the most serious domestic threat to the New World Order.[18] Moreover, in response to this threat, pedagogy and the issue of cultural representation have become strategic forces used by the New Right and other conservative groups in mobilizing an authoritarian populist movement. Three important issues are at stake here. First, the New Right has developed a powerful new strategy for abstracting cultural difference from the discourse of democracy and social justice. Central to such a strategy is the attempt to fuse culture within a tidy formation that equates the nation, citizenship, and patriotism with a racially exclusive notion of difference. Second, it is crucial to recognize that conservatives have given enormous prominence to waging a cultural struggle over the control and use of the popular media and other spheres of representation in order, according to Howard Winant, to "articulate contemporary racial meanings and identities in new ways, to link race with more comprehensive political and cultural agendas, to interpret social structural phenomena (such as inequality or social policy) with regard to race."[19] Third, it is imperative that the Left not only construct a new politics of difference but extend and deepen the possibilities of critical cultural work by reasserting the primacy of the pedagogical as a form of cultural politics.

In what follows, I will analyze more specifically the ideological contours of the old and new politics of difference. I will then examine how some of the basic assumptions of the new politics of difference are used in the film *Grand Canyon* (1992) to refigure dominant social and racial identities. I will conclude by considering the implications my discussion of these issues has for a critical pedagogy of representation. In doing so, I will stress the importance of reworking the relationship between cultural workers and pedagogy as part of a broader politics of representation, political practice, and emancipatory change.

REPRESENTATION, DIFFERENCE, AND THE NEW POLITICS OF RACE

> The culturalism of the new racism has gone hand in hand with a definition of race as a matter of difference rather than a question of hierarchy. In another context [Frantz] Fanon refers to a similar shift as a progression from vulgar to cultural racism.... Culture is conceived along ethnically absolute lines, not as something intrinsically fluid, changing, unstable, and dynamic, but as a fixed property of social groups rather than a relational field in which they encounter one another and live out social, historical relationships. When culture is brought into contact with race it is transformed into a pseudobiological property of communal life.
>
> —Paul Gilroy, "One Nation under a Groove"

The old racism developed within the historical legacy of colonialism and modern slavery and rested on a blatant ideological appeal to pseudobiological and scientific theories of race to justify inequality, hierarchies, and exploitation as part of the universal order. In this racism, the Other's identity warrants its very annihilation because it is seen as impure, evil, and inferior. Moreover, whiteness represents itself as a universal marker for being civilized and in doing so posits the Other within the language of pathology, fear, madness, and degeneration.[20]

Within dominant regimes of representation, the old racism trades in classic stereotypes, grounds otherness in fixed, transhistorical and cultural categories, and refuses to address the structural and ideological foundations of racist cultural practices.[21] Racist ideology in this case collapses the meaning of being the Other into the representation of otherness.[22] In its various forms, there is little effort to make inequality or powerlessness problematic, open to discussion—in other words, this is a racism that refuses to engage critically in ethical and political terms its own privileged site of enunciation. It is the racism of *The Birth of a Nation*, the black exploitation films of the 1960s, the school textbooks filled with grotesque stereotypes of blacks. It is a racist practice that offers no apologies and focuses on how one inhabits dominant representations/beliefs rather than on the beliefs themselves as the basis for constructing common sense. The old racism is organized through the epistemic discourse of the violence of the Other. Based on fear and desire, the old racism attempts to construct blacks as the objects rather than the subjects of representation—a process that allows whiteness to remain unproblematic even as it projects onto black subjects its own fantasies of noble primitiveness and reckless violence. The old racism, in the words of Stuart Hall, "operates by constructing impassable symbolic boundaries between racially constituted categories, and its typically binary system of representation constantly marks and attempts to fix and naturalize the difference between belongingness and Otherness."[23]

We are now witnessing in the United States (and in Europe) the emergence of a new racism and politics of cultural difference expressed both in the reconfiguration of the relationship between otherness and difference, on the one hand, and meaning and the politics of representation, on the other.[24] Underlying the emergence of the new politics of racism and difference is a deep ambivalence on the part of liberals and conservatives about the traditional categories that have been used to defend racist practices. Identifications grounded in the racial superiority of whites, the fixing of Anglo-European culture as synonymous with civilization itself, and the civilizing mission of patriarchal, Eurocentric discourse are no longer easily maintained within mainstream ideologies and regimes of representation. The new social movements of the 1960s, the reception of feminist, postmodernist, and postcolonialist discourses in the 1970s, the development of critical popular cultural forms in the 1980s, and the rise of the new ethnicities, with their challenge to liberal pluralism in the 1990s, have necessitated a new politics of difference and representation of racial politics on the part of both the Left and the New Right.[25] As American life becomes more hybridized, the distinctions between what Emily Hicks calls "original and alien cultures" have become more difficult to maintain theoretically and politically.[26] As new cultural boundaries and spaces emerge crisscrossed with a diversity of otherness, dominant strategies of representation are abrogated and struggled over through an ongoing process of negotiation, translation, and transformation. The sensibility that informs the relationship between cultural borders reorders the codes of reference for engaging cultural differences and their related networks of hierarchy, power, and struggle.

With these qualifications in mind, any analysis of the new cultural politics of difference and race must acknowledge the shift in what Hall calls the "dominant regimes of representation" around race and multiculturalism that has occurred in the national and popular press within the last few years. In theoretical terms, the new politics of difference points to a proliferation of competing discourses that not only challenge the old vocabulary on race but also expand the sites from which notions of whiteness and blackness, among others, are made visible, rewritten, and circulated. At the same time, since there is no longer any single articulating principle defining the racial dimensions of cultural work and life, the audiences which are the subject and object of racial enunciations have become more complex, contradictory, and multilayered. On one level this has led to what Stuart Hall calls the end of the innocent black subject. At stake here is the recognition that "'black' is essentially a politically and culturally constructed category, which cannot be grounded in a set of fixed trans-cultural or transcendental racial categories and which therefore has no guarantees in Nature."[27] Hence, issues of being black are abstracted from the language of essentialism and scientism and shifted to the terrain of representation. As Hall puts it, "The end of the essential black subject . . . entails a recognition that the central issues of race always appear historically in articulation, in a formation, with other categories and divisions and are constantly crossed and recrossed by the categories of class, of gender, and ethnicity."[28]

Within this discourse the relationship between identity and being "black" is no longer fixed, static, or secure. Hall's position offers cultural workers new opportunities to rewrite the politics of representation around race and difference by deconstructing in historical and relational terms not only the central categories of "otherness," but also the dominant discourses and representations that secure "whiteness" as a universalizing norm.[29] At stake here is the need to create a new political vocabulary and project for rethinking a politics of cultural difference predicated on broader conceptions of race and identity. In this case, cultural workers need to construct a notion of border identity that challenges any essentialized notion of subjectivity while simultaneously demonstrating that the self as an historical and cultural formation is shaped in complex, related, and multiple ways through its interaction with numerous and diverse communities.[30] Needless to say, such a project poses a serious threat to the hegemonic politics of race and representation practiced by Reagan/Bush conservatives. The challenge has not been lost on the New Right.

Whereas the Bush era began with the image of Willie Horton and the implication that black criminality offered the principal signifier to underscore the cultural concerns of racism, the new cultural racism has shifted the emphasis from a notion of difference equated with deviance and cultural deprivation to a position that acknowledges racial diversity only to proclaim that different racial formations, ethnicities, and cultures pose a threat to national unity. Racial privilege is no longer maintained primarily through the use of terror or other traditional neofascist techniques (though one cannot overlook the upsurge in police brutality against blacks and the increases in police and prison budgets of late). The struggle for racial privilege based on an implicit model of white supremacy or cultural nationalism takes many forms among conservatives and right-leaning liberals, but underlying all of these efforts is an attempt, according to Howard Winant, to "rearticulate racial meanings, to reinterpret the content of 'whiteness' and the politics that flows from it."[31] One instance of this hegemonic project is a politics of representation that suggests that whites are the victims of racial inequality. In this discourse the social gravity of poverty, economic exploitation, and class divisions is removed from any analysis of race. The strategy for such a politics gathered a powerful momentum during the Reagan era with the practice of "coding" racial meanings so as to mobilize white fears. Hence, the use of terms such as quotas, busing, welfare, and multiculturalism as signifiers to arouse the insecurities and anger of whites. Another instance of the new politics of racism consists of displaying racial difference as a significant aspect of American life, but doing so only to pose it as a threat that has to be overcome. This strategy became particularly clear in the aftermath of the Los Angeles uprising. The dominant press repeatedly labeled the uprising a riot, and consistently referred to the events that took place as acts of lawlessness. In this case, the politics of the new racism revealed itself shamelessly in the Bush administration's efforts to respond to the L.A. uprising by claiming that it was caused by the failed liberal social programs inaugurated by President Lyndon Johnson in the 1960s. What is really under assault here are not the social, economic, and political conditions that made the uprising possible, but the Voting Rights Act of 1965 and various programs that launched Aid to Families with Dependent Children, Head Start, Chapter 1, Food Stamps, and other public reform efforts. The most disgraceful response to the uprising, one which fully embodied the sentiments of the new racism, came from the *National Review*, which claimed that the main lesson of the insurrection was that law-abiding people (read whites) need more police to protect them and that the real cause of the uprising was, in Harold Johnson's words, "bitterness nursed by many blacks [which] is largely the bequest of people like Reverend Jackson and Representative Waters, who have a stake in formenting [*sic*] divisive race-consciousness."[32]

Surprisingly, these two strategies are not fundamentally at odds with each other. In the first instance, conservatives invoke racial separation in order to mobilize white fears and to organize a constituency for implementing mainstream policy initiatives. In the second instance, racial difference is attacked as something to be overcome. In this discourse, whiteness as a signifier of power and privilege becomes the unspoken referent for naming and passing judgment on the continuing efforts of radicals, minorities, and others to organize around racial and class differences in pressing for political, educational, cultural, and social reforms. Evoking the racially coded language and images of national unity, conservative groups have attempted to dismantle the progressive elements of racial politics by advocating standardized testing in the public schools, attacking multiculturalism as a threat to a "common culture," and deploying cultural pluralism as a slogan which displays difference without mentioning dominant relations of power and class oppression. Winant argues that the new racial politics of the New Right and neoconservatism are articulated with a wider cultural and political agenda that resist any policy which threatens "the fundamentally integrative, if not assimilationist, character of the 'American ethnic pattern,' market rationality, anti-statism, the merits of individualism, and respect for the 'high culture' of the West."[33]

In what follows, I want to analyze the film *Grand Canyon* in order to illustrate how the new politics of difference and race is being constructed within a Hollywood version of identity politics. This analysis is intended to examine how a representational politics actively marks its subjects through racially coded forms of address and enunciation in which subject positions are made available and desires mobilized and where, in Stuart Clarke's words, "spectacles of identity politics interact with the construction of common sense."[34] In the last section of the chapter, I will develop some central elements of a pedagogy of representation that offers possibilities for developing a decolonizing educational practice in which the act of representing can be addressed historically and semiotically as part of an emancipatory attempt to situate relations between the self and others within a broader struggle for a more just and democratic society.

NEW AGE WHITENESS AND THE POLITICS OF DIFFERENCE

> America's sense of its own "radical innocence" has its most profound origins in [the] belief that there is a basic humanity unaltered by the diversity of the citizens who share in it. Democracy is the universal quantifier by which America—the "melting pot," the "nation of immigrants"—constitutes itself as a nation. If *all* our citizens can be said to be Americans, this is not because we share any positive characteristics, but rather because we have all been given the right to *shed* these characteristics, to present ourselves as disembodied before the law. I divest myself of my positive identity, therefore I am a citizen.
>
> —Joan Copjec, "The Unvermögender Other"

As we move into an age in which cultural space becomes unfixed, unsettled, porous, and hybrid, it becomes increasingly difficult either to defend notions of singular identity or to deny that different groups, communities, and people are increasingly bound to each other in a myriad of complex relationships. Modes of representation that legitimated a world of strict cultural separation, collective identities, and rigid boundaries seem hopelessly outdated as the urban landscape is being redrawn within new and shifting borders of identity, race, and ethnicity. New cultural spaces, borderlands, identities, texts, and crossings have created something of a panic among those groups who control dominant regimes of representation. Whereas in the past, the response to racial inequality was to pretend it didn't exist, the current reaction is to re-present it without changing the social, economic, and political conditions that create it. Indifference and silence, or even worse, an appeal to outright racial supremacy, have reluctantly given way to forms of negotiation and translation as varied ethnicities, races, and cultural differences assert themselves both within and between diverse communities. Dominant society no longer resorts to exterminating or silencing Others; nor can it simply erase them. Cultural difference has descended on America like a fog. Dominant groups are now driving very carefully over a cultural terrain in which whiteness can no longer remain invisible as a racial, political, and historical construction. The privilege and practices of domination that underlie being white in America can no longer remain invisible through either an appeal to a universal norm or a refusal to explore how whiteness works to produce forms of "friendly" colonialism.[35]

Los Angeles seems to exemplify the changing nature of the metropolitan urban terrain and the cultural politics that appear to besiege it.[36] The hybridized cultural landscape of Los Angeles has been mythologized in Dennis Hopper's depiction of gang life in *Colors* (1988), rendered as a borderland where cyborgs and humans rewrite the meaning of identity and difference in Ridley Scott's *Bladerunner* (1982), and brilliantly taken up through the complex relations that constitute the coming-of-age experiences of mostly black young men in a neighborhood in South Central Los Angeles in John Singleton's *Boyz N the Hood* (1991). In all of these films, Los Angeles is portrayed against a gritty reality in which cultural differences produce a borderland where an apocalyptic vision of the future is played out amid growing forms of daily violence, resistance, fear, and struggle. Difference in these films is neither innocent nor removed from wider social and political articulations.

In *Grand Canyon* (1992), directed by Lawrence Kasdan, Los Angeles once again becomes a prophetic site for understanding how the language and relations of cultural difference are reshaping public culture in the happy boutique neighborhoods of the rich and the privileged. As in the films mentioned above, Los Angeles becomes an important signifier in order to comment on fear, violence, and racial politics as they are rewritten within the changing understanding of otherness and the growing self-consciousness of what it means to be white in America. What is interesting about *Grand Canyon* is that it goes beyond the empty pluralism that always racializes the Other but never makes whiteness visible. In fact, Kasdan presents a narrative in which whiteness becomes the major referent for defining and acknowledging the responsibility that whites have in a world in which they define themselves as racially and culturally under siege.

Grand Canyon embodies the reactionary side of identity politics, but it does not echo the shrill fanaticism of a Pat Buchanan, Jesse Helms, or Pat Robertson. Instead, it mobilizes the fears and desires of white folks who recognize that cultural differences are here to stay but don't want to be positioned so as to call their own racism or complicity with economic, social, and political inequalities into question. The central white characters in Kasdan's film want to exercise good conscience, retain their property values, and still be able to jog without being mugged. Their racism is more subtle, clean, and New Age. Racial otherness represents a pragmatic rather than an ethical dilemma for them. Border crossings become an excuse for acknowledging the collapse of public life without having to take responsibility for it.

Kasdan's *Grand Canyon* attempts to erase the problem and politics of representation by refusing to portray the complexity of social, political, and cultural forces that structure relationships between whites and blacks, on the one hand, and men and women, on the other. But it is important to note, particularly with regard to white-black relations, that Kasdan does not rely on traditional modes of representation. That is, he does not resort to addressing the issue of cultural difference by simply including the Other in the script. He does not attempt to secure filmic legitimacy simply by covering the story and including the requisite number of blacks. On the contrary, Kasdan is more vigilant and intent on rewriting and reimaging how otherness is presented in ways, in the words of Phil Mariani and Jonathan Crary, that don't "permit or make for interventions on the part of those (Others) represented."[37] In this case, Kasdan's view of racial conflict, poverty, sexism, and public life is defined within a monolithic notion of whiteness which fails to question the place of white racism as an historical and social construction. Consequently, Kasdan provides a celluloid mapping of racial conflict and cultural differences that are resolved in a dystopian politics. His worldview does two things: it subordinates human agency to the grand forces of nature and it allows whites to feel good about themselves while simultaneously absolving them of any responsibility in either constructing or maintaining those ideological and structural forces that privilege agency for some groups and greatly limit it for others. Goodwill and choice combine in this film to create a New Age sense of possibility which in the final analysis collapses irreducible differences among blacks, whites, men, and women into the airy recognition that we are all secondary to the larger cosmic forces of good and evil. Thus, the film provides a common ground on which to recognize how goodness can flow out of despair, how agency is limited by nature, and how ethics is powerless against nature's unfolding.

What is missed in Kasdan's New Age ideology, as Michael Dyson points out in a different context, is "how choice itself is not a property of autonomous moral agents acting in an existential vacuum, but rather something that is created and exercised within the interaction of social, psychic, political, and economic forces of everyday experiences."[38] Of course, it could be argued, since Kasdan refuses in *Grand Canyon* to disrupt the ideological, textual, and structural codes that inform race relations in this country, that his approach simply reflects the traditional colonial policy of reinscribing potentially disruptive social relations in order to contain them. But where Kasdan takes a different theoretical and political twist is in his attempt to produce forms of cultural self-representation in which whites are simultaneously portrayed as both the victims of cultural change and the only gatekeepers of a society which appears to be on the verge of self-destruction. In this form of cultural representation, radical innocence becomes the signifier for a hegemonic practice that colonizes the normal through a notion of common sense in which race, inequality, and power are eventually erased in a New Age vision of goodwill where luck and chance rather than struggle and agency police the present and predict the future. Though willing to admit that the landscape of cultural difference has radically changed in America in the last twenty years, Kasdan presents his audiences with a hegemonic notion of cultural "innocence" in which it is argued that, in Joan Copjec's words, there "still exists a precious, universal, 'innocent' instance in which we can all recognize ourselves."[39]

ENCOUNTERS WITH OTHERNESS

> Historically speaking, every community has felt forced to accept change, to at least come to terms with other communities. The question is, when do communities become frozen? When do they say that they will not change any more? I think that happens when they feel besieged, threatened, when no space is left for them to grow.
>
> —Homi K. Bhabha and Bhikhu Parekh, "Identities on Parade"

Grand Canyon is most importantly about whites becoming self-consciously aware of race and otherness as central determinants in shaping the existing social, political, and cultural landscape, but also in providing a referent for a new politics and form of ethical address. This referent combines for whites the opportunity to acknowledge the new cultural landscape without having to give up their power or privilege. At the heart of the story is an attempt to define what being white, male, and privileged means when the encounter with the harsh colonial terrain of American society can no longer be avoided by the rich and the powerful. *Grand Canyon* attempts to mediate the traditional white phobia of race mixing through the liberal assertion of the right to be different. Couched in the discourse of pluralism, this particular notion of cultural difference presents whiteness, in Richard Dyer's words, "more as a case of historical accident, rather than a characteristic cultural/historical construction, achieved through white domination."[40] Whiteness as a category is rendered invisible as a symbol of ethnicity while simultaneously avowed as a major category to normalize definitions of class, race, gender, heterosexuality, and nationality.[41] Similarly, *Grand Canyon* does not address cultural differences by acknowledging the wider grid of social relations marked by existing systems of inequality and discrimination. Hence, there is no sense in this film of how, as Sharon Welch writes, "different groups are related to each other within networks of hierarchy and exploitation."[42] Understood in these terms, the film attempts first to renegotiate the possibilities for whites to acknowledge those Others who have been marginalized in American society less as human beings caught in the vice of oppression and exploitation than as a threat to a unitary sense of white identity and national unity. Second, *Grand Canyon* attempts to develop an articulation between unity and difference that reinforces whiteness as a discourse, referent, and practice of power. Third, the film uses racism as the basis for white self-criticism but in doing so is silent about the mutuality of responsibility between whites and blacks in addressing issues of ethnicity and social change. These points can be more fully developed by analyzing how the overarching narrative that structures *Grand Canyon* is organized around three different sets of relations: the social divisions between whites and blacks, the relationship between men and women, and the relationship between human beings and nature.

Black and white relationships are primarily developed by the encounter that Mack (Kevin Kline), a wealthy immigration lawyer, has with Simon (Danny Glover), a mechanic who virtually saves Mack from being assaulted by a black gang after he gets lost while driving home from a Lakers basketball game. The context of the meeting is central to their relationship.

In order to avoid heavy traffic after the game, Mack tries taking a shortcut and drives into a black neighborhood that immediately appears to be both alien and menacing. Difference looms up before Mack as strange, unfamiliar, and ominous. As Mack drives along the streets of the neighborhood with its boarded-up houses, numerous liquor stores, and mix of homeless, poor, and roaming youth, he hears the sound of rap music exploding all around him. A car drives by filled with four black youths who wave menacingly to him. Suddenly, his new Lexus dies and he is trapped in a zone of difference coded with racial fear and danger. He uses his car phone to call for a tow truck, but the phone stops working and he is forced to leave the safety of his Lexus and use a public phone. In a state of panic, he tells the tow truck dispatcher that if a driver doesn't show up soon he may lose his life and not just his car. His fear has reached the point of desperation, and he races back to his car to wait for the tow truck. Within minutes, the car playing the rap music, surely a signifier of danger to the yuppie lawyer, pulls up behind Mack's Lexus. Four young men get out of the car and begin to taunt him. Clearly, Mack's life is in danger. One of the young men has a gun tucked in his belt and gestures to it while telling Mack to get out of the car. Mack gets out and tells them they can have whatever they want. The young man snarls at him. The juxtaposition of Mack as the model of decency and the young black men as a threatening symbol of social savagery skillfully works to portray whites as a besieged group while simultaneously portraying inner-city black youths as a signifier of danger and social decay.[43]

Chance and danger, another major subtext of the film, emerge when Simon, the black tow truck driver, arrives on the scene. Exhibiting street-wise savvy and courage, Simon convinces the young men to cool out and go back to roaming the streets. Simon is the model of the cool, tough yet responsible black man. He lives alone. Not only does he support a deaf daughter who attends a college in Washington, D.C., he also helps support his sister, who lives with a son who is gradually being lost to the L.A. black gang culture. Simon's life is complicated. Trapped within the limits imposed by poverty, racism, and the culture of survival, Simon maintains a view of society that allows him to go on with his life, but undercuts his own sense of individual and collective agency.

Sitting with Mack while the Lexus is being repaired, Simon tells him that he once visited the Grand Canyon. He recalls how it made him realize how insignificant life is in the long haul. For Simon, the message is clear: humans within the larger scheme of nature are minute and transitory. Humbled before the long duration of history and time that inscribes the vastness and wonder of the Grand Canyon, Simon substitutes a New Age naturalism for a notion of critical agency and social possibility.

Mack is so grateful to Simon for saving his car and life that he later takes him out to breakfast, develops a friendship with him, and in doing so crosses over a racial boundary—a crossing that allows him to recognize difference as part of daily life. At the same time, however, he refrains from questioning his own place in the larger economy of power and privilege that largely relegates blacks to a subaltern status in contemporary American society.

The relationship between Simon and Mack is mutually reinforced through their understanding that the world is organized through a random sense of chance, luck, and danger. For Mack, this is an important insight that allows him to assuage his liberal conscience by helping Simon's sister find an apartment in a safer neighborhood and fixing Simon up with a black woman who works for Mack's law firm. In this context, Mack's whiteness is not understood through the evocation of a critical reading of history, an invocation of dangerous memory, or an understanding of how social relations that reproduce privileges and power must be unlearned and transformed. On the contrary, whiteness for Mack becomes a referent for self-sacrifice buttressed by the liberal assumption that as a privileged white man he can solve the problems of marginalized and subordinate Others. For Simon, Mack exemplifies how history turns merely on luck and circumstance. After all, what are the chances of an inner-city black mechanic either meeting or becoming friends with a high-powered, privileged yuppie white lawyer? Simon displays his gratitude to Mack at the end of the film by driving his sister and her young boy along with Mack and his family to the Grand Canyon. It is here in the face of the wonder of nature that the immensity of the racial, cultural, political, economic, and social differences that separate these families are erased in a New Age notion of unity and spirituality.

The relationship between whites and blacks/Others is also revealed through the coming-of-age narrative of two young men in the film. Mack and Claire's son, named after Roberto Clemente, the famous Puerto Rican baseball player, is portrayed in terms that suggest he leads a relatively untroubled life. Roberto is from a rich family, goes to a decent school, develops a romance with a young woman in summer camp, and appears to be on his way to a successful future. The most serious tension in his life appears to be learning how to drive and coping with a name that contradicts his own refusal to view himself as ethnic. Learning how to make a left turn in traffic appears to be the most pressing test he will face in the near future.

On the other hand, Simon's nephew is portrayed as a young black male who has given his life up to the L.A. gang culture. This black teenage boy's problems come from living with a single parent who cannot contain him and residing in a community filled with crime and despair over which he has no control. Kasdan presents the film audience with a view of black urban life that is as one-dimensional as the stereotypes and tropes he uses to construct the coming-of-age odyssey of a black youth growing up in a poor, inner-city neighborhood. The suffocating conditions of urban decay, rampant poverty, and random violence are frozen by Kasdan in a series of images that refuse to analyze the historical, cultural, economic, and political conditions that provide some dialectical grounding for understanding how domination, power, resistance, and identity come together to reveal the complexity of life in such a setting. The binarism created by Kasdan of growing up "black" and "white" does not suggest what these two young men have in common, how one form of life relates to the other, or how new identities might be constructed by transforming these related sites of privilege and oppression. In this scenario, whiteness is not only privileged, it is also the only referent for social change, hope, and action. Within the rigid binarism portraying these two very different coming-of-age experiences cast in racial terms, blacks are equated with lawlessness while whites are seen as paragons of rationality, compassion, and stability. Once again, what is revealed here is a fundamental disrespect for marginalized Others manifest in the refusal to analyze what whiteness as a category of power means (or suggests) in terms of its ethical relations with Others. This type of disrespect for the Other is also manifested throughout the film in the refusal of allowing those who are oppressed—blacks, women, and children—to speak for themselves, to be the subject of resistance and historical agency, and to be complexly represented within rather than outside of the specificity of their daily lives.

Otherness as both a marker of deficit and a resource to redefine whiteness as a universal symbol of unity and hope is displayed in a number of other relations throughout the film. Race and gender intersect in a dominating fashion through the portrayal of Mack's wife, Claire (Mary MacDonnell). Caught in a midlife crisis, Claire appears to solve her problem while taking her daily jog. Passing the nearby woods, she finds and takes possession of an abandoned Third World baby. Even if we ignore the concrete identities of the child and the woman involved (Why was the baby abandoned? What history, memories, and pain inform Claire's act?), we cannot fail to ask: What does such an act suggest about the ethical relations between the wealthy and the poor in terms of their respective problems, hopes, and plans for the future? Kasdan uses this intersection of "chance and luck" to suggest that Claire's identity is entirely dependent on her providing nurturance to others, particularly since she can no longer provide such nurturance to her husband and teenage son. Claire eventually adopts the baby she found and in doing so not only secures her own identity but also affirms the notion of self-sacrifice, guilt, and duty that appears to be endemic to Kasdan's conception of how responsible action is constituted for whites. A subtext of this relationship is that Third World families are not responsible enough to raise their own children. Conversely, in this case, colonialism is seen as having its benefits.

Claire doesn't differ much from all the other women who inhabit the celluloid landscape of *Grand Canyon*. Mack's mistress, Simon's lover, and Claire are women whose identities are largely shaped in the images of men. Kasdan suggests that their only desires are rooted in the patriarchal demands for women (not men) to nurture, raise children, or find a "good" man. Deprived of a complex identity and voice, all of the women in this film lack any sense of agency or any urge to redefine their lives outside of the imperatives of a patriarchal culture. Moreover, Kasdan also uses a debilitating binarism in framing what differences there are among the women in *Grand Canyon*. Either they are viewed as little more than prostitutes, as is the case with Mack's mistress, Dee (Mary-Louise Parker), or they are viewed as selfless saints, an image embodied in Claire (who is viewed in a number of scenes through the figure of the Madonna rocking the baby Jesus).

Finally, all of the main characters in this film share the belief that some miraculous force establishes connections between people who inhabit the planet and that this force expresses itself through the circumstances of luck, chance, and fate. Mack tells Simon, for instance, that he believes that God once appeared to him in the form of a woman wearing a baseball cap and saved him from being hit by a bus. Clearly, his time to die had not come. Simon reveals his own infatuation with nature and the insignificance of human life and agency in the face of the wonder and awe of the Grand Canyon. Claire believes that finding the baby she adopted was orchestrated by some higher force. Thus, she doesn't have to bother with the social, political, and ideological consequences of either the abandonment of a Third World child or her adopting a baby under such circumstances. In the end, the primacy of the social, political, and cultural as they are manifested in various problems informing cultural differences, gender issues, and the problematic of ethnicity are wiped away in a New Age adoration of the mysteries and wonders of nature. All of life's riddles are seemingly resolved when all the central players end up in the final scene of the film staring with amazement and awe at the aesthetic wonder of the Grand Canyon. Clearly, in this scenario, nature and social Darwinism are on the side of white domination as all of the differences that brought together these various men, women, and children are removed from the systemic injustices which influence their respective lives. History, power, and agency now dissolve into the abyss of liberal goodwill, New Age uplift thinking, and a dead-end pastoralism; and cultural differences dissolve into a regime of representations that universalizes harmonizing systems while eliminating the discourse of power, conflict, and struggle.

TOWARD A PEDAGOGY OF REPRESENTATION

The question I want to take up here is how cultural workers might engage a politics and regime of representations in pedagogical terms. In what follows, I want to elaborate on this issue by developing both in the remainder of this chapter and in chapter 5 what I call a pedagogy of representation. In part, the starting point for such a pedagogy stresses the importance of illuminating the various ways in which representations are constructed as a means of comprehending the past through the present in order to legitimate and secure a particular view of the future. Pedagogically, this raises the question of how students might learn to interrogate the historical, semiotic, and relational dynamics involved in the production of various regimes of representation and their respective politics. In other words, a pedagogy of representation focuses on demystifying the act and process of representing by revealing how meanings are produced within relations of power that narrate identities through history, social forms, and modes of ethical address that appear objective, universally valid, and consensual. At issue here is the task of both identifying how representational politics works to secure dominant modes of authority and mobilize popular support while also interrogating how the act of representing is developed within forms of textual authority and relations of power, according to Edward Said, "which always involve choice, selectivity, exclusions, and inclusions."[44]

Central to a pedagogy of representation is providing students with the opportunities to deconstruct the mythic notion that images, sounds, and texts merely express reality.[45] More specifically, a critical pedagogy of representation recognizes that students inhabit a photocentric, aural, and televisual culture in which the proliferation of photographic and electronically produced images and sounds serve to actively produce knowledge and identities within particular sets of ideological and social practices. By granting the concept of representation a formative and not merely an expressive place in the constitution of social and political life, questions of subjectivity, power, and politics take on an increasing significance as a pedagogical practice in which the relationship between difference and identity must be located within rather than outside of the mediations of history, culture, and ideology.[46]

On one level, this suggests that students must analyze those institutions that constantly work through the power of representations and social practices, in Chandra Mohanty's words, to "produce, codify, and even rewrite histories of race and colonialism in the name of difference."[47] Representations are not simply forms of cultural capital necessary for human beings to present themselves in relation to others and human nature, they also inhabit and sustain institutional structures that need to be understood and analyzed within circuits of power that constitute what might be called a political economy of representations. In this case, a pedagogy and politics of representation would highlight historically how "machineries of representation" within the growth of new mass communication and information technologies are inextricably linked to the emergence of corporate-controlled and knowledge-based societies in which a politics of representation must be partly understood within the imperatives of the newly emerging transnational market economies of the postmodern age.[48] This insight has provoked Trinh T. Minh-ha to remark: "To address the question of production relations . . . is endlessly to reopen the question: how is the real (or the social ideal of good representation) produced? Rather than catering to it, striving to capture and discover its truth as a concealed or lost object, it is therefore important also to keep asking: how is truth being ruled?"[49] In part, Stuart Hall further extends this insight in arguing that cultural workers must address not only the relations among representations, how their machineries work to actively produce common-sense notions of identity and difference, but also how dominant regimes of representation actively "structure conditions of existence . . . outside of the sphere of the discursive."[50] By providing students with critical tools to decode dominating machineries of representation, cultural workers can help them understand their own locations and social formations in terms that allow them to introduce into their discourse what Joan Borsa calls "a sense of the political which ultimately leads to a consideration of power."[51]

In more specific terms, a pedagogy of representation can be used to take up some of the following issues as they relate to analyzing cultural texts such as *Grand Canyon* as part of a broader politics of difference. First, a pedagogy of representation would give students the opportunity not simply to discover their hidden histories but to recover them. This means, as Richard Kearney writes, "retrieving the betrayed stories of history . . . through a critical deployment of imagination . . . able to discriminate between reality as a fact and existence as a possibility."[52] As part of the politics of cultural representation and identity formation, such a retrieval would suggest that cultural workers offer students the tools to challenge any notion of subjectivity grounded in a view of history as unchanging, monolithic, or static. Identities are always subject, as Stuart Hall points out, "to the 'play' of history, culture, and power."[53] Consequently, identities undergo constant transformations.

The relationship between history and identity is a complex one and cannot be reduced to unearthing hidden histories that are then mined for positive images. On the contrary, educators need to understand and develop in their pedagogies how identities are produced differently, how they take up the narratives of the past through the stories and experiences of the present. Understood in these terms, a pedagogy of representation is not wedded to the process of narrating an authentic history, but to the dynamics of cultural recovery, which involves rewriting the relationship between identity and difference through a retelling of the historical past. Such a pedagogy is rooted in making the political more pedagogical by addressing how a critical politics can be developed between a struggle over access to regimes of representation and using them to re-present different identities as part of the reconstruction of democratic public life. Stuart Hall alludes to this problem as the struggle around positionalities and the struggle for a politics of difference. For him, the important issue here is how a "politics can be constructed which works with and through difference, which is able to build those forms of solidarity and identification which make common struggle and resistance possible but without suppressing the real heterogeneity of interests and identities, and which can effectively draw the political boundary lines without which political contestation is impossible, without fixing those boundaries for eternity."[54]

Second, critical educators need to understand more clearly how to construct a pedagogy that is attentive to how the incorporation of the everyday is mobilized within the text of mass culture to produce particular relations between the margins and the centers of power.[55] In part, this means providing students with the analytical tools to challenge those representations that produce racism, sexism, and colonialism through the legacy of ethnocentric discourses and practices.

At issue here is the need to develop pedagogical practices that do more than read off ideologies as they are produced within particular texts. Central to such an approach is the need to develop analyses which illustrate how particular representations emerge out of and legitimate particular institutions, economies of power, and sites of struggle. Representations need, in part, to be located not merely in the ideologies they produce but also in the material structures of power they legitimate. Similarly, a pedagogy of representation needs to focus on how different ways of reading, writing, listening, and viewing are determined within broader social and cultural formations and how these contain what can be understood and said about identity, cultural democracy, and social struggle. By engaging representations as historically and socially constructed texts, cultural workers can provide a site for students to create counternarratives of emancipation in which new visions, spaces, desires, and discourses can be developed that offer them the opportunity for rewriting their own histories differently within rather than outside of the discourse of power and social struggle.

Within this perspective, the struggle over identity can be addressed or understood, in the words of Anne Balsamo, to "be a struggle about the politics of representation and the relations of power that organize knowledge; this not only concerns the form and content of representations in books or films, but more broadly in the university curriculum, social movements, and global economic relations (among other things)."[56] Pedagogically, Balsamo's comments suggest that students analyze how relations of power historically inform the narratives, experiences, and positions from which such students construct their own identities and relationships to others. In doing so, they would critically engage their own ethnicities and gain some sense of those complex and diverse cultural locations that have provided them with a sense of voice, place, and identity. This pedagogical practice also suggests providing students with the opportunity to move beyond the search for an authentic identity. Instead, a pedagogy of representation establishes "spaces" where meaning can be rewritten, produced, and constructed rather than merely asserted.

Representation in this sense becomes an interpretative act that reveals a cultural practice. As such, it points to cultural practices that both include and exclude, that unsettle, for instance, what Biddy Martin and Chandra Mohanty call "the seeming homogeneity, stability, and self-evidence of 'white identity.'"[57] I am particularly concerned here about a pedagogy of representation that makes whiteness visible as an ethnic category, about making white students understand how their own identities are beyond neither ethnicity, history, privilege, nor struggle. Cultural difference, in this case, must be taken up as a relational issue and not as one that serves to isolate and mark particular groups. This has important pedagogical implications. For example, Bob Suzuki discovered that in a class he was teaching on multicultural education, many of his white students were ignorant of their own Irish, working-class histories. He writes:

> When I asked my students to share what they knew about their ethnic and cultural backgrounds with the rest of the class, students of color —especially African-American students—usually had the most knowledge of their family histories. White ethnic students were generally the least knowledgeable, and after they listened to the long narratives of the students of color, they would be somewhat intimidated and say—sometimes rather forlornly—"I wish I had something to contribute, but I don't even know much about my background. In fact, I don't even have a culture." At first, I found such statements astonishing because I hadn't realized the extent to which ethnic experience has been literally obliterated for many white ethnics. Once I gained that realization, however, I could deal much more effectively with these students.[58]

The pedagogical practice illustrated by Suzuki rejects the notion that the systemic violence of racism and difference as negative identity can only be addressed by focusing on alleged Others. Ethnicity becomes a constantly traversed borderland of differences in which identities are fashioned in relationship to the shifting terrains of history, experience, and power.[59] Ethnicity as a representational politics pushes against the boundaries of cultural containment and becomes a site of pedagogical struggle in which the legacies of dominant histories, codes, and relations become unsettled and thus open to being challenged and rewritten. This suggests at the most general level that a pedagogy of representation must be a pedagogy of place, that is, it must address the specificities of the experiences, problems, languages, and histories that students and communities rely upon to construct a narrative of collective identity and possible transformation.

In conclusion, I want to reiterate that if a pedagogy of representation is to address the challenge of the new cultural racism, it will have to rework the relationship between identity and difference as part of a broader struggle over institutions and ideologies designed to extend and deepen greater forms of political, economic, and cultural democracy. Such a struggle demands a critical understanding of how ideological and material conditions can generate theoretical discourses and practices that produce plural identities and public spaces for students and others to engage and negotiate those representations that enable concrete possibilities for collective agency and social justice. At the very least, any attempt to connect the issues of agency and ethical responsibility with a pedagogy of representation must be rooted in a politics which is utopian yet always suspicious of its own tenets.

5

Pedagogy and the Critical Practice of Photography

Roger I. Simon, Co-author

In the view of this chapter's coauthors, expanding the possible contribution schooling might make to citizens and their communities requires a renewed attention to the practices which constitute our social imaginations. As particular ways of naming and ordering social and physical realities, these practices simultaneously enable and constrain options for practical action. Framing the "possible and desirable," they shape the terrain of cultural politics informing notions of knowledge, significance, and desire. Included in such practices are the creation of particular modes of symbolic and textual expression as well as the means by which such expressions are placed within systems of distribution, display, and engagement. For this reason, the production of various forms of image, text, gesture, and talk—as well as their ordered presentation and structured efforts to influence their mediation—has to be understood as integral to the possibility of either the reproduction or the transformation of any social order. In other words, cultural work matters and its effects and modes of production deserve close attention.

As teachers we function explicitly within the realm of cultural work. Our attempts to engage students are constructed within specific modes of textual, verbal, and visual practices which we hope will provoke particular forms of communication, comprehension, and interest. How we fashion this engagement, within what value-based projects and with what corresponding strategies and questions, defines much of our pedagogical practice. In education, dominant modes of production often attempt to normalize "truthful" or "useful" textual practices and image repertoires, as well as what counts as their adequate display and mediation. Such normalizations are efforts to regulate particular ways of seeing the world and defining "common sense." However, from our vantage point as cultural workers such modes of production and regimes of representation are problematic, to say the least, particularly as they help maintain unjust inequalities and are implicated in the daily symbolic and physical violence which diminishes the possibility of human dignity. This is why many of our efforts over the last decade have been devoted to enabling varieties of critical pedagogical practice, varieties intended to support efforts at social transformation and contribute to discussions of what moral commitments and economic and social forms might enliven our communities.

In this respect Abigail Solomon-Godeau's work in photography offers reflections central to our pedagogical concerns.[1] First of all, Solomon-Godeau reminds us of the importance of theorizing the photographic image as an "event."[2] This does not simply reference the image as a factual record but requires attention to its intervention in the narrativization of the past, an intervention most often characterized by the erasure of the marks of its own "making and maker." Bearing the sign of the "real," that something must have taken place *right there*, a photograph simultaneously poses questions and provides the terms to be met by the writing of answers. If historiography, in Michel de Certeau's words, "aims at calming the dead who still haunt the present by offering them scriptural tombs,"[3] photography makes the dead nervous by its ceaseless demand for intelligibility. This is an intelligibility conditioned but not fulfilled by the photograph. Thus we agree with Solomon-Godeau's suggestion that an adequate history of photography would be "not the history of remarkable men, much less remarkable pictures, but the history of photographic uses."[4]

As educators and cultural workers, our interests extend beyond pedagogies that address the value or compositional character of the image and how the viewer might be educated to "see more" (or at least differently). Rather, our interest—coincident with Solomon-Godeau's—given the status of images as "events," is in what people narratively do with the photographs[5] they encounter in books, family albums, newspapers, galleries, museums, on postcards, posters, advertisements, compact discs, record albums, and so on. Such a concern is quite consistent with a notion of pedagogy that includes provoking questions about and reconsideration of how images are created, circulated, and mediated. But provocations of this type do not exhaust the pedagogical concerns that intersect with the representational medium of photography. As we will argue, how one theorizes the dynamics of the use of photographic images is decisive for elaborating a fundamental theme woven through Solomon-Godeau's theoretical work: the question of what constitutes a critical practice adequate to both producing and deploying photographic images. That is, given the possibility of a photographic practice which might rupture and re-form hegemonic visions of the actual, desirable, and possible, what images or modes of circulation and display would constitute a critical approach? While necessarily referencing the particular technological limits and discursive frames of photography, the question of what constitutes a critical photographic practice remains inherently pedagogical. This is why, as educators, we have begun to study the work of people as diverse as Lewis Hine, John Heartfield, Martha Rosler, and Connie Hatch.[6] Solomon-Godeau provides an extensive consideration of what constitutes an adequate critical practice. We read her to enhance our understanding not only of how we might produce and employ photographs which would aid in the reformation of a social and political imagination but also for how such efforts inform more generally the possibilities for critical cultural work.

WHAT CONSTITUTES AN ADEQUATE CRITICAL PRACTICE OF PHOTOGRAPHY?

For Solomon-Godeau, critical practice is always multilayered, mobile, and self-conscious. On one level, she recognizes it as a discourse whose aim is to disrupt, rupture, and render visible how power works to promote relations of domination through the established ordering of institutional forms, representational practices, and social relationships. On another level, she is concerned with what might be called the politics of representation. That is, as part of a broader project to understand how politics is inscribed within the form and act of representing itself, she wants to make critical practice consistently self-conscious about its own organizing principles, structuring codes, and shifting oppositional salience. Rejecting the orthodoxy of a politics that refuses to be skeptical of itself, Solomon-Godeau offers a critical practice that destabilizes and unsettles not only dominant regimes of representation but also the ideological edifice and technological apparatuses that provide the context, content, and positioning of the radical gaze or event of criticism itself. Recognizing that critical practice, as embodied in documentary practice, cannot be premised on subject matter alone, Solomon-Godeau takes great pains to make the politics of the photographer/cultural worker as much an object of critical scrutiny as the texts and subject matter that traditionally come under critical analysis. For Solomon-Godeau, this is an attempt to construct a cultural politics that serves to deepen and extend the possibilities of critical practice by recognizing that it is always indebted to changing and complex historical conditions; thus such practices cannot live in the comfort of a secure definition of what form art production or cultural criticism might take. In this case, critical practice is haunted and invigorated by the paradox of being an active agent in the production of places, practices, and spaces but lacks the benefit of guaranteeing its own politics and effects in advance. Hence, critical practice, along with the political project which frames it, must always be struggled over and consistently redefined. It is precisely this caution mediated by a strong sense of politics that makes Solomon-Godeau's notion of critical practice so important and yet so elusive.

What we wish to stress is that Solomon-Godeau offers a theoretical service in arguing that the politics of representation and the representation of politics cannot be separated from each other. In this case, critical practice becomes a referent for self-critique as well as social criticism. Similarly, critical practice must also be concerned with engaging the historically informed and specifically situated conditions of domination. At stake here is a notion of critical practice that can sustain the conditions which make it possible, in part, by being vigilant against becoming complicitous with the very forms of domination which it attempts to disrupt. In a succinct, revealing, and controversial instance, Solomon-Godeau asserts the value of particular cultural sites and discourses as an arena for struggle while at the same time suggesting that the discourse of ethics is not important to a critical practice.

> Whether artists choose to publicly define their positions in opposition to, or in strategic alliance with, dominant modes of cultural production is important only insofar as such definitions may contribute to a collective space of opposition. But in the absence of a clearly defined oppositional sphere and the extreme rarity of collaborative practice, attempts to clarify the nature of critical practice must focus on the art work's ability to question, to contest, or to denaturalize the very terms in which it is produced, received, and circulated. What is at stake is thus not an ethics or a moral position, but the very possibility of a critical practice within the terms of art discourse. And as a fundamental condition of possibility, critical practices must constantly address those economic and discursive forces that perpetually threaten to eradicate their critical difference.[7]

In what follows, we analyze several aspects of Solomon-Godeau's notion of critical practice and develop its implications for educators and cultural workers who must engage pedagogy as a struggle over assigned meanings, modes of expression, and directions of desire as these bear on the formation of the multiple and ever-contradictory versions of the "self" and its relationship to the larger society. We will do this by highlighting the importance of some of the central issues that Solomon-Godeau develops in her notion of critical practice.

ALWAYS HISTORICIZE

One of the striking features of Solomon-Godeau's project is her recognition that critical practice and historical analysis are inseparable. Attempting to provoke an active and analytic viewing as opposed to a passive and contemplative one, she rejects modernism's rendering of the photograph as a thing in itself, an artifact of high culture privileged by virtue of a reified aesthetics and legitimated as a unique expression of "genius." By highlighting historical, semiotic, and relational analyses, Solomon-Godeau does not erase material economies of cultural and social production through an exclusive emphasis on demystifying hegemonic representations and codes. Power, for Solomon-Godeau, is more than a floating signifier. She makes quite clear in her analysis of the canonization of Eugene Atget that power is to be found inscribed in bodily disciplines, in cultural and political institutions, and in the political apparatuses of the state. By examining the canonization of Atget's work, not only does Solomon-Godeau rewrite history as a form of cultural criticism that robs mainstream photographic history of its transcendental claims to subjectivity, originality, and authorship, she also reconstructs history within a politics and system of representation that makes visible a sense of location of those who engage history but refuse to acknowledge their complicity in organizing it as a hegemonic text. In her critical analysis of the political and institutional implications of canonicity, Solomon-Godeau both reveals how Atget's canonization calls into question modernism's cherished principles of authenticity, originality, and privileged vision and relates the construction of a canon to the securing of power through the "converging interests of the individuals—curators, critics, scholars, dealers, and collectors—who promoted him at the historical moment most propitious for the establishment of a new canon."[8]

In this context, history as a form of critical practice is not merely reinvented or resurrected, it is reconstituted as a form of cultural recovery aimed at demystifying how domination works through a view of history that presents itself as disinterested, objective, and authoritative. For Solomon-Godeau, any viable critical practice must contextualize the history of photographic uses not only as a legacy of struggle and disruptions but also as a practice capable of mobilizing agency to effect changes or differences in the world. What is so important about Solomon-Godeau's approach to history is her understanding that historical agency is not only found in the dynamics of ruling groups but also in an insurgent subjectivity and a politics of representation that provide an enunciative energy, a dialectic of negotiation and translation, that marks agency not simply as a location but as an engaged critical practice.[9]

DECONSTRUCTION AND BEYOND

In her attempt to develop a critical practice of photography, Solomon-Godeau goes to great pains to deconstruct the dominant concept of the aesthetic employed by the discourses and institutional apparatuses of high culture. Employing familiar postmodern critiques of authorship, genius, aura, and self-referentiality, she deftly discloses the primary importance of photographic users and usage as a starting point for revealing how the material and ideological functions of power work on and through the organization, presentation, and circulation of images, identities, and social relations. Furthermore, she also recognizes that active analytic viewing requires something more than deconstructing the ideological character of the image. Solomon-Godeau is concerned with how images engender forms of investment, negotiation, and translation on the part of the maker and viewers. Ideological critique is crucial to any critical practice, but it is not enough.

To understand what is at stake here we return for a moment to the notion of the image as an event. The "event" status of a photographic image is constituted in the concrete conditions of its viewing. It is here, in the discursively saturated materiality of the specific circumstances in which a photograph is seen[10] that the image makes its demand for intelligibility. It is here, too, that the appearance of an image both encumbers and informs our social imagination and its associated "structure of feeling." Yet, paradoxically, this *image-event* presents itself not just as the requirement and point of departure of comprehension but as a potential "blind spot," a limit condition on, and perhaps a caesura of, the frames and "facts" which constitute our knowledge.

Much of Solomon-Godeau's writing is structured by her recognition that photographs are the consummate nexus of power and knowledge, given their indexical relationship to reality and their mutability by caption and context. In addition, she acknowledges that an understanding of *photographic use* must begin with the recognition that the photograph is a building block in a larger structure. This larger structure, whether manifest in a textbook or newspaper or on a gallery wall, is defined by the ideologically structured material and semiotic field in which the photograph appears. However, the key question here is how, within this larger structure, a photograph functions in respect to the demand for intelligibility which itself provokes in its appearance an image-event. How one answers this question is a crucial determinant of any conception of critical practice that seeks to shift how photographs are seen and (more ambitiously) refashion their contribution to the social imagination of diverse publics.

Throughout her essays on art and documentary photography as well as in her discussions of photography and sexual difference, Solomon-Godeau develops a notion of photographic use that centers on its confirmatory function. She begins by positioning herself over and against a naive view that the indexical character of the photograph functions as a "proof-text," bearing a transparent truth that confirms assertions and positions itself outside of the historical, ideological, and material mediations in which it is constructed. Rather than confirming the "real," Solomon-Godeau sees photography functioning to ratify and affirm the complex ideological web that is the taken-for-granted frame with which one perceives reality. The photographic image here is a provocation for the writing of its truth. That is, the demand of intelligibility requires that signs reproduced in the image become the limit conditions against which its associational and contextual structure must work in order to render both the meaning and emotional resonance of that which is pictured. Of central importance in this stance is the assumption that the viewer must take up a position within a discursive frame that simultaneously references and explains the image. It is this positioning which implicates the photograph in the process of subject formation and hence in the problematics of pedagogy. It is also in this sense that Solomon-Godeau refers to the notion of "photographic agency" as a central subtext addressed throughout her book. What is critical here is that one understand that this agency does not *work on* subjects but rather *through* them. Suppression of this understanding can only function to reproduce a subject/object dichotomy which restrains viewers from asking questions about their own complicity in the specific ways the "truth" of a photograph is written.

It is in this sense that Solomon-Godeau wants to understand photographic practice within the interrelated modalities of audience, reception, and address. What is implied in this interrelation is the notion that a critical practice of photography must address how the province of the subjective is constructed and challenged not only within the alleged facticity of the photograph, but also through its related moments of production and reception. The pedagogical and political importance of this framework is demonstrated by the way Solomon-Godeau elaborates three central moments of her critique. First, the act of imaging as a reality effect hides the historically and socially constructed nature of a photograph's form, content, and maker. Solomon-Godeau illustrates this issue by addressing how the documentary photography of Dorothea Lange, Jacob Riis, and others depoliticized the visual by framing pictures of the poor as pictorial spectacles. In such work, the process of securing the truth of an image can render a photograph emblematic. This emblematic rendering of an image has consequent ideological effects which must be taken into account in any analysis of photographic use. For example, as Solomon-Godeau (echoing Martha Rosler) suggests, when visual facts of individual victimization or subjugation are written as a metonym for the conditions that produce it, there is the potential for slippage from the political to the anecdotal or emblematic. "The photographer's desire to build pathos or sympathy into the image, to invest the subject with either an emblematic or archetypical importance, to visually dignify labor or poverty, is a problem to the extent that such strategies eclipse or obscure the political sphere whose determinations, actions and instrumentalities are not in themselves visual."[11]

Second, relying upon the work of Connie Hatch and others, Solomon-Godeau attempts to reveal the importance of a cultural practice that foregrounds those photographic operations that position the subject as a commodity, aestheticize the politics of poverty, or fix women as the object of patriarchal desire. In this case, Solomon-Godeau wants to problematize the camera's fixing of subject/object positions and make visible how the photographer and viewer are implicated in a complex grid of power relations. In other words, she wants to do more than reveal what mainstream photography leaves out; her notion of critical practice is neither formulated on making visible the "lack" in particular photographs or exhibitions nor exclusively devoted to the strategy of offering positive counterimages. While these are important issues concerning power, politics, and the use of photography, Solomon-Godeau wants to extend the dynamic of power that informs them by addressing the issue of how power operates outside of its mere expression in the image; that is, she wants to contest the very terms of representation.

This leads to her third important insight. For Solomon-Godeau, a viable critical practice must address the embeddedness of photography's production, exhibition, circulation, and distribution within a broader economy of power and politics. For example, drawing upon feminist debates on pornography, Solomon-Godeau argues that the problem of

> the covert circulation of erotic and pornographic images cannot be understood to occupy a space apart from mainstream imagery. . . . it may well be that the most insidious and instrumental forms of domination, subjugation, and objectification are produced by mainstream images of women rather than by juridically criminal or obscene ones. . . . the pressing need, it seems to me, is not to locate and censor a "worse offender" class of images, but rather to better understand—in order to effectively combat—the complex network of relations that meshes power, patriarchy, and representation.[12]

This is more than an attempt to recover a dialectical relationship between the specific and the wider web of relations with which it articulates. More specifically, it points to Solomon-Godeau's important recognition that if critical practice is to be transformative it must address questions of access and control over photographic work in terms of its exhibition, publication, and distribution.

SUSTAINING CRITICAL PRACTICE

While Solomon-Godeau is primarily concerned with the substance of critical practice, she also pays considerable attention to the issue of how it might be sustained. In several chapters she is concerned about the cooptive absorption of such practices. She implicitly poses the question of what conditions could sustain a critical practice, particularly one which incorporates the production and use of images. Partial answers are suggested throughout the book, many of which provide valuable insights regarding the conditions that need to be addressed to keep alive the constant renewal of critical practice. It is to these that we now turn.

For Solomon-Godeau, it is crucial that art critics, producers, and other cultural workers actively address the intersection of their own location as cultural critics, the shifting and different terrains of audience reception, and those hegemonic forces, both ideological and institutional, that are constantly attempting to depoliticize and reappropriate critical work. In the first instance, Solomon-Godeau argues that cultural workers need to constantly engage what is at stake in the epistemological battles over what constitutes art and art criticism. This is a crucial issue that not only makes modernist aesthetics the ongoing subject of critique but also provides a basis for informing the critic about his or her own relations to those institutions of power that are constantly struggling to reinscribe the autonomy, nonutility, purity, and alleged self-reflexivity of the work of art. Of course, false claims to universality and transcendence do not serve merely to reinforce such concepts; they also actively work to construct the notion of the Promethean artist and to erase politics and power amid the appeal to the timeless authority of aura, genius, and oeuvre.

Secondly, Solomon-Godeau is acutely aware of the need to understand how practices of production, circulation, and reception are deeply enmeshed in the commodified character of the image. Resisting such commodification raises important questions about developing a radical aesthetic that highlights rather than makes invisible the politics in a work of art. This means not only making problematic the content of the image, but also developing images that consistently problematize the politics of location of both the maker and the viewer of the image. Like the Russian formalists who wanted to establish modes of perception that would unsettle the visioning of everyday life, Solomon-Godeau wants cultural workers to refuse the seduction of style. Moreover, she is intent on encouraging textual and contextual strategies that expose how complicity and power intersect in the acts of making and looking. Offering as examples critical practices drawn from the work of contemporary artists such as Richard Prince, Richard Baim, Connie Hatch, Cindy Sherman, Louise Lawler, Francesca Woodman, and others, Solomon-Godeau attempts to appropriate the most critical insights from postmodern and feminist discourses. In this she endows her work with a political edge that suggests the importance of recognizing the politics of one's own location as both a set of orienting assumptions and a problematic that consistently needs to be interrogated and made visible and, hence, subject to ongoing debate.

Finally, Solomon-Godeau's important concern with the politics of recuperation provides the basis for the dialectical interplay of self and social criticism, that is, criticism that is both internal and external, that unravels how as cultural workers we have been grounded in the shifting terrain of history, identity, and place. Not only is this necessary in order to arrive at a larger understanding of our roles as cultural workers; it is also essential in order to construct the alternative spaces and projects necessary for nourishing the conviction, in Richard Kearney's words, "that things can be changed . . . [in order that we may] begin to imagine that the world as it is could be otherwise."[13]

ETHICS, POSSIBILITY, AND THE PEDAGOGY OF REPRESENTATION

Abigail Solomon-Godeau provides invaluable theoretical insights for educators attempting to invent strategies of critical practice. Specifically, her work bears on the concerns of what we call a pedagogy of representation: that complex and inherently political intersection of the production and selection of image and text, the specification of their context and mode of presentation, and the formation of structures within which their engagement can be extended and challenged. We shall now briefly summarize our appropriation of these insights, extending their application while indicating where we depart from Solomon-Godeau's critical vision.

First, Solomon-Godeau's work underscores the importance of cultural workers identifying practices which help make apparent the historically contingent nature of the form and content of a particular form of representation. Such practices would be concretized in a search for approaches through which, for example, a book, film, or photograph can be problematized for the ways in which it both produces and covers over forms of cultural self-representation that are constructed within dominant historical, hierarchical, and representational systems. This is not merely a matter of recovering lost historical narratives; it is a matter of asserting the need for a pedagogical practice that addresses the issue of how forms of cultural identity are learned in relation to the ordering and structuring of dominant practices of representation. At stake is not only how representational practices efface the "marks of [their] making" but also how those excluded from the means of representation are actually represented.

Second, Solomon-Godeau's work also suggests the importance of going beyond the identification of representations that do violence to those who are either represented or erased from time and space. Her work suggests that cultural workers need to find practices that refuse the voyeuristic reception of texts by providing a variety of critical methodologies and approaches through which people may explore how issues of audience, address, and reception configure within cultural circuits of power to produce particular subject positions and secure specific forms of authority. This is a search for practices which make problematic those representations that legitimate certain strategies of inclusion and exclusion, subject formation, and affective investment and expression. Of particular interest here would be how forms of representation create and mobilize desires that secure varieties of affective investment. Such an approach suggests more than taking up how representations work to police desires; more important, it points to how we actively produce and mobilize our own desires within particular historical and social contexts as forms of identification and agency.

Third, Solomon-Godeau's work is also helpful for clarifying our understanding that representations are always produced within cultural limits and theoretical borders, and as such are necessarily implicated in particular economies of truth, value, and power. These insights challenge cultural workers to find ways of provoking questions such as: Whose interests are being served by the representations? Where can we situate such representations ethically and politically with respect to questions of social justice and human freedom? What moral, ethical, and ideological principles structure our reactions to such representations?

Fourth, it is important to take Solomon-Godeau seriously in her concern with how audiences, students, and others learn to identify, challenge, and rewrite the representations through which they inscribe themselves. More specifically, this means developing pedagogical practices that allow students to engage the means by which representational practices can be portrayed, taken up, and reworked subjectively so as to produce, reinforce, or resist certain forms of cultural representation and self-definition.

These appropriations indicate the value of Solomon-Godeau's approach for cultural workers both in and outside of the arts. However, if critical practice is to do more than provide a genealogy of how power works as part of a politics of representation, it is not enough to relegate progressive cultural work to the reflexive deconstruction of the institutional and discursive apparatuses of social and cultural reproduction. What is also needed is a social imaginary that configures a third space, one that offers normative notions or forms of ethical address that not only indicate, as Nancy Fraser has written, "what is wrong with the power/knowledge regime and why we ought to oppose it,"[14] but also points to a horizon of possibility in which the terms for self-definition and social agency offer new sets of social relations and a more compelling ethics of political and social responsibility.

For example, in the context of practices in which people are encouraged to take up and rework representations, there is a need for cultural workers to accentuate the mutually reinforcing moments of pedagogy and politics as primary to the practice of representing as an act of resistance and transformation. Richard Kearney has addressed, in part, this issue by posing the postmodern problematic of representation as an issue at once of politics, ethics, and pedagogy. The central question for him, as for us, is "how to imagine a set of relations which will do justice to the postmodern imaginary . . . to render due account of the complexities of our civilization of images; and to judge it justly according to adequate ethical criteria."[15] In attempting to partially respond to Kearney's concerns, we would propose that a pedagogy of representation firmly address the ethical imperative of providing a normative grounding for constructing relationships between ourselves and others.

Unlike Solomon-Godeau, we believe that more is demanded than an understanding of the content and context of representations and how they are used to fix identities within relations of domination and subordination. At issue here is the need to develop pedagogical practices that attempt to understand how knowledge, ethics, and desire come together to promote particular forms of cultural production, investments, and counternarratives that invoke communities of memory that are lived, felt, and interrogated. Within this context, a pedagogy of representations actively attempts to produce what Walter Benjamin called the "dream work" of dialectical images. It is precisely these images which serve to provide the grounds for counternarratives in which new visions, spaces, desires, and discourses can be developed that, in Kearney's words, "involve the power to unrealize repressive realities in favor of emancipatory possibilities."[16] In this way, students could be made more attentive both to the struggles that inform their own identities and to other struggles around culture and voice that often seem to have no relationship to their own lives.

At the very least, a representational pedagogy must renounce the notion of aesthetic autonomy and fully engage the social and political realities that shape the larger society; moreover, the knowledge, skills, and values that students acquire in rewriting the relationship between pedagogy and a representational politics must also be used to constantly interrogate the politics of their own locations and modes of understanding. One pedagogical qualification needs to be made here. A representational pedagogy and politics of representation must do more than promote self-understanding and an understanding of others, it must also work to create the institutional, political, and discursive conditions necessary so that power and privilege are not merely exposed or eliminated but, in R. S. Khare's words, are "consciously rendered reciprocal (and put to good use)."[17]

In conclusion, we believe that Solomon-Godeau's work is invaluable in fashioning important theoretical elements for a pedagogy of representation. Hers is a body of work whose significance for critical practice far exceeds the boundaries of art history; it is invaluable for understanding the ideological nature of the debate over the canon, the politics of feminist representation, and the rewriting of cultural criticism through a variety of postmodern discourses. But as part of a larger political project, it lacks the productive dynamics of a utopian discourse that can bear witness to representations that narrate cultural legacies which favor emancipatory possibilities and offer cultural workers, students, and others the opportunity to represent themselves in ways which suggest that they can imagine differently in order to act differently.

Cultural Studies and Pedagogical Strategies

6
The Turn Toward Theory

Theory has never fared well in educational circles. Highly pragmatic and behavioristic in both its assumptions and practices, the field of education historically has always viewed theory as something of an unnecessary intrusion. So maligned is the term that teachers often confuse it with methods, while summarily dismissing its value by arguing that they have never found it useful in their classes. Academics in colleges of education often debunk theory as the refuge of an elite who are hopelessly out of touch with reality. Even theorists in other disciplines appear to believe that theory has nothing to do with education. This is evident in the endless number of reviews in social theory journals that hold to a double standard. Theoretical discourse is encouraged for intellectuals writing in sociology, history, political science, and other areas in the humanities and liberal arts, but when it comes to judging the writing of educational theorists, it is often made quite clear that they have no right to write in complex theoretical terms.

This may be more than simply a matter of disciplinary elitism. Of course, it may be that theory becomes too dangerous when undertaken by people working in applied fields like education and thus demands a closer scrutiny in order for its borders to be policed. Or it may be that the canonization of the disciplines dictates for many theorists that education is simply a vocationalized field not worthy of serious theoretical work. Regardless of the characterization, I believe that with the pluralization of theoretical discourses, identities, and public spaces in the 1980s and '90s it is becoming increasingly more difficult to hold to such positions. Education has become a site of enormous contention and struggle popularized, in part, by the right-wing assault of the last fifteen years. Discourse is central to pedagogy, and pedagogy deepens its political possibilities by recognizing and acting upon those critical, theoretical discourses that broaden the capacity of educators and cultural workers to both understand and transform the related conditions of knowledge, power, collective agency, and social struggle. In what follows, I want to extend this argument by addressing the importance of appropriating selective aspects of literary theory and poststructuralism as part of a broader attempt to develop (an) insurgent pedagogy/ies aimed at reconstructing and animating numerous critical public cultures.

Within the last decade, the disciplines of literary theory and critical pedagogy have undergone major transformations.[1] With the advent of the attack on higher education by Reagan/Bush conservatives, it is clear that literary theory no longer serves unproblematically as the academic gatekeeper of a narrowly defined cultural tradition transmitted through the auspices of a largely white, patriarchal professorate. Influenced by the emerging critical discourses of feminism, poststructuralism, postmodernism, and postcolonialism, literary theory has developed a number of insurgent strands that offer rhetorical resistance to the diverse ways in which higher education secures authority and promotes dominating social relations.[2] Challenging existing disciplinary boundaries, rejecting the authorizing voice of the canon, and decentering traditional views of the subject and human agency, literary theory has burst upon the academic and popular scene with a vengeance.

Embroiled in what has been called the canon wars, right-wing and left-wing critics have launched a full-scale attack on critical theorists whom they deem responsible for what has been labeled as a "crisis" in the humanities. For conservatives such as William Bennett, Lynne V. Cheney, John Silber, and E. D. Hirsch, critical literary theory represents nothing less than a "barbaric" assault on the tradition of the Great Books, the humanist subject, and the allegedly universal values and prominent ideas of Western civilization.[3]

Critical strands of literary theory have also been criticized from a variety of left critics, particularly Marxists and feminists. Both groups have argued that the turn in literary theory toward analyzing processes of symbolization, representation, textual authority, and the construction of identity and sexuality represents a theoretical and political retreat into liberalism or, even worse, careerism.[4] In this case, literary theory is charged by some left critics of undermining the importance of addressing pressing political, material concerns such as poverty, rape, economic exploitation, the state, oppressive social structures, and global capitalism.[5]

The intersection between literary theory and critical pedagogy has its own narrative which I will address throughout this chapter, but it is worth noting that critical pedagogy as a separate and diverse movement has also undergone some major theoretical changes within the last decade. Once restricted to a few critical theorists in the field of education, critical pedagogy as both a theoretical discourse and a practical form of politics is now taken up in a variety of disciplines.[6] Moreover, like literary studies, pedagogy is generating something of a boom industry, and has found its way into a vastly expanding number of publishers' book lists. Of course, the proliferation of these two fields has not gone on unproblematically. There is widespread public debate over the central categories, premises, and practices being legitimated within various discourses that address the respective parameters that constitute these fields and the point at which they intersect in a kind of postdisciplinary borderland of theory and practice. More specifically, there is widespread disagreement not only over the meaning and purpose of literary studies and critical pedagogy, but also over the degree to which these fields are complicitous with the oppressive political and pedagogical practices they attempt to challenge and transform.

While a number of books have been published that attempt to integrate critical pedagogy into the disciplinary terrain of literary studies, few attempt to *make problematic* both the terrain of literary studies and its diverse appropriations of critical pedagogy. The desire to either adapt critical pedagogy to an existing body of literary theory or reduce pedagogy to a method for delivering literary studies more critically to students appears to be, for most theorists, an unavoidable inclination. However, what is crucial to this task is, in short, the reinsertion of the political into literary studies by defining it within the borders of critical pedagogical practice. Hence, unlike most "critical" notions of literary theory, this challenge cannot be taken up as a mere rearticulation of the call for the addition of heretofore excluded writers to the syllabus; nor can it be reduced to a call for a "new and improved" methodology in which critical pedagogy becomes one more approach to the arts that competent teachers and cultural workers must include in their professional repertoire. Instead, literary theory and pedagogy need to be seen as mutually informing discourses that produce conditions for learning and teaching that must be understood, engaged, and transformed if academics are to provide both an oppositional rhetoric and an insurgent practice in the classroom. What is refreshing to find among the diverse positions in literary studies with regard to certain aspects of poststructuralism is an overall agreement that the texts of everyday life can serve as reliable objects of social knowledge. Given this concurrence, theorists can begin to address the importance of literary studies not as a canonical body of knowledge but as a contested site of historical, aesthetic, and sociological categories that transcend conventional notions of disciplinary structure. In this way, the explosion of traditional notions of "the text" and poststructuralism's implicit challenges to textual authority provide an important interruption, a moment when theory can begin to be taken seriously both as a body of knowledge to be studied and as a form of pedagogical production in which students must engage.

I want to argue that the relationship between literary theory and critical pedagogy can be organized around four intersecting concerns. First, there is the need to define theory as central to any viable pedagogical practice. Second, there is the need to address critically the debate on the meaning and appropriation of poststructuralism in literary studies and its viability as a pedagogical practice. Third, it is essential to address the meaning and purpose of critical pedagogy as a concrete practice which informs both the disciplinary structure of the curriculum and the conditions for empowering students as what Maria-Regina Kecht calls "socially and historically inscribed subjects who can be agents of social transformation."[7] Fourth it is necessary to extend the debate over the principles that structure the disciplinary politics of the university, a debate which by implication raises important questions regarding how educators might mediate between their role as academics and their obligations as public intellectuals. Before turning to these issues, I want to make some general comments about poststructuralism since it is a discourse that references many of the concerns I will address.

THE POSTSTRUCTURALIST TURN

The turn to poststructuralism is rooted in an overall critique of materialism, the alleged coherence and meaning of texts, the Cartesian concept of the unified human subject, and an Enlightenment notion of foundationalism. In the first instance, poststructuralism in its various forms rejects the Marxist assumptions that consciousness is ultimately a refraction of matter and that economic relations constitute the primary organizing principle of a social order. Arguing that reality must be read as a text, poststructuralism reasserts the importance of language as a mode of representation that constitutes rather than merely expresses what counts as reality. At the same time, poststructuralism cannot be solely identified with the claim that nothing exists outside of language; on the contrary, various poststructuralist theorists reaffirm Michel Foucault's insight that nondiscursive forces have their own social and material gravity, but that they can only be understood within language and discourse. In this respect, power does not exist outside of language but is seen as an attribute of discourse in its capacity as a signifying practice to actually construct reality. Central here is the presupposition that any viable notion of critical agency has to be conscious of how power and authority are secured in the languages through which individuals speak and are spoken.

But poststructuralism does more than attempt to undermine theories of economic and material causality rooted in the legacy of Marxism. Equally destabilizing is its attack on the Cartesian notion of the humanist subject. Poststructuralist theorists have pointed to at least three major destabilizing forces. First, they have borrowed from Marx in arguing that history creates material and ideological conditions in the formation of individual and collective identities of which human beings have neither complete control nor a full understanding. Adding an important theoretical twist to this insight, history becomes less a search for the founding moment that will explain the present and the future than it does a text that needs to be interpreted and rewritten as an act of cultural recovery in which, as Michele Barrett writes, "one looks for meaning to the ongoing inner representations of experience, with current repetitions being seen as more significant than any 'original' moment."[8]

Second, poststructuralism has appropriated Freud's discovery of the unconscious in claiming that the self cannot completely know its own identity because its self-formation is never completely produced or revealed in consciousness. In this instance, rationality and consciousness provide only partial definitions of what constitutes human action and subjectivity.

Third, poststructuralists have argued powerfully that the self is constructed within and against language and that identity, like language, is always contingent, shifting, and deferred.[9] Within this formulation, the notion of an essentialized and fully transparent identity and universalized subject is replaced by one that is partial, decentered, and grounded in the particularities of history, place, and language. From this perspective, there is no subject or identity fashioned outside of its own history and contingency.[10] Ernesto Laclau comments on the importance of this insight in claiming that identity is only meaningful through an assertion of its own history. The implication being that "if something is essentially historical and contingent, this means that it can always be radically questioned."[11] If identity can only be understood in political and historically relational terms, this perspective suggests, then the entire modernist metaphysics of Western logocentrism is subject to question, subject to being viewed less as a civilizing discourse, as conservatives would argue, than as a colonizing practice that represses differences and the recognition of multiple identities. It is also important to acknowledge that the poststructuralist critique of the humanist subject is not tantamount to doing away with human agency or reducing human behavior to a function of shifting signifiers. What is at stake here is an attempt to interrogate how the subject is constructed, to more fully understand its constructed nature as the precondition of its agency, and to recognize that if the subject is formed through a social grid of exclusions and differentiations constitutive of multiple subject positions, then the crucial political issue becomes how such positions are actually negotiated.

Another important challenge that poststructuralism has brought to bear on literary studies and a number of other fields centers around its support of a radical antifoundationalism as a precondition for politically engaged critique and practice. Arguing against essentialism, poststructuralists have challenged versions of foundationalism and the illusion of a universality that masks the power relations inscribed in dominating claims for securing specific forms of authority, inclusion, and social relations. This is particularly true in the poststructuralist refusal of totalizing narratives that subsume complexity, specificity, and contingency while simultaneously rendering their own discourse as unquestionable. At stake here is a critique of any principle which, because of its claim to universal status, denies human agency by foreclosing decisions about how it is constituted and how it is to locate itself in the grid of social reality. In other words, universalism is denounced because it demands reverence rather than skepticism, recognition rather than critical engagement, and transmission rather than suspicion. Judith Butler raises serious questions about foundationalism as "an insidious cultural imperialism [which] legislates itself under the sign of the universal" and views the poststructuralist critique of this position as less an instance of "nihilistic relativism incapable of furnishing norms" than the precondition for a radical democratic feminism. She writes:

> A social theory committed to democratic contestation with a postcolonial horizon needs to find a way to bring into question the foundations it is compelled to lay down. It is this movement of interrogating that ruse of authority that seeks to close itself off from context that is, in my view, at the heart of any radical political project. Inasmuch as poststructuralism offers a mode of critique that effects this contestation of the foundationalist move, it can be used as part of such a radical agenda.[12]

For Butler and other theorists, the appeal to foundationalism undercuts the precondition for agency and political action. Agency in this case is undermined by being constituted outside of rather than within history. In a similar manner, Ernesto Laclau has argued that the critique of foundationalism is not a surrender to relativism, but a willingness to view exchange, dialogue, and critical analysis as conditions for the radicalization of democracy itself. As Laclau points out, "Practices such as that of deconstruction . . . accomplish the function of increasing our awareness of the socially constructed character of our world and open up the possibility of a foundation through collective decisions of what was before conceived as established forever by God, or by Reason, or by Human Nature—all those equivalent names that function by placing the destiny of human beings beyond the reach of their decisions."[13]

Of course, poststructuralism has also played an enormous role in developing a new politics of difference, one that not only resulted in the widespread adoption of a new conception of plural identities but that also pluralized public space itself, especially where cultural trends that emerged from the margins are concerned. The 1980s witnessed, for example, the emergence of black women's writing in the United States, the insertion of people of color in the production of film, photography, and aesthetic criticism, and the development of a vibrant cultural terrain constituted through the work of black lesbians and gay men in England.[14]

While there are any number of additional assumptions and practices that can be associated with the broad theoretical movement known as poststructuralism, it is impossible for me to develop them in this chapter, but I do want to make a qualification regarding poststructuralist theory that might seem either ironic or contradictory to some. Poststructuralism as a unified field does not exist. While there are central assumptions regarding language, identity formation, and representation that mark its theoretical borders, it is a diverse and fragmented collection of discourses that simply cannot be lumped together as a synthetic whole. Poststructuralist insights have been taken up by literary theorists, postcolonialists, feminists, critical educators, and a number of other academics and political activists. What is important to note is that poststructuralism comes in a variety of forms, be they radical, liberal, conservative, or downright apolitical. As a method, it can be used to legitimate an interest in textual analysis that is as narrow as it is depoliticized. It can also be used to buttress an elitist, "clever" aesthetic formalism that erases the marks of institutional power and concrete social conflicts. But poststructuralism is more than a retreat from politics and social engagement or an overbearing form of relativism. In the hands of different theorists, it has been used to highlight the representative spaces from which institutions construct dominant and subordinate voices. For example, many feminists have used it to deconstruct gendered representations and to make visible strategic exclusions in dominant narratives, texts, and practices.[15] Moreover, many educators have drawn upon poststructuralist insights to deconstruct the vanguardism of theory and the complex ways in which truth is produced to uphold relations of domination in the schools and other institutions.[16] In all of these cases, poststructuralism has attempted to make visible the relationship between violence and discourse, to illuminate how social groups are formed within relations of inequality, and to reveal how cultural hegemony is secured and contested.[17]

At stake here is a highly schematic rendering of poststructuralism that contests any attempt to position it as an artificially constructed whole in order that it then be summarily dismissed as what Judith Butler has called an "impending nihilism."[18] In accordance with Butler, I believe that "to install the term as that which can only be affirmed or negated is to force it to occupy one position within a binary."[19] Poststructuralism in this approach becomes an easy target. Moreover, this type of criticism undermines our ability to accomplish the more difficult task of appropriating those elements of poststructuralist discourse that might be useful for expanding the possibilities of critical pedagogy and cultural resistance. It is precisely in the intersection between poststructuralism and pedagogy that we must attempt to open up a dialogue and make such an appropriation an object of debate.[20]

THEORY AS A PEDAGOGICAL PRACTICE

One of the more disturbing aspects of critical pedagogy in the last few years has been a rising anti-intellectualism which subordinates theory to practice, conflates authority with authoritarianism, and reduces language to a vehicle of clarity. Almost without exception, recent work in this area has challenged these positions and made a strong case for the importance of theory as both a political and pedagogical practice.[21] Theory is understood here as central to any notion of critical pedagogy, but at the same time there is the recognition that an innovative theory does not necessarily constitute a radical approach to pedagogy. Many theorists address this tension by attempting to combine what I will call a pedagogy of theory and a pedagogy of theorizing. Moreover, students need to be exposed to a variety of theories but not in a way that reinforces the privileged authority of the teacher. Put simply, if educators make a distinction between teaching theory as a body of knowledge that informs students' understanding of the world and the practice of theorizing as a pedagogical activity in which students actually participate, it becomes possible to assert the mutual importance of both practices without one erasing or canceling out the other. Central to a pedagogy of theory is the assumption that teachers have a responsibility to teach theory, in David Shumway's words, as "a postdisciplinary practice . . . characterized by an attitude of skepticism toward accepted beliefs, a willingness to play with alternatives, a focus on what is entailed and not merely stated."[22] But at the same time, educators should not posit theory as something to be absorbed, on the contrary, they should define a pedagogical space where students become agents by doing theory. And this entails a pedagogy of theorizing.

Taken a step further, a pedagogy of theorizing insists that students need to be self-conscious about the theories that guide their perceptions. However, such a noble pedagogical goal is often vitiated when theory is taught through the banking concept of education, less as a basis for dialogue than as a quantifiable content to be stockpiled. Educators such as Joseph Harris want to rethink the pedagogy of theorizing around a set of reversals. Instead of teachers merely teaching theory, he wants students to theorize about how they as subjects are simultaneously produced, situated, and contained within the classroom. Instead of canonizing the teaching of theory through the lecture method, he wants to engage students in critical discussions, collaborative work, and postdisciplinary inquiries that put both classroom texts and the teacher's authority into question.[23] Theorizing in this case becomes more than an affirmation of student voice, it becomes a form of critical insurgency, a space of the possible in which intellectual responsibility is summoned in order to continually clarify questions of consciousness, desire, self, and social identity.

Central to a concern about the importance of theory as a discourse to be learned and theory as an activity to be practiced is the role of poststructuralist pedagogy in making it possible for such work to take place. It is to this issue that I will now turn.

IS THERE A POSTSTRUCTURALIST PEDAGOGY?

The intersection between poststructuralism and pedagogy represents a point of division and contention for and among many educational theorists. In one camp there are Marxists who view this conjuncture as lacking any referent for political and ethical guidance in an age marked by growing forms of despair and oppression. While such authors tend to present positions that are severely undialectical and often resort to forms of theoretical overkill, they do provide a number of criticisms that challenge the limits of a postructuralist pedagogy.[24] For example, one can argue that such a pedagogy often places power in the background because of its focus on interrogating texts and its overemphasis on reading strategies. Some theorists have argued that, by diverting attention from the social economy of power, poststructuralist pedagogues ignore the classroom as a site of contestation, power, and conflict. More specifically, when the classroom becomes merely a text to be read, the poststructuralist pedagogy that informs such a position places the school, knowledge, and power beyond the reach of history, suspended in a web of textual signifiers that simply need to be decoded. In this instance, poststructuralist pedagogy covers up its own authority and erases any trace of the relationship between power and knowledge, in the words of Mas'ud Zavarzadeh, by substituting "difference for contestation and replacing conflict with pluralism."[25]

Constituting a second camp are liberal critics who focus their criticisms on the shortcomings of "close reading" strategies that explore the how and what of the content of texts. These critics argue that poststructuralist educators fail either to interrogate how students learn or to make problematic the teacher's own relationship to power and knowledge. More specifically, critics have argued that the poststructuralist rupturing of the text often turns subversion into an aesthetic practice that fails to address how teachers, schools, and students are implicated in and subjected to various forms of oppression. The concern expressed in this case is that poststructuralist pedagogues rightfully recognize the power of the text, but in doing so they fail to render their own beliefs vulnerable to student interrogation. Critical attention is also given to the failure of poststructuralist pedagogy to focus on the myriad ways in which students learn, work collaboratively, and understand how institutions work politically.[26]

In opposition to the Marxist and liberal dismissal of poststructuralism, a third camp of critics attempt to define what might be called a "resisting" poststructuralism. For these theorists, the classroom is primarily concerned with struggles over the meaning and use of language. While harboring some reservations about poststructuralist pedagogy, these theorists believe that, in the long run, poststructuralism offers the tools and skills to call into question the boundaries of the academic disciplines and the ways in which different theoretical discourses both reinforce and police boundaries as well as transgress them. Thus, a new space might possibly be opened up to the construction of new forms of theory unobstructed by old regimes of truth, power, and authority. One of the central tasks of educators, in this view, becomes analyzing how language works when we undertake pedagogical practices. According to theorists such as Susan Horton, this involves more than insisting on the primacy of language in poststructuralist intervention; that is, literacy itself should be seen as a "relationship between an individual and a signifying practice."[27] For Horton and others, this means pedagogically that literacy becomes a way of investigating not only what students know and how they learn, but also what it means to enlarge the object of classroom study. Hence, to work with texts means enlarging the range of cultural significations that can be taken up as classroom texts, whether they be film, literature, music, or any other cultural object. The poststructuralist emphasis on deconstructing language invokes the necessity to take seriously the kind of literacy that students bring into the classroom; it means having students read their own writing as expressions of particular historical and social legacies, and it means helping students understand the different implications of diverse readings including their own.

Moreover, a poststructuralist pedagogy involves the learning of particular analytical skills that need to be taught by teachers and understood by students. For example, the demands of a poststructuralist pedagogy necessitate that teacher authority be invoked in order to provide the conditions for students to learn how to read complex materials, to understand why they are reading, and to make teacher authority the subject of an ongoing debate. In this case, teacher authority becomes a form of ethical address that provides a normative grounding for the conditions through which the relations of power and knowledge structure teacher/student practices.[28]

TOWARD A POLITICALLY ENGAGED PEDAGOGY

There are at least three ways in which the confluence of literary theory and pedagogy bears directly on the principle and practices of emancipatory education. Mas'ud Zavarzadeh has outlined what he calls a pedagogy of enablement. For Zavarzadeh, a pedagogy of enablement is premised on making the relationship among authority, power, and knowledge visible as these are concretely expressed in "relations between the teacher and the student and among the students in the classroom."[29] While Zavarzadeh is sketchy on how this is to happen, he is helpful in reminding educators that the classroom needs to be a place where the practices of the world must be interrogated, particularly as they shape, produce, and contain identities and experiences. Mistrustful of the humanist celebration of experience, Zavarzadeh wants educators to problematize how the act of knowing is related to the power of self-definition, how experience can be understood within its discursive construction. Joan Scott, in a different context, raises this issue provocatively in claiming that "it is not individuals who have experience, but subjects who are constituted through experience. Experience in this definition then becomes not the origin of our explanation, not the authoritative evidence that grounds what is known, but rather that which we seek to explain, that about which knowledge is produced."[30]

While various writers offer different strategies regarding the role of language in constructing a critical pedagogy, they largely believe that the prevailing system of power and authority, in part, resides in the ways in which language is produced, distributed, and circulated in the classroom. For Zavarzadeh, this insight suggests pedagogical practices based on Bertolt Brecht's use of epic theater. In this context, Zavarzadeh wants to reveal the social uses of language as it frames the production of classroom knowledge and social practices. By revealing the "situatedness" of representation and reception, Zavarzadeh wants to denaturalize how power works in the classroom in order to enable students to "make the world intelligible."[31] For Zavarzadeh all resistance to theory by educators and teachers simply becomes a trope for reproducing the status quo. In opposition to this view, he calls for a theory of intelligibility, "an inquiry into the grids of social intelligibilities produced by the discursive activities of a culture."[32]

How such a theory of intelligibility might work itself out pedagogically can be taken up in several ways. One intervention suggests that all pedagogy has to address what it means to promote "sane historical sense." That is, as Richard Ohmann writes, "it has to define itself as critical of both official history and the power relations that sustain it and are sustained by it."[33] This demands teaching about texts as subversive historical narratives. Taking seriously Walter Benjamin's admonition "to brush history against the grain,"[34] Ohmann illustrates how teachers might draw texts from popular culture and then historicize them in order to analyze them more critically. In this instance, he organizes a pedagogical lesson around the Virginia Slims ads comparing them historically with the flapper image used in 1920s advertising. Moreover, Ohmann skillfully poses questions to his students while encouraging them not only to engage in theoretically sophisticated forms of textual interrogation, but also to interrogate how domination actually works. Poststructuralism is valuable pedagogically in its use as a "crap detector," but he argues that "we need a more sensitive instrument that will identify the dangerous crap."[35] In other words, a critical pedagogy needs to overcome versions of a poststructuralist pedagogy that "makes possible a radicalism without the messy implications of engagement."[36]

The question becomes, thus, in addition to that of developing a critical sense of history, What constitutes a politically engaged pedagogy? There are at least two crucial pedagogical issues to take up here. First, teacher authority provides the normative space that organizes much of what is taught in classrooms. Unless this authority is problematized by both teachers and students, the crucial practices of naming and listening will not take place in classrooms. Problematizing teacher authority is far from an original issue for critical educators.[37] An interesting twist to this argument suggests that authority must be analyzed in part as a form of teacher resistance forged in the unwillingness of educators to open up their own values and use of power to classroom dialogue and exchange. In this way, student resistance is analyzed as a form of knowledge that must become visible. The "knowledge" that informs such resistance is viewed as an invitation for teachers and other cultural workers to make the students' desires, experiences, and stories an integral aspect of our teaching. But the call to bring the themes and texts of students' everyday lives into the classroom demands more than affirming and problematizing student resistance; it also means reordering the curriculum to allow the force and affective energy of other kinds of "texts," including films, videos, and music, to combine with the critical activity often allotted to written texts. Using various popular texts, teachers can begin to break down student resistance, promote collaborative engagement, and destabilize fixed notions of what constitutes valuable social knowledge. The texts of everyday life, when constituted as objects of social knowledge, provide the possibility for combining textual, historical, and ideological analyses that transcend the narrow limits of discipline-based inquiry and also serve to challenge the disciplinary function of canonical texts. A constant vigilance regarding teacher authority coupled with a respect for student knowledge mediates the obligations teachers have for expanding the possibility of public discourse such that the latter might engage how learning can be used to promote not merely varied forms of resistance but new subject positions and practices that encourage civic courage and radical, democratic citizenship in a postmodern, global world.

It seems to me that the importance of relating classroom knowledge to the everyday lives of students cannot be overemphasized. For example, theorists such as John Clifford strongly urge teachers to use student writing as a springboard not only for understanding how students construct themselves, but also for "helping students bring the authority of their own experience to bear on the texts they encounter."[38] Clifford believes that writing offers students an opportunity to rewrite the texts of the dominant culture by bringing to bear not merely their own experiences but a sharply tuned theoretical consciousness. For it is in the process of writing that the possibilities exist for students to understand how they are inscribed in language, what it means to rewrite language as an act of critical engagement, and to learn how to write in a variety of literacies. According to Clifford, the traditional call to reduce language to the trope of clarity is nothing more than an expression of masculine values, a retreat from the unsettling space of discursive ambiguity, uncertainty, and experimentation. Clarity in this case not only represents the privileging of appearance over rigorous inquiry, it also serves as an invitation for students and others to deskill themselves. That is, it positions human agency and cultural production outside of the struggle over language and meaning. But writing for many cultural workers is about more than a critical pedagogy of representation, it is also a way to read the larger culture in political, ideological, and historical terms.[39] These theorists want to find ways to use the classroom as a place to interrogate and resist the outside world. That is, they want to reassert pedagogy as a set of conditions within the context of a call for responsibility, freedom, and critical inquiry.[40]

CONCLUSION

While it is of no small importance to investigate the recent incorporation of theoretical trends such as poststructuralism in the service of critical pedagogical practice, the linking of literary theory and critical pedagogy addresses what I believe has become one of the central issues in education: the need for a better conception of the relationship between agency and subjectivity. While it has become commonplace to speak of the death of the subject, many theorists refuse to assume that since the subject is multiple it can only be presumed that there is no basis for recognizing agency in one's self or in others. On the contrary, one of the central theoretical issues raised in this crucial debate has been clearly articulated by Judith Butler:

> Agency is always and only a political prerogative. As such, it seems crucial to question the conditions of its possibility, not to take it for granted as an a priori guarantee. We need instead to ask, what possibilities of mobilization are produced on the basis of existing configurations of discourse and power? Where are the possibilities of reworking that very matrix of power by which we are constituted, of reconstituting the legacy of that constitution, and of working against each other those processes of regulation that can destabilize existing power regimes? For if the subject is constituted by power, that power does not cease at the moment the subject is constituted, for that

> subject is never fully constituted, but is subjected and produced time and again.[41]

Butler's notion that the subject is produced "time and again" raises some issues that highlight what is missing from this debate, and it is to these concerns that I want to turn.

In spite of the recent theoretical gains made in literary and cultural studies regarding the emphasis on decentering authority, exploring the relationship between language and experience, and the pedagogical conditions for teacher and student agency, there is a strange silence surrounding these investigations regarding the context in which education finds itself in the wake of the Reagan/Bush years. If schooling is primarily about context, why is it that theorists in these fields when addressing issues of pedagogy, almost without exception, say nothing of the right-wing assault on schools as democratic public spheres? Is it possible to talk about education in the 1990s and not mention the emergence of nativism, racism, and censorship in higher and public education? While there is a debate being waged around the struggle over the canon, there are few attempts to link any of the problems and possibilities of pedagogy to a viable, democratic political project.

Granted, critical educators take a great interest in interrogating authority, sharing power with students, and implementing postdisciplinary curricula, but what for? Why should domination be resisted? What are the ethical criteria or normative notions that allow us to make important political discriminations about what is worth knowing and doing in our classrooms? What do curricula and classroom practices presuppose about the nature of the political project that serves as a referent for what we do as engaged and committed intellectuals? Nancy Fraser has suggested that a "critical social theory frames its research program and its conceptual framework with an eye to the aims and activities of those oppositional social movements with which it has a partisan, though not uncritical, identification."[42] Fraser's point is important because it highlights two lacunae in current theoretical work. First, there are few attempts on the part of many of the theorists in the fields of cultural studies and literary studies to link their own work as intellectuals to larger social movements and struggles. Hence, there is no broader sense of the relationship between the pedagogical and the political in much theoretical writing. More specifically, there are few attempts to address university and school reform as part of a larger project for reconstituting a public culture that is democratic and socially just. Ironically, the vast majority of writers, while offering a brilliant critique of the dominant notions of received traditions and canonical knowledge, fail to accentuate the specificity of broader political projects that would challenge the ethical, political, and social nature of education from being overrun by right-wing fundamentalism and neoliberal vocationalism.

Second, the abstract quality of the language used in much of this writing rarely provides a focus on concrete, moral suffering.[43] There is no substantive indication of what is at stake here besides the fate of deconstruction, critical teaching, or the reform of literary studies. Thus, there is a tendency not only to contain some of the more brilliant insights to be found currently within poststructuralism, but also to inadequately challenge the very professionalism that has continually worked to depoliticize literary studies in spite of some of its most radical advocates.

Unfortunately, the newfound concern with pedagogy in academic departments outside the discipline of educational theory and practice is often characterized by a refusal to engage the diverse work that has been undertaken in this field by a number of critical educational theorists. For example, while pedagogy has become a "hot" topic in literary, French, gender, and English studies, the books produced in these disciplines largely suggest, by virtue of their theoretical gaps and structured silences, that pedagogy as a form of critical and political practice is a new theoretical invention discovered and developed within the narrow confines of each of these respective disciplines.[44] The resulting work often expresses itself in both reductionistic theories of pedagogy and as an indictment of specialized scholarly work; at the same time, this work implicates itself in the disciplinary elitism that haunts the overall structure of academic disciplines. In this case, the field of education is the "Other," marginalized and displaced as a serious source of theory, resistance, and cultural politics. This suggests not only a commentary about the academic status of educational theory as a discipline, but also the fear and loathing handed out to any area that is politically engaged and "closely" intersects with the everyday problems of public life. Unfortunately, few theorists writing both within and outside education escape the effects of this form of disciplinary terrorism.

It is ironic that, while many authors list among their primary objectives the challenge to existing disciplinary boundaries, there is little understanding of the work that has been done in pedagogy throughout the 1980s and early 1990s in critical educational studies. Disciplinary terrorism works in subtle ways. For example, what are we to make of one literary theorist's comment that "the relationship between theory and curriculum has remained largely undiscussed and unquestioned"?[45] These issues were being discussed by Roger Simon, Jonathan Kozol, Bill Pinar, Maxine Greene, and Herb Gintis in the 1970s. This is not to suggest that the theoretical gains currently being made across a variety of fields simply recycle existing work in critical pedagogy. All translations offer something new, open up further opportunities for examining the specificity of how pedagogy addresses problems that often cut across disciplines. Moreover, this work provides a number of valuable insights regarding how critical pedagogy is being fashioned in different ways in English departments in the United States. For those educators who are merely intellectual tourists, these are not comforting thoughts. But for those educators who are willing to struggle over language and expand the democratic imperatives for critical cultural workers, recent writing that takes up the relationship between literary studies and pedagogy is worth reading and engaging. At stake here are the theoretical and practical opportunities for educators and other cultural workers to cross over the disciplinary divide, explore new theoretical territories, and further understand how critical pedagogy is reconstituting itself in a postdisciplinary context.

7

Does Anybody Write in the Cultural Studies Classroom?

It is becoming increasingly difficult to assess what cultural studies is either as a political project or as a postdisciplinary practice.[1] For some theorists, it is precisely the emergence of cultural studies outside of the university and its articulation with various social movements, such as feminism, rather than its academic location that have helped to prevent it from being incorporated into the university as merely an additive to the established canon.[2] For others, cultural studies must be developed with regard not only to the changing nature and specificity of the problems and conflicts it addresses, but also to the legacy of its history as a preeminently political and oppositional practice.[3]

It is not my intention here to replay the debate regarding what the real history of cultural studies is, though this is an important issue. Instead, I want to analyze how certain features of the history of cultural studies might inform its present and future politics. More specifically, I want to focus on the importance of pedagogy as a central aspect of cultural studies and writing as a pedagogical practice. In doing so, I want to develop a notion of border writing as a form of cultural production forged among the shifting borderlands of a politics of representation, identity, and struggle. In part, I am concerned with a notion of cultural recovery in which the production of knowledge, subjectivity, and agency can be addressed as ethical, political, and pedagogical issues. This suggests critically appropriating from cultural studies the insights it has accrued as it has moved historically from its narrow concerns with class and language to its more recent analysis of the politics of race, gender, ethnicity, and colonialism. This is not meant to suggest that the history of cultural studies needs to be laid out in great detail as some sort of foundational exegesis. On the contrary, cultural studies needs to be approached historically as a mix of founding moments, transformative challenges, and self-critical interrogations.[4] And it is precisely the rupturing spirit that informs elements of its postdisciplinary practice, social activism, and historical awareness that prompts my concern for the current lacunae in cultural studies regarding the theoretical and political importance of pedagogy as a founding moment in its legacy. At the same time, it is important to stress that the general indifference on the part of many theorists to the importance of pedagogy as a form of cultural practice does an injustice to the politically charged legacy of cultural studies, one which points to the necessity for combining self-criticism with a commitment to transforming existing social and political realities.

Neither critical educators nor cultural studies theorists can ignore the relationship of pedagogy to cultural studies at the current historical juncture. Indeed, the indifference to pedagogy warrants a deep suspicion of the viability of the political project that informs such a view of cultural studies. Central to my analysis as well as to the politics of my own location as a teacher and cultural worker is the assumption that cultural studies must be grounded, in part, in a project that deepens and expands the possibilities for radical democracy both in the United States and abroad. Democracy in this sense is the discursive face and lived experiences of struggling to expand the conditions for social justice, freedom, and equality across all the major economic, political, and social spheres that shape, position, and locate people in everyday life. It is within this project that I want to address the importance of writing and pedagogy as central elements of an insurgent cultural studies.

In what follows, I want to argue that, while cultural studies represents an ensemble of diverse discourses, it is an important historical, political, and cultural formation that points to a number of issues that need to be addressed in pedagogical terms. I then want to provide a rationale for putting the language of pedagogy and politics back into the discourse of cultural studies as part of a broader attempt to expand and deepen what I will call a pedagogy of cultural studies. Finally, I will explain how I take up the issue of pedagogy as a cultural practice through the use of writing in my class. In part, this section not only discusses border writing as a form of pedagogical practice, but also suggests a connection between some of the central themes of cultural studies and writing as a cultural practice.

CULTURAL STUDIES AND THE ABSENCE OF PEDAGOGY

It is generally argued that cultural studies is largely defined through its analysis of the interrelationship between culture and power. This is particularly evident in two areas. First, cultural studies has strongly influenced a shift in the terrain of culture, as Stuart Hall has noted, "toward the popular."[5] Second, it has broadened the traditional idea of reading to encompass a vast array of cultural forms outside of the technology and print culture of the book. Not only has this resulted in a critical approach to the production, reception, and diverse uses of popular texts, but it has also expanded the meaning of more conventional works.

Texts, thus, in this case constitute a wide range of aural, visual, and printed signifiers; moreover, such texts are often taken up as part of a broader attempt to analyze how individual and social identities are mobilized, engaged, and transformed within circuits of power informed by issues of race, gender, class, ethnicity, and other social formations. All of these concerns point to the intellectual and institutional borders that define and contain meaning, marking it off as a site of social struggle. Moreover, one of the emerging theoretical features of cultural studies is its refutation of the notion that the struggle over meaning is primarily about the struggle over language and textuality.[6] On the contrary, a number of cultural studies theorists have named terror and oppression in concrete terms and have addressed how domination is manifested in a variety of sites, on a number of different levels, and how it can be understood in historical and relational terms through a variety of articulations and categories.[7] In fact, cultural studies draws its theoretical inspiration from feminism, postmodernism, postcolonialism, and a host of other areas. Lawrence Grossberg claims that cultural studies as a strategic practice performs two functions: first, it keeps alive the importance of political work in an "age of diminishing possibilities." That is, it radicalizes the notion of hope by politicizing rather than romanticizing it. Second, it refuses to collapse a commitment to political work into the frozen theoretical winter of orthodoxy. In this case, it responds to the specificity of history and in doing so leaves open the political cartography that informs how it names both its own strategies and the "world of political struggle."[8] The notion that cultural studies is unstable, open, and always contested becomes the basis for its rewriting as both the condition for ideological self-criticism and constructing social agents within rather than outside historical struggles. Grossberg writes:

> For cultural studies assumes that history—its shape, its seams, its outcomes—is never guaranteed. As a result, doing cultural studies takes work, including the kind of work deciding what cultural studies is, of making cultural studies over again and again. Cultural studies constructs itself as it faces new questions and takes up new positions. In that sense, doing cultural studies is always risky and never totally comfortable. It is fraught with inescapable tensions (as well as with real pleasures). In the U.S., the rapid institutional success of cultural studies has made it all a bit too easy. Cultural studies has to be wary of anything that makes its work too easy, that erases the real battles, both theoretical and political, that have to be waged, that defines the answers before it even begins.[9]

I want to take Grossberg at his word and argue that cultural studies is still too rigidly tied to the modernist academic disciplinary structures that it often criticizes. This is not to suggest that it does not adequately engage the issue of academic disciplines. In fact, this is one of its most salient characteristics.[10] What it fails to do is to critically address a major prop of disciplinarity, which is the notion of pedagogy as a transparent vehicle for transmitting truth and knowledge. Lost here is the attempt to understand pedagogy as a mode of cultural criticism for questioning the very conditions under which claims to authority are secured and knowledge produced. Of course, theorists such as Gayatri Spivak, Chandra Mohanty, bell hooks, Stanley Aronowitz, and others do address the relationship between cultural studies and pedagogy, but they constitute a small minority.[11] The haunting question here is, what is it about pedagogy that allows cultural studies theorists to ignore it?

One answer may lie in the refusal of cultural studies theorists to either take schooling seriously as a site of struggle or to probe how traditional pedagogy produces particular identities, how it constructs students through a range of social forms. Of course, within radical educational theory, there is a long history of developing critical discourses of the subject around pedagogical issues.[12]

Another reason cultural studies theorists have devoted little time to pedagogy may be the disciplinary terrorism that leaves the marks of its legacy on all areas of the humanities and liberal arts. Pedagogy is often deemed unworthy of being taken up as a serious subject; in fact, even popular culture has more credibility than pedagogy. This can be seen not only in the general absence of any discussion of pedagogy in cultural studies texts, but also in those studies in the humanities that have begun to examine pedagogical issues. Even in these works there is a willful refusal to acknowledge some of the important theoretical gains in pedagogy that have been made in the last twenty years.[13] Within this silence lurks a disciplinary policing, a refusal to cross academic borders, and a shoring up of the imperatives of careerism, competitiveness, and elitism. Of course, composition studies, one of the few fields in the humanities that does take pedagogy seriously, occupies a status as disparaged as the field of education.[14] Hence, it appears that the legacy of academic elitism and professionalism still exercises a strong influence on the field of cultural studies, in spite of its alleged democratization of social knowledge.

RECLAIMING PEDAGOGY

In what follows, I want to make a case for the importance of pedagogy as a central aspect of cultural studies. In doing so, I first want to analyze the role that pedagogy played in the early founding stages of the Birmingham Centre for Cultural Studies in England. I then want to define more specifically the central dimensions of pedagogy as a cultural practice. But before I address these two important moments of critical pedagogy as a form of cultural politics, I think it is important to stress that the concept of pedagogy must be used with respectful caution. Not only are there different versions of what constitutes critical pedagogy, but there is no generic definition that can be applied to the term. At the same time, there are important theoretical insights and practices that weave through various approaches to critical pedagogy. It is precisely these insights which often define a common set of problems that serve to delineate critical pedagogy as a set of conditions articulated within the context of a particular political project. Moreover, it is precisely such a project that takes up these problems differently within the specificity of particular contexts. These problems include but are not limited to the relationships between knowledge and power, language and experience, ethics and authority, student agency and transformative politics, and teacher location and student formations.

This is precisely how Raymond Williams addressed the issue of pedagogy in his discussion of the emergence of cultural studies in Britain. For Williams, pedagogy offered the opportunity to link cultural practice with the development of radical cultural theories. Not only did pedagogy connect questions of form and content, it also introduced a sense of how teaching, learning, textual studies, and knowledge could be addressed as a political issue which foregrounded considerations of power and social agency. According to Williams, the advent of cultural studies in the 1930s and 1940s directly emerged out of the pedagogical work that was going on in adult education. The specificity of the content and context of adult education provided cultural studies with a number of issues that were to direct its subsequent developments in Birmingham. These included the refusal to accept the limitations of established academic boundaries and power structures, the demand for linking literature to the life situations of adult learners, and the insistence that schooling be empowering rather than merely humanizing. Williams is quite adamant in refuting "encyclopedia articles dating the birth of Cultural Studies from this or that book in the late 'fifties." He goes on to say that "the shift of perspective about the teaching of art and literature and their relation to history and to contemporary society began in Adult Education, it didn't happen anywhere else. It was when it was taken across by people with that experience to the Universities that it was suddenly recognized as a subject. It is in these and other similar ways that the contribution of the process itself to social change itself, and specifically to learning, has happened."[15] For Williams there is more at stake here than reclaiming the history of cultural studies; he is most adamant in making clear that the "deepest impulse [informing cultural studies] was the desire to make learning part of the process of social change itself."[16] It is precisely this attempt to broaden the notion of the political by making it more pedagogical that reminds us of the importance of pedagogy as a cultural practice. In this context, pedagogy deepens and extends the study of culture and power by addressing not only how culture is shaped, produced, circulated, and transformed, but also how it is actually taken up by human beings within specific settings and circumstances. In this instance, pedagogy becomes an act of cultural production, a form of "writing" in which the process by which power is inscribed on the body and implicated in the production of desire, knowledge, and values begins not with a particular claim to postdisciplinary knowledge but with real people articulating and rewriting their lived experiences within rather than outside of history.

The importance of pedagogy to the content and context of cultural studies lies in the relevance it has for illuminating how knowledge and social identities are produced in a variety of sites, including schools. Pedagogy, in this sense, offers an articulatory concept for understanding how power and knowledge configure in the production, reception, and transformation of subject positions, forms of ethical address, and what Roger Simon calls "desired versions of a future human community."[17] By refuting the objectivity of knowledge and asserting the partiality of all forms of pedagogical authority, critical pedagogy initiates an inquiry into the relationship between cultural work, authority, and the securing of particular cultural practices. In this sense, as a mode of cultural politics, pedagogy takes as an object of study the relationship between the possibilities for social agency expressed in a range of human capacities and the social forms that often constrain or enable them. At stake here is not only the necessity to recognize pedagogy as a cultural practice, but also to address what Lawrence Grossberg has called the pedagogy of cultural practices.[18]

The politics of critical pedagogy is radical but not doctrinaire. That is, critical pedagogy self-consciously operates from a perspective in which teaching and learning are committed to expanding rather than restricting the opportunities for students and others to be social, political, and economic agents. As agents, students and others need to learn how to take risks, to understand how power works differently as both a productive and a dominating force, to be able to "read" the world from a variety of perspectives, and to be willing to think beyond the commonsense assumptions that govern everyday existence. Critical pedagogy engages experience in order to inquire into the conditions of its production, authorization, and effects. What is radical about the relationship between pedagogy and the issue of experience is that pedagogy addresses the inner workings of experience, how it functions to produce knowledge, and how it might be implicated in the construction of forms of subjectification. Politicizing the relationship between thought and experience points to a pedagogical practice in which cultural workers can offer, in Simon's words, "questions, analyses, visions and practical options that people can pursue in their attempts to participate in the determination of various aspects of their lives. . . . Required is a practice rooted in an ethical-political vision that attempts to take people beyond the world they already know but in a way that does not insist on a fixed set of altered meanings."[19]

Defined as an attempt to alter experience in the interest of expanding the possibilities for human agency and social justice, critical pedagogy makes visible the need for social relations that inform a number of considerations that cut across the diverse terrain of cultural studies.

WRITING AS A PEDAGOGICAL PRACTICE

In what follows, I want to describe how I use writing as a pedagogical practice to challenge certain dominant assumptions about the meaning of schooling, the discourse of authority, the relationship between language and experience, and the role of social responsibility within the politics of my own location as a university teacher. Most of the classes I teach at Penn State University are graduate courses in education and cultural studies. The students who take my courses are mostly working-class males and females, generally between the ages of twenty-five and sixty. Very few of the students are familiar with the theoretical discourses of cultural studies and critical pedagogy. In the past, I have tried to organize my courses around selected critical texts, combining introductory lectures with a seminar format in which students were asked to actively engage the texts by reading them oppositionally. Though this approach attempted to make the class more democratic, it failed to unsettle the kinds of social relations that characterize teacher-centered environments. The reasons are numerous and they include the following: first, many students felt intimidated by the language of theory. They often noted at some point in the class that the assigned texts were too difficult to read, that they didn't understand their practical application to education, or that they simply did not feel comfortable speaking through a discourse that seemed foreign to them. Second, many students have not problematized the ways in which traditional schooling has shaped their perceptions of power, learning, and identity. Many of the students in my classes believed that either their own voices did not count for much or that the only role for students in the class was to accept what was dispensed to them as knowledge rather than either raise questions about taking control over the conditions of the production of knowledge or approach the classroom texts critically in light of their own experiences, histories, and concerns. Third, whenever class discussion did occur, it was more often than not dominated by males, especially white males, in spite of the fact that women often constituted over fifty percent of my classes. Moreover, when students did speak they often looked at me rather than direct their remarks to other students. In this instance, they were positioning me as the authorizing agent for their discourse and for feedback.

It became clear to me very quickly that in spite of my use of oppositional material and the seminar format of the class, I was reproducing a set of pedagogical relations that did not decenter authority, undermined my attempts both to provide students with the opportunity to speak in a safe space and to appropriate power in the class in order to deconstruct the texts, and engage in collective self-criticism and a critique of the politics of my own location as a teacher.

In the first semester of the 1992-93 school year, I taught a new course called Postcolonialism, Race, and Critical Pedagogy. In this course, I attempted to address some of the above problems by organizing a series of pedagogical practices around particular writing assignments that helped to create what can be called, to use Homi Bhabha's phrase, a "third space" in the classroom. But before I articulate the details of the pedagogical practices that I employed, I want to mention a specific tension that I had already encountered in the classroom and in my own teaching.

Like many teachers, academics, and other cultural workers, I felt that the most substantive aspect of my pedagogy centered on defining my own goals for education along with the politics of my own location as a teacher. For example, my overriding pedagogical project was rooted in an attempt at majority democratic education—that is, an education whose aim is to advance the ideological and lived relations necessary for students to at least interrogate the possibility of addressing schooling as a site of ongoing struggle over what Judith Butler calls the "social and political task of transformation, resistance, and radical democratization."[20] This is a project that has continually driven my own politics and pedagogy regardless of the specific courses I have taught in the university. In looking back at this project, I have fewer reservations about its political importance than I do about the pedagogical practice of removing it from the actual social formations that shaped students' histories and lived experiences and which served to undo its most promising possibilities. In other words, by not paying more attention to what it meant to give students more control over the conditions of their own knowledge production, I reproduced the binarism of being politically enlightened in my theorizing and pedagogically wrong in my organization of concrete class relations. My wish to overcome this binarism was a major factor behind the reorganization of my pedagogy in the Postcolonialism, Race, and Critical Pedagogy class. Developing a series of reading and writing activities as the basis of the new course helped me to work through and resist the negative effects of my own authority as a teacher. In what follows, I want to spell out how I used border writing less as a technical exercise in skill development than as a form of cultural production that more closely articulated with the tenets of my political project as a progressive teacher and the underlying principles and practices informing the organization and character of my class.

My use of writing assignments was closely linked to getting students to theorize about their own experiences rather than articulate the meaning of other people's theories. The assignments were designed to get students to examine how representations signify and position learners through the institutional and ideological authority they carry in the dominant culture. Moreover, the writing assignments were constructed so as to give students the opportunity to acknowledge their own emotional and affective investments in issues related to race, colonialism, and the politics of representation. In addition, writing was not merely used as an ideological marker for locating specific biographical interests and forms of identification; it was also viewed as a rupturing practice, as an oppositional pedagogy in which one pushes against the grain of traditional history, disciplinary structures, dominant readings, and existing relations of power.

Raymond Williams has rightly pointed out the need for cultural workers to be attentive to the formations out of which specific projects arise. As part of an attempt not to reproduce the pedagogical practices that positioned students as the objects rather than the subjects of learning, I attempted to organize the writing assignments in my seminar around a number of structuring principles conducive to the success of my own political and pedagogical project. For instance, I introduced the course by talking about power in the classroom and how it was implicated in all aspects of classroom teaching, including the development of a syllabus, the organization of classroom relations, and the method of evaluation. I also made clear the rationale for the authority I exercised in the course and how that authority was to be used, or so I hoped, to expand rather than restrict the possibilities for student agency. In part, I made the form and content of my authority as a teacher visible in order to problematize and debate the moral vision and social ethic I used to justify my organization of the syllabus and the pedagogical practices that informed my class.

In doing so, I relinquished all claims to objectivity, and I attempted to refute the traditional notion that teachers are disinterested, that knowledge is unproblematic, and that teaching is merely a methodology for transmitting information to students. I argued that the latter positions are often used to obscure the ideological and political interests that regulate dominant versions of schooling and the role that teachers play in actively regulating the production of knowledge and values. By presenting a view of schools as sites of conflict and contestation, I attempted to open a space for students to engage political, social, and cultural differences in ways that would highlight pedagogy as an oppositional rather a merely a dominating practice.

In addition, I stressed the need for social relations in the class that would give students the opportunity to produce and appropriate knowledge as part of an ongoing struggle to represent themselves in terms of their interests, lived experiences, and wider political concerns. Two issues derived from the more political and emancipatory theoretical insights of cultural studies guided my pedagogical strategies. First, I wanted to make clear than any pedagogical process could not be located outside of the intellectual and affective investments I brought to the class. Hence, the politics of my own location had to be subjected to extensive critique and dialogue in the written assignments and class debates. Second, the class had to become a site where writing offered the opportunity, in the words of Meaghan Morris, to "engage rather than displace the voices of aggressive, theorizing [student] subjects."[21] I further suggested that some of the major elements structuring teacher-student relations in the class would be taken up around some of the following considerations: how do language and experience intersect? That is, how do different discourses shape, address, and deconstruct the experiences and stories told by ourselves and others? Second, what conditions are necessary to develop a sense of political, moral, and social agency in the classroom? For example, what pedagogical practices might be necessary to promote collaborative work? To examine dominant and subordinate traditions critically? To get students to question the partiality of both their own knowledge and the knowledge presented by the teacher? Third, how might teacher authority be manifested without being inimical to the issue and practice of student freedom?

By making my own theoretical and pedagogical concerns visible at the beginning of the semester, I was attempting to be up-front about the parameters of the course, especially in a school of education where students often believe that they will not have to read intellectually challenging work or that educational theory is mainly about learning methodologies. But there was more at stake here than exercising authority in the spirit of promoting rigorous intellectual work and providing a call for self-discipline; I also posited the goals and project of the course as an invitation for the students to rethink how they might want to take up and transform certain aspects of their own learning. For instance, in an effort not to remove all traces of their own socially and historically constructed voices, I asked students to form groups after my introductory remarks in order to respond to the issues I had raised. I was particularly interested in whether the principles and rationale I had offered for the course were suited to their own perception of what the course would be. I also invited the students to suggest specific readings beyond the assigned texts that we might take up in the class.

Within an hour the students convened their respective groups and a debate took place over the shape and format of the class. It became instantly clear to me that the students also wanted the class to be participatory, critical, attentive to immediate and global concerns regarding racial politics, and they wanted to both provide their own list of readings for the course and evaluate their own performance for a course grade. Gently exercising my own authority, I mediated their concerns with three qualifications. First, I suggested that the course be organized around a series of writing assignments that reproduced the principles they had articulated in the discussion. Second, in order to relieve the immediate fear that students often express about writing in a class, I suggested that, as a major precondition for discussing the student writing presented to the class, it was imperative for all of us to create the conditions for a "safe space" for each other. Since students often feel that their identities are on trial when they either speak from their writing or share it with the rest of the class, I considered it crucial that students be given every opportunity to speak, argue, take risks, and position themselves without fear of intimidation, humiliation, or outright pedagogical terrorism from either the teacher or other students. In this case, issues of trust and respect for difference became paramount in structuring classroom relations. In addition, I suggested that students make every attempt to use their writing as a pedagogical tool to present their theoretical position, to promote class discussions, to engage other texts, and to work collaboratively with others. Third, while they would be given the opportunity to evaluate their own final projects, those projects should be organized around an attempt to integrate the theoretical discourses taken up in the class with an analysis of some aspect of popular culture. For example, an individual or a group might decide to write about how the legacy of colonialism frames much of the racial discourse in a film like Lawrence Kasdan's *Grand Canyon* (1992). Students might also want to mix media in compiling a critical commentary on racism in the university, the town, or the national media. Or they might want to focus on popular magazines as a source of social knowledge, use ethnographic approaches to conducting oral histories, construct their own video, and so on.

As part of an attempt to pay close attention to the political and pedagogical dynamics that structured the class, three major writing assignments were used to organize how texts were to be taken up and rewritten in an effort to register differences, analyze diverse arguments, and cross disciplinary borders.

The writing assignments were organized in the following ways. The initial three weeks of the course were developed around analyzing the reading material largely selected by the class. The readings in this case were taken up through the thematics of "Orientalism, Difference, and Multiculturalism," "Postcolonialism, Race, and Feminism," and "Nationalism and the Politics of Speaking for Others." The class was divided into three groups. Each group was assigned the task of developing a position paper on the readings for one of the three thematics. The papers would then be duplicated for the rest of the class and used as a basis for class discussion.

Each group worked collaboratively to produce a paper that was then duplicated and read by the rest of the class the evening the reading assignment was due. The group assigned to present a paper for a given class first talked about how they came to address a particular aspect of the assignment, how they worked out the collaborative process, and why they thought the issues they addressed were important to them in terms of their own experiences. For example, the first group developed a paper that was a transcript of a dialogue they collectively held in analyzing certain aspects of the readings they had done on Orientalism and the politics of multiculturalism. The paper clearly demonstrated those issues over which individual members of the group disagreed, what concerns they shared, and what questions they wanted to take up with the rest of the class. It is important to note that students who did not present a group paper during any one class meeting had to prepare journal entries on the readings assigned and in doing so worked from their own notes in responding to both the group paper and other questions that arose from the readings. Since the readings ranged from sources as diverse as Cornel West's "The New Politics of Difference" to Diane Ravitich's "Multiculturalism," there was a range of ideological positions to engage, which made for lively discussions.[22]

But in discussing the papers the emphasis was not merely on taking up conflicting positions. Students had to insert themselves into the texts by taking a position on the readings, talking about the consequences of their positions in terms of how they addressed questions of race, freedom, justice, and so on. Moreover, the group constantly talked about how the university itself was implicated in reproducing some of the racial problems they discussed and how the racial problems in the school articulated with and reinforced larger societal problems.

During the second part of the course, students paired up and each week for the remainder of the course one pair of students would teach the text assigned for that particular week. Books discussed ranged from "*There Ain't No Black in the Union Jack*" by Paul Gilroy to *Black Looks* by bell hooks and *Learning to Question* by Paulo Freire and Antonio Faundez. In this assignment, students had to "write" the book; that is, they had to present a paper that provided an exegesis, offer a critical reading of the text's major assumptions, and analyze the relevance of the text to their own experiences as future educators. Moreover, they could present their analysis in a variety of mixed formats but had to use a substantial portion of their time for dialogue with the rest of the class. The presentations were on the whole amazingly imaginative. Most students combined a short lecture with some other medium to illustrate their analysis of the texts. Most prepared open questions to give some structure to the debates, and in certain cases provided the rest of the class with alternative or supplementary readings.

The third writing assignment consisted of a collaborative position paper based on applying some aspect of what the students had learned about race and pedagogy in the class to a particular problem in the wider university community. The activities undertaken ranged from an analysis of the textbooks used in the local secondary school to an interrogation of the racial-sensitivity seminars conducted by some faculty in the university. In each case, the students had little trouble in linking some of the theoretical issues addressed in the class with wider practical and pedagogical concerns.

The final writing project in the class enlisted writing as a pedagogical practice by getting students not only to analyze popular texts that extend the range of what constitutes social knowledge, but also to be self-reflective about their own engagement with the course and what its implications were for rethinking the ways in which power works through diverse regimes of representation, institutional structures, and the larger spaces of social power.

All of these writing assignments positioned students as cultural producers and enabled them to rewrite their own experiences and perceptions through an engagement with various texts, ideological positions, and theories. In all cases, the students consistently attempted to learn from each other, to decenter the power in the classroom, to challenge disciplinary borders, to create a borderland where new hybridized identities might emerge, to take up in a problematizing way the relationship between language and experience, and to appropriate knowledge as part of a broader effort at self-definition and ethical responsibility. Border writing in this case became a type of hybridized, border literacy, a form of cultural production and pedagogical practice where otherness becomes comprehensible, collective memory rewrites the narratives of insurgent social movements, students travel between diverse theoretical and cultural zones of difference and in doing so generate a space where new intersections between identity and culture emerge. It is precisely in this space informed by the critical imperatives of cultural studies and the ongoing demands of a restless critical pedagogy, that teachers and students can rewrite, reaffirm, and struggle over the central issue of modern politics and life in the United States—the goal of achieving a multicultural and multiracial democracy.

8

Paulo Freire and the Rise of the Border Intellectual

> Yet we have different privileges and different compensations for our positions in the field of power relations. My caution is against a form of theoretical tourism on the part of the first world critic, where the margin becomes a linguistic or critical vacation, a new poetics of the exotic.
>
> —Caren Kaplan, "Deterritorializations"

The work of Paulo Freire continues to exercise a strong influence on a variety of liberal and radical educators. In some quarters his name has become synonymous with the very concept and practice of critical pedagogy. Increasingly, Freire has become the standard reference for engaging in what is often referred to as teaching for critical thinking, dialogical pedagogy, or critical literacy. As Freire's work has passed from the origins of its production in Brazil through Latin America and Africa to the hybrid borderlands of North America, it has been frequently appropriated by academics, adult educators, and others who inhabit the ideology of the West in ways that often reduce his work to a pedagogical technique or method. Of course, the requisite descriptions generally invoke terms like "politically charged," "problem-posing," or the mandatory "education for critical consciousness" and often contradict the revolutionary nature of

Freire's pedagogical practice.[1] But in such a context, these are terms that speak less to a political project constructed amid concrete struggles than they do to the insipid and dreary demands for pedagogical recipes dressed up in the jargon of abstracted progressive labels. What has been increasingly lost in the North American and Western appropriation of Freire's work is the profound and radical nature of its theory and practice as an anticolonial and postcolonial discourse. More specifically, Freire's ideas are often appropriated and taught, as Robert Young has written, "without any consideration of imperialism and its cultural representation. This lacuna itself suggests the continuing ideological dissimulation of imperialism today."[2] This suggests that Freire's work has been appropriated in ways that denude it of some of its most important political insights. Similarly, it testifies to how a politics of location works in the interest of privilege and power to cross cultural, political, and textual borders so as to deny the specificity of the Other and to reimpose the discourse and practice of colonial domination.

I want to argue that Paulo Freire's efforts must be read as a postcolonial text and that North Americans, in particular, must engage in a radical form of border crossing in order to reconstruct Freire's work in the specificity of its historical and political construction. More specifically, this means making problematic a politics of location situated in the privilege and power of the West and engaging the question of how the ideological weight of such a position constructs one's own reading of Freire's work. At the same time, becoming a border crosser engaged in a productive dialogue with others means producing a space in which those dominant social relations, ideologies, and practices that erase the specificity of the voice of the Other must be challenged and overcome.

In order to understand the work of Paulo Freire in terms of its historical and political importance, I want to explore what it means for cultural workers to become border crossers. Border crossing suggests that teachers and other intellectuals both problematize and take leave of the cultural, theoretical, and ideological borders that enclose them within the safety, in Joan Borsa's words, of "those places and spaces we inherit and occupy, which frame our lives in very specific and concrete ways."[3] Being a border crosser suggests that one has to reinvent traditions not within the discourse of submission, reverence, and repetition, but, as Ernesto Laclau writes, "as transformation and critique. [That is,] . . one must construct one's discourse as difference in relation to that tradition and this implies at the same time continuities and discontinuities."[4] Border crossing engages intellectual work in its specificity and partiality, as part of a discourse of invention and construction rather than a discourse of recognition whose aim is reduced to revealing and transmitting universal truths. In this case, it is important to highlight intellectual work as being forged at the intersection of contingency and history arising not, according to Laclau, from the "exclusive hunting grounds of an elite [but] from all points of the social fabric."[5]

This task becomes all the more difficult with Paulo Freire because the borders that define his work have shifted over time in ways that parallel his own exile and movement from Brazil to Chile, Mexico, the United States, Geneva, and back to Brazil. Freire's work draws heavily not only upon European discourses, but also upon the thought and language of theorists in Latin America, Africa, and North America. Freire's ongoing political project raises enormous difficulties for educators who situate Freire's work in the reified language of methodologies and in empty calls that enshrine the practical at the expense of the theoretical and political.

Freire is an exile for whom being home is often tantamount to being "homeless" and for whom personal identity—one's own and that of Others—is viewed as a site of struggle over the politics of representation, the exercise of power, and the function of social memory.[6] It is important to note that the concept of "home" being used here does not refer exclusively to those places in which one sleeps, eats, raises children, and sustains a certain level of comfort. For some, this particular notion of "home" is too mythic, especially for those who literally have no home in this sense; it also becomes a reification when it signifies a place of safety which excludes the lives, identities, and experiences of the Other, that is, when it becomes synonymous with the cultural capital of white, middle-class subjects.

"Home," the way I am using it, suggests a critical destabilizing gesture. It refers to the cultural, social, and political boundaries that demarcate varying spaces of comfort, suffering, abuse, and security that define an individual or group's location and positionality. To move away from "home" is to question in historical, semiotic, and structural terms how the boundaries and meanings of "home" are often constructed beyond the discourse of criticism. "Home" is about those cultural spaces and social formations which work hegemonically and as sites of resistance. In the first instance, "home" is safe by virtue of its repressive exclusions and privileged location of individuals and groups outside of the flux of history, power, and ethics. In the second case, "home" becomes a form of "homelessness," a shifting site of identity, resistance, and opposition that enables conditions of self- and social formation. Abdul JanMohamed captures this distinction quite lucidly.

> "Home" comes to be associated with "culture" as an environment, process, and hegemony that determine individuals through complicated mechanisms. Culture is productive of the necessary sense of belonging, of "home"; it attempts to suture . . . collective and individual

> subjectivity. But culture is also divisive, producing boundaries that distinguish the collectivity and what lies outside it and that define hierarchic organizations within the collectivity. "Homelessness," on the other hand, is . . . an enabling concept . . . associated with . . . the civil and political space that hegemony cannot suture, a space in which alternative acts and alternative intentions which are not yet articulated as a social institution or even project can survive. "Homelessness," then, is a situation wherein utopian potentiality can endure.[7]

For Freire, the task of being an intellectual has always been forged within the trope of homelessness: between different zones of theoretical and cultural difference; between the borders of non-European and European cultures. In effect, Freire is a border intellectual[8] whose allegiance has not been pledged to a specific class and culture, as in Antonio Gramsci's notion of the organic intellectual; instead, Freire's writings embody a mode of discursive struggle and opposition that not only challenges the oppressive machinery of the state but is also sympathetic to the formation of new cultural subjects and movements engaged in the struggle over the modernist values of freedom, equality, and justice. In part, this explains Freire's appeal for educators, feminists, and revolutionaries in Africa, Latin America, and South Africa.

As a border intellectual, Freire disrupts the humanist relationship between individual identity and collective subjectivity. He makes visible a politics that links human suffering with a project of possibility, not as a static plunge into a textuality disembodied from relations of power and human struggles, but as a critical literacy forged in the political and material dislocations of regimes that exploit, oppress, expel, maim, and ruin human life. As a border intellectual, Freire occupies a terrain of "homelessness" in the postmodern sense that suggests there is little possibility of ideological and hegemonic closure, no relief from the incessant tensions and contradictions that inform one's own identity, ideological struggles, and dreams of future possibility. It is this sense of "homelessness," this constant crossing over into terrains of otherness, which characterizes both Freire's life and his work. It is as an exile, a border being, an intellectual posed between different cultural, epistemological, and spatial borders that Freire has undertaken to situate his own politics of location as a border crosser.

It is to Freire's credit as a critical educator and cultural worker that he has always been extremely conscious of the intentions, goals, and effects of crossing borders and of how such movements offer the opportunity for new subject positions, plural identities, and insurgent social relations that can produce resistance to and relief from structures of domination and oppression. While this insight has continuously invested his work with a healthy "restlessness," it has not meant that Freire's work has developed unproblematically. For example, in his earlier writing, Freire attempted to reconcile an emancipatory politics of literacy and a struggle over identity and difference with certain problematic elements of modernism. Freire's incessant attempts to construct a new language, produce new spaces of resistance, and imagine new ends and opportunities to reach them were sometimes constrained by totalizing narratives and binarisms that deemphasized the mutually contradictory and multiple character of domination and struggle. In this sense, Freire's earlier reliance on emancipation as being one and the same with class struggle sometimes erased how women were subjected differently to patriarchal structures; similarly, his call for members of dominating groups to commit class suicide downplayed the complex, multiple, and shifting nature of human subjectivity. Finally, Freire's reference to the "masses," or oppressed, as being inscribed in a culture of silence appeared to be at odds with both the varied forms of domination these groups labored under and Freire's own belief in the diverse ways in which the oppressed struggle and manifest elements of practical and political agency. While it is crucial to acknowledge the theoretical and political brilliance that informed much of this early work, it is also necessary to recognize that it bore slight traces of vanguardism. This is evident not only in the binarism that informs *Pedagogy of the Oppressed* but also in *Pedagogy in Process: The Letters to Guinea-Bissau*, particularly in those sections where Freire argues that the culture of the masses must emulate and develop on the model of science, and that emancipatory pedagogy must be aligned with the struggle for national reconstruction.

Because it does not adequately address the contradictions these issues raise between the objectives of the state, the discourse of everyday life, and the potential for pedagogical violence being done in the name of political correctness, Freire's work is open to the charge made by some leftist theorists of being overly totalizing.[9] But this assessment can be read less as a reductive critique of Freire's work than as an indication of the need to subject it and all forms of social criticism to analyses that illuminate its strengths and limitations as part of a wider dialogue in the service of an emancipatory politics. The contradictions raised by Freire's work suggest a number of questions that need to be addressed by critical educators and cultural workers about not only Freire's earlier efforts but also their own. For instance, what happens when the language of the educator is not the same as that of students or subordinate groups? How is it possible to be vigilant against taking up a notion of language, politics, and rationality that undermines recognizing one's own partiality and the specificity of the voices and experiences of Others? How does one explore the contradiction between validating certain forms of "correct" thinking and the pedagogical task of helping students become critical agents rather than simply follow the dictates of authority. Of course, it cannot be forgotten that the strength of Freire's early discourse rests, in part, with its making visible not merely the ideological struggle against domination and colonialism but also the material substance of human suffering, pain, and imperialism. Forged in the heat of life-and-death struggles, Freire's use of binarisms such as the oppressed vs. the oppressor, problem solving vs. problem posing, science vs. magic, and so on raged bravely against dominant languages and configurations of power that refused to address their own politics by appealing to the imperatives of politeness, objectivity, and neutrality. Here Freire strides the boundary between modernist and anticolonialist discourse; he struggles against colonialism, but in doing so he often reverses rather than ruptures its basic problematic. Benita Parry locates a similar problem in the work of Frantz Fanon: "What happens is that heterogeneity is repressed in the monolithic figures and stereotypes of colonialist representations. . . . [But] the founding concepts of the problematic must be refused."[10]

In his later writing—particularly in his work with Donaldo Macedo—in his numerous interviews, and in his talking books with authors such as Ira Shor, Antonio Faundez, and Myles Horton, Freire undertakes a form of social criticism and cultural politics that pushes against those boundaries that invoke the discourse of the unified, humanist subject, universal historical agents, and Enlightenment rationality.[11] Refusing the privilege of home as a border intellectual situated in the shifting and ever-changing universe of struggle, Freire invokes and constructs elements of a social criticism that shares an affinity with emancipatory strands of postmodern discourse. That is, in his refusal of a transcendent ethics, epistemological foundationalism, and political teleology, he further develops a provisional ethical and political discourse subject to the play of history, culture, and power. As a border intellectual, he constantly reexamines and raises questions about what kinds of borders are being crossed and revisited, what kinds of identities are being remade and refigured within new historical, social, and political borderlands, and what effects such crossings have for redefining pedagogical practice. For Freire, pedagogy is seen as a cultural and political practice that takes place not only in schools but in all cultural spheres. In this instance, all cultural work is pedagogical and cultural workers inhabit a number of sites that include but are not limited to schools. Most recently in a dialogue with Antonio Faundez,

Freire talks about his own self-formation as an exile and border crosser. He reflects:

> It was by travelling all over the world, it was by travelling through Africa, it was by travelling through Asia, through Australia and New Zealand, and through the islands of the South Pacific, it was by travelling through the whole of Latin America, the Caribbean, North America and Europe—it was by passing through all these different parts of the world as an exile that I came to understand my own country better. It was by seeing it from a distance, it was by standing back from it, that I came to understand myself better. It was by being confronted with another self that I discovered more easily my own identity. And thus I overcame the risk which exiles sometimes run of being too remote in their work as intellectuals from the most real, most concrete experiences, and of being somewhat lost, and even somewhat contented, because they are lost in a game of words, what I usually rather humorously call "specializing in the ballet of concepts."[12]

It is here that we get further indications of some of the principles that inform Freire as a revolutionary. It is in this work and his work with Donaldo Macedo, Ira Shor, and others that we see traces, images, and representations of a political project that is inextricably linked to Freire's own self-formation. It is here that Freire is at his most prescient in unraveling and dismantling ideologies and structures of domination as they emerge in his confrontation with the ongoing exigencies of daily life as manifested differently in the tensions, suffering, and hope between the diverse margins and centers of power that have come to characterize a postmodern/ postcolonial world.

Reading Freire's work for the last fifteen years has drawn me closer to Theodor Adorno's insight that "it is part of morality not to be at home in one's home."[13] Adorno was also an exile, raging against the horror and evil of another era, but he was also insistent that it was the role of intellectuals, in part, to challenge those places bounded by terror, exploitation, and human suffering. He also called for intellectuals to refuse and transgress those systems of standardization, commodification, and administration pressed into the service of an ideology and a language of "home" that occupied or were complicitous with oppressive centers of power. Freire differs from Adorno in that there is a more profound sense of rupture, transgression, and hope, intellectually and politically, in his work. This is evident in his call for educators, social critics, and cultural workers to fashion a notion of politics and pedagogy outside of established disciplinary borders, outside of the division between high and popular culture, outside of what Biddy Martin and Chandra Mohanty call "stable notions of self and identity . . . based on exclusion and secured by terror,"[14] outside of homogeneous public spheres, and outside of boundaries that separate desire from rationality, the body from the mind.

Of course, this is not meant to suggest that intellectuals have to go into exile to take up Freire's work, but it does suggest that in becoming border crossers, it is not uncommon for many of them to engage his work as an act of bad faith. Refusing to negotiate or deconstruct the borders that define their own politics of location, they have little sense of moving into an "imagined space," a positionality from which they can unsettle, disrupt, and, in Carol Becker's words, "illuminate that which is no longer home-like, *heimlich*, about one's home."[15] From the comforting perspective of the colonizing gaze, such theorists often appropriate Freire's work without engaging its historical specificity and ongoing political project. The gaze in this case becomes self-serving and self-referential, its principles shaped by technical and methodological considerations. Its perspective, in spite of itself, is largely, as JanMohamed writes, "panoptic and thus dominating."[16] To be sure, such intellectuals cross borders less as exiles than as colonialists. Hence, they often refuse to hold up to critical scrutiny their own complicity in producing and maintaining specific injustices, practices, and forms of oppression that deeply inscribe the legacy and heritage of colonialism. Edward Said captures the tension between exile and critic, home and "homelessness," in his comment on Adorno, though it is just as applicable to Paulo Freire:

> To follow Adorno is to stand away from "home" in order to look at it with the exile's detachment. For there is considerable merit in the practice of noting the discrepancies between various concepts and ideas and what they actually produce. We take home and language for granted; they become nature and their underlying assumptions recede into dogma and orthodoxy. The exile knows that in a secular and contingent world, homes are always provisional. Borders and barriers, which enclose us within the safety of familiar territory can also become prisons, and are often defended beyond reason or necessity. Exiles cross borders, break barriers of thought and experience.[17]

Of course, intellectuals from the First World, especially white academics, run the risk of acting in bad faith when they appropriate the work of a Third World intellectual such as Paulo Freire without what JanMohamed calls "mapping the politics of their forays into other cultures,"[18] theoretical discourses, and historical experiences. It is truly disconcerting that First World educators rarely articulate the politics and privileges of their own locations, in any case, so as at the very least to be self-conscious about not repeating the type of appropriations that inform what Said calls "Orientialist" scholarship.[19]

I want to conclude by raising some issues regarding what it might mean for cultural workers to resist the recuperation of Freire's work as an academic commodity, a recipe for all times and places. Additionally, I want to offer some broad suggestions for reinventing the radicality of Freire's work within the emergence of a postcolonial discourse informed by what Cornel West terms the "decolonization of the Third World" and characterized by "the exercise of . . . agency and the [production of] new . . . subjectivities and identities put forward by those persons who had been degraded, devalued, hunted, and harassed, exploited and oppressed by the European maritime empires."[20] The challenge presented by Freire and other postcolonial critics offers new theoretical possibilities to address the practices, authority, and discourses wedded to the legacy of a colonialism that either directly constructs or is implicated in social relations that keep privilege and oppression alive as active constituting forces of daily life within the centers and at the margins of power.

Postcolonial discourses have made clear that the old elements of the political Left, Center, and Right can no longer be as easily defined as they once were. Indeed, postcolonial critics have gone further and provided important theoretical insights into how partisan discourses either actively construct colonial relations or are implicated in their construction. From this perspective, Robert Young argues that postcolonialism is a dislocating discourse that raises theoretical questions regarding how dominant and radical theories "have themselves been implicated in the long history of European colonialism—and, above all, the extent to which [they] continue to determine both the institutional conditions of knowledge as well as the terms of contemporary institutional practices—practices which extend beyond the limits of the academic institution."[21] This is especially true for many of the theorists in a variety of social movements who have taken up the language of difference and a concern for the politics of the Other. In many instances, theorists within these new social movements have addressed political and pedagogical issues through the construction of binary oppositions that not only contain traces of racism and theoretical vanguardism but also fall into the trap of simply reversing the old colonial problematic of oppressed vs. oppressor. In doing so, they have often unwittingly imitated the colonial model of erasing the complexity, complicity, diverse agents, and multiple situations that constitute the enclaves of colonial/hegemonic discourse and practice.[22]

Postcolonial discourses have both extended and moved beyond the parameters of the debate on identity politics and difference in a number of ways. First, postcolonial critics have argued that the history and politics of difference are often informed by a legacy of colonialism that warrants analyzing the exclusions and repressions that allow specific forms of privilege to remain unacknowledged in the language of Western educators and cultural workers. At stake here is the task of demystifying and deconstructing forms of privilege that benefit maleness, whiteness, and property as well as those circumstances that have disempowered Others from speaking in places where those who are privileged by virtue of the legacy of colonial power assume authority and impose the conditions for human agency. This suggests, as Gayatri Spivak has pointed out, that more is at issue here than problematizing discourse. More important, educators and cultural workers must be engaged in "the unlearning of one's own privilege. So that, not only does one become able to listen to that other constituency, but one learns to speak in such a way that one will be taken seriously by that other constituency."[23] In this view, postcolonial discourse extends the radical implications of difference and location by making such concepts attentive to providing the grounds for forms of self-representation and collective knowledge in which the subject *and* the object of European culture are problematized.[24]

Second, postcolonial discourse rewrites the relationship between the margin and the center by deconstructing the colonialist and imperialist ideologies that structure Western knowledge, texts, and social practices. In this gesture, there is an attempt to demonstrate how European culture and colonialism, according to Robert Young, "are deeply implicated in each other."[25] This suggests more than rewriting or recovering the repressed stories and social memories of the Other; it means understanding and rendering visible how Western knowledge is encased in historical and institutional structures that both privilege and exclude particular readings and voices, certain aesthetics and forms of authority, specific representations and modes of sociality. The West and otherness relate not as polarities or binarisms in postcolonial discourse but in ways in which both are complicitous and resistant, victims and accomplices. In this instance, criticism of the dominating Other returns as a form of self-criticism. Linda Hutcheon captures the importance of this issue with the question: "How do we construct a discourse which displaces the effects of the colonizing gaze while we are still under its influence?"[26]

While it cannot be forgotten that the legacy of colonialism has meant large-scale death and destruction as well as cultural imperialism for the Other, the Other is not merely the opposite of the Western colonialist, nor is the West a homogeneous trope of imperialism. This observation suggests a third rupture provided by postcolonial discourses. The current concern with the "death of the subject" cannot be confused with the necessity of affirming the complex and contradictory character of human agency. Postcolonial discourse reminds us that it is ideologically convenient and politically suspect for Western intellectuals to talk about the disappearance of the speaking subject from within institutions of privilege and power. This is not to suggest that postcolonial theorists accept the humanist notion of the subject as a unified and static entity. Conversely, postcolonial discourse agrees that the speaking subject must be decentered; but this does not mean that all notions of human agency and social change must be dismissed. Judith Butler has illuminated this position by arguing that the critique of the subject as constructed and decentered is tantamount neither to doing away with the issue of human agency nor to claiming that subjectivity is ready-made, fixed, and overdetermined. On the contrary, the critique of the subject is essential to analyzing the subject's "construction as a pregiven or foundationalist premise. . . . the constituted character of the subject is the very precondition of its agency . . . [and] agency can be presumed only at the cost of refusing to inquire into its construction . . . . As such, it seems crucial to question the conditions of its possibility, not to take it for granted as an a priori guarantee."[27] Understood in these terms, the postmodernist/poststructuralist notion of the subject must be accepted and modified in order to extend rather than erase the possibility of creating the enabling conditions for human agency. At the very least, this would mean coming to understand the strengths and limits of practical reason, the importance of affective investments, the discourse of ethics as a resource for social vision, and the availability of multiple discourses and cultural resources that provide the very grounds and necessity for agency.[28]

Of course, while the burden of engaging these postcolonial concerns must be taken up by those who appropriate Freire's work, it is also necessary for Freire to be more specific about the politics of his own location and what the emerging discourses of postmodernism and postcolonialism mean for a self-reflective engagement with both his own work and his current location as an intellectual aligned with the state (Brazil). If Freire has the right to draw upon his own experiences, how do these get reinvented so as to prevent their incorporation by First World theorists within colonialist rather than decolonizing discourses and practices? In raising this question, however, I want to emphasize that what makes Freire's work important is that it doesn't stand still. It is not a text for but against cultural monumentalism, one that offers itself up to different readings, audiences, and contexts. Moreover, Freire's work has to be read in its totality to gain a sense of how it has engaged the postcolonial age. Freire's writing cannot be separated from either its history or its author, but it also cannot be reduced to the specificity of intentions or historical location. Maybe the power and forcefulness of Freire's works are to be found in the tension, poetry, and politics that make it a project for border crossers, those who read history as a way of reclaiming power and identity by rewriting the place and practice of cultural and political resistance. Freire's work represents a textual borderland where poetry slips into politics, and solidarity becomes a song for the present begun in the past while waiting to be heard in the future.

9

Traveling Pedagogies

INTRODUCTION

Lech Witkowski is an internationally renowned scholar who holds the chair of Contemporary Philosophy at Nicolas Copernicus University in Torun, Poland. He is a prolific writer, actually a border intellectual, who writes as fluently about literary theory and philosophy as he does about education. Professor Witkowski and I have been collaborating since 1986. We share a common concern about the dynamics of educational reform as it works itself out in the vastly complex postmodern world of the 1990s. In collaboration with his colleague Professor Zbigniew Kwiecinski, editor of the Polish journal *Absent Discourses*, Professor Witkowski has written cogently about the need for a new educational discourse. For him the legacy of Marxism and the increasingly vocationalized language of the free market offer little hope for addressing and transforming the educational system in Poland. Passionately eager to invent a discourse that promotes rather than closes down schooling for critical and responsible citizenship in Poland, Professor Witkowski and his associates invited me to Poland in April of 1992 to discuss the history of critical educational discourse in the United States. In my conversations with him, Professor Kwiecinski, and the minister of education, pedagogy, postmodernism, multiculturalism, and a host of other concerns often missing from the debates in the United States were discussed. In what follows, I present an interview that Professor Witkowski conducted with me and later published in Poland.[1] The interview is important less for what I say than for the sharpness of the questions and concerns that Witkowski expresses in his questions and comments. I present this interview as an example of collaborative work and a tribute to the Polish educators I met during my short time in Warsaw and Torun.

LECH WITKOWSKI: To start our interview, Henry, the first question I would like to ask you concerns the basic definition of your idea of pedagogy. As one of the leading representatives of this important stream of educational theory which is called critical or radical pedagogy, don't you feel sometimes uneasy with people's reaction toward the notions of radicalism or criticism? How would you defend intellectually this "radicalism" in terms of your pedagogy in a way that permits you at the same time to avoid accusations of being an extremist (in a political sense)?

HENRY A. GIROUX: I believe that the notion of radical needs to be appropriated for furthering the necessary conditions human beings need in order to imagine living in a society that expands the range of their potentialities and desires as part of the advancement of democratic public life. In this sense, the concept of "radical" points to a number of considerations for creating the possibilities for human agency and for developing public spaces organized around issues of dialogue, social justice, freedom, and equality. Radical in these terms signals for me the assumption that all forms of teaching, learning, and knowledge contribute to the possibility for people not only to understand the world but to also act in the world, to transform it. This suggests a definition of radical that is unsettling and destabilizing. Such a definition of radical points to practices, ideas, and social relations that provide the basis for people to think beyond the given, that they may engage what I would call horizons of possibility, thus placing themselves within the contexts of history so as to be able not simply to be moved by history but also to change it. In these terms, the notion of "radical" does not take on a disparaging connotation that suggests that it is at odds with human struggle, agency, and projects of possibility. On the contrary, this reappropriation of the notion of radical demands that we recover its most emancipatory moments historically, articulate the diverse conditions under which it points to practices that open up rather than close down democratic practices, and use it as a signifier to insert the ethical and political back into the struggle over schooling and the construction of a democratic society. Hence, the concept of radicalism and the concept of democracy essentially become synonymous.

LECH WITKOWSKI: OK. When I look through your books and your papers I get a feeling that what you mean by pedagogy is specific and expansive, linking forms of educational theory, social theory, and cultural studies in a way that, as I understand, is not casual. At the same time I think that the term "struggle" is one of the key terms for your perception of a pedagogical framework. How would you define your position and how would you explain, from your point of view, the need for the term "struggle" in your program of pedagogy?

HENRY A. GIROUX: I think that when you begin with a definition of pedagogy as the production of knowledge, identities, social relationships, and values that takes place in a variety of cultural sites, one important question becomes, whose values, whose identities, whose knowledge, whose social relationships? In other words, who speaks for whom and under what conditions? If pedagogy serves to point to specific conditions in which knowledge, power, and identities come into play as part of a larger conception of social life, it is imperative *not* to view it as a disciplinary subject, methodology, or process that simply has to be transmitted. Once pedagogy is reduced to a set of absolute truths, methodologies, or standards, the ethical and political referents that give it meaning appear to exist outside of history, struggle, and human intervention. This is a prescription for legitimating authoritarian knowledge; it is a pedagogy without any self-criticism regarding the politics of its own representation. Pedagogy should always be addressed as a site of conflict and dialogue. It should be treated with respect, not reverence. Far from being a totalizing narrative or monolithic set of ready-made practices, pedagogy is a complex, shifting set of theoretical and political interventions into the relationship between knowledge and authority and how the latter are expressed and taken up within specific contexts. In part this means that questions concerning teaching, learning, desire, and power should always be taken up as part of a set of guiding narratives concerning what kind of future one wants to build for future generations, what it means to create a world without injustice, and so on. If all pedagogical practice is implicated in the production of stories, then it becomes imperative to raise the questions: Whose stories are being produced under what circumstances? What social relations do they legitimate? What histories do they exclude or include? How are they complicitous with legacies of patriarchy, colonialism, racism, and other forms of oppression? As Roger Simon has pointed out, such stories are never innocent. By removing schooling from the shield of objectivity, it becomes more clear how the terrain of pedagogy, with its intersection of politics, power, and morality, must always be viewed as the site of contestation and struggle. Pedagogy is not something that is merely transmitted, it's always something that is struggled over.

LECH WITKOWSKI: But keeping in mind that notion of struggle, how would you see the possibility for linking this progressive notion with more traditional pedagogical concerns that are of considerable importance, like those of objectivity, those of autonomy, those of compromise and coexistence of diversity . . . ?

HENRY A. GIROUX: Well, let me place the question in a somewhat different context. I believe that issues of objectivity, autonomy, and consensus are tied to a modernist project that has subordinated, on the one hand, the central issues of how values and ideologies work through our scholarship, subjectivities, and the production of different forms of representation. In the name of science and objectivity, such discourses often fail to locate their own politics and in doing so become unaccountable politically and ethically. Certainly pedagogy needs to be rigorous, fair, aware of its own theoretical limitations, and be willing to engage its assumptions through interactions with the world. But at the same time, we need a new language for this type of understanding, engagement, and analysis of what intellectual work is and does. For example, I don't believe that one can talk about pedagogy unless you talk about a particular project: that is, what's the project that critical pedagogy emerges out of, or what is the location of its politics and the politics of its location? And in this sense my argument would be that pedagogy is always a struggle against what I call forms of monumentalism and totalitarianism, specifically those narratives that deny the existence of difference, assault the possibilities of democracy, and often promote forms of infantilism, demagoguery, oppression. More specifically, the concept of struggle has at least two very important defining elements; first it emerges out of an ethical discourse, the ability to imagine the "not-yet" in the Blochian sense; second, it is always linked not simply to the question of individual consciousness and action but also to the promise of solidarity in struggle. In other words, pedagogy is linked to how as educators we both understand and act collectively to promote forms of radical tolerance, civic courage, good judgment, justice, and rational discourse in the service of creating the good life for all citizens.

LECH WITKOWSKI: Yes, I see. But, of course, as I understand it, the pedagogue is not concerned with struggle in an overt sense—organizing political parties, going to clashes in the streets, etc., and you share this observation. There are a lot of forms of oppression and symbolic violence which are hidden within sometimes very soft, very gentle methods of manipulation in human interactions. Therefore it seems to me that the idea of struggle must take into consideration this particular aspect of hidden confrontation which actually takes place.

HENRY A. GIROUX: I think that the notion of oppression operates both in a hard and a soft sense. It operates in the hard sense in that it takes place on the *terrain of the visible:* those oppressive practices such as police brutality, the use of government torture, assaults on the bodies of workers, women, and people of color (wage slavery, homelessness, rape, racist attacks). All of these practices point to sites of struggle that are easily recognizable. But what has often happened in the late twentieth century, as Antonio Gramsci brilliantly pointed out, is that people often find themselves positioned within forms of knowledge, institutional structures, and social relationships that have a "creeping or quiet" kind of hegemony about them. The forms of domination they produce and sustain are not so obvious, they're not so clear. For instance, dominant groups often invite people to deskill themselves by promoting what might be called regimes of common sense; in this case, people are presented with narratives about their lives, society, and the larger world that naturalize events in order to make it appear as if particular forms of inequality and other social injustices are natural, given, or endemic to questions of individual character. In this case, social problems are decontextualized historically and politically and defined through the narrow landscape of essentialism, fate, or destiny. And I think that pedagogy needs to both demystify those kinds of hidden forms of domination, but at the same time go beyond a simple hermeneutics. A critical pedagogy must address how meanings get mobilized in the interest of domination by linking the questions of knowledge and power not simply to the most visible kinds of struggle, though that's very important, but also to struggles that take place at the interstices of everyday life. I mean specifically social relations forged in the classroom, tracking the hidden curriculum—the ways in which students are sorted out by virtue of class, race, gender—as well as all those spaces which people inhabit that shape their identity in a particularly harmful way. I think critical pedagogy needs to make the operations of domination visible through analysis of the structured absences that shape texts, social forms, and institutional structures. For example, texts of all sorts must be read critically not only in terms of what they say, but also in terms of what they leave out, exclude, and deny.

LECH WITKOWSKI: To understand better the progress of critical pedagogy, it is useful to situate it, as you do, in contexts of two other dominating streams in American pedagogy, namely one that you call neoconservatism and the other one that you call neoliberalism. Now, could you articulate your understanding of the basic disagreement with these two alternative ways of thinking about educational institutions and initial pedagogy?

HENRY A. GIROUX: First, it is important not to underestimate the complexity and diverse positions that characterize political ideologies such as conservativism and liberalism. These are not unified ideologies and they contain within and across their parameters many similarities and differences. In another words, there is no absolute sign under which both can be categorically inserted. In the more general sense, I want to draw upon a distinction first used by Philip Corrigan between what he called human capacities and social forms in order to talk about neoconservatism, neoliberalism, and the issue of pedagogy. Human capacities refer to the abilities students and others have to think, learn, act, desire, and engage in a variety of performative skills that define their horizons of agency and possibility. Social forms refer to the home, the school, the workplace—all those institutional places and public forms that people inhabit in daily life. Neoconservatives in the United States generally argue from the ideological perspective of functionalism; that is, they believe that the role of education is to promote those human capacities in students that enable them to adapt to existing social forms such as schools, the state, and the workplace. Therefore the kind of pedagogy that often emerges out of the conservative position is usually one of transmission as opposed to critically engaged inquiry. Knowledge in this case is often objectified, standardized, and atomized as part of a management pedagogy. Moreover, culture is treated less as an ongoing social and historical production than as an artifact. Once again, learning is reduced to simply the act of reverence. Similarly, the appeal to knowledge is often made in terms that are universal or transcendent. This does not translate into a pedagogy of struggle; on the contrary, it supports what I would call a pedagogy of adaptation.

Liberal pedagogy, on the other hand, operates from the humanist assumption that there is a unified subject, that such a subject is a source of all actions, that the experience of self is constituted as transparent and given. In this scenario, there is no conflict between thought, experience, and reality. What is missing in the liberal paradigm is the necessity to explore how identity and experience are constructed through a variety of subject positions. There is no sense here of how experiences are produced, authorized, and exercised within conflicting terrains of power, ideology, and discourse. Nor is there any sustained analysis of how identities are fashioned socially, under conditions of inequality, and what this suggests for understanding the role that schooling and pedagogy might play in such a process. Hence, without any attempt to explore the constituted character of experience, subjectivity, and agency, neoliberals are too quick to attribute all behavior and learning solely to the sutured and privatized world of the individual. In this formulation, the social as a dynamic political and formative assemblage of pedagogical and ethical practices simply is erased. Hence, the neoliberal emphasis on universal standards, national curriculum, and testing. The notion of the unified subject supports the suppression of difference as a relational category forged within asymmetrical relations of power and in doing so treats culture as a unified category, and schooling as its unproblematic dispenser. Within this perspective, liberals often depoliticize knowledge, dehistoricize knowledge, and refuse to engage classroom knowledge as an object of contestation that links schools to other social phenomena. Schools appear too innocent in this formulation. There is little sense of the powerful role that schools play in maintaining and sustaining certain relations of domination.

LECH WITKOWSKI: I see. But I now want to raise an issue concerning your perception of culture as both a sphere of human behavior and a symbolic universe which is not coherent but full of contradictions. Intolerance and injustices make up a part of everyday life for individuals and, moreover, they take on a kind of insistent necessity for various individuals or groups. The traditions of such groups are rooted in the everyday practices of their cultures and inscribed in ways that promote long-lasting hatreds and intolerance. If we take, for example, any radical group of youngsters who clash among themselves—for example, youth gangs, which certainly constitute part of existing school populations: How might a radical pedagogy address these historically inscribed capacities, hatreds, and conflicts? One only has to look at the seething nationalist and ethnic conflicts emerging all over Europe to get a sense of the divisions that pedagogically and politically fracture cultural life. How do we engage students in terms of the contradictions that arise when intolerance is supported by different cultural traditions and practices?

HENRY A. GIROUX: I want to approach this issue from another perspective, and in doing so, hopefully, I will create the grounds for my answer. One starting point in responding to these difficult questions is to address how culture as a category is often taken up within the conservative approaches to schooling. For conservatives, culture is often treated as not only uniform but also stable, right? So that you often have an educational system based on a notion of culture that is both uniform and elitist. Difference in this view of culture often is seen as either a threat or as an object of assimilation. Moreover, this position, more often than not, supports a view of high culture that disdains popular culture. One pedagogical consequence of this is that schools tend to refuse to take the different voices of various groups seriously; that is, they reproduce the pedagogical tendency to refuse to recognize that there are diverse cultures, multiple literacies, and that people speak from within a wide range of contradictory and multiple positions. Pedagogy in this instance often defines students categorically through tracking, racism, sexism, and other practices of "otherness" in which students who are "Other" are placed at a pedagogical and institutional disadvantage by virtue of their differences. This is no small problem because ideologies are then developed which serve to blame these students for the very prejudices they suffer in schools. If their identities are not part of the dominant culture, students very quickly learn that their histories and voices have been erased—they are not affirmed, they are not taken up, they are not built into the culture itself. And it seems to me that if you are going to make knowledge critical you first have to make it meaningful. In other words, those identities have to be affirmed so that they can be then interrogated and extended to address other discourses and cultural traditions. But even more important, it seems to me that what we often find in dominant pedagogy is a rigid refusal to deal with difference—cultural, political, sexual, class—as in fact something that expands the possibility for dialogue and human rights. Difference is also generally seen as deviance, so that any attempt to incorporate difference into the curriculum is often seen as a threat, a subversive gesture that undermines the fiction of what I want to call a kind of coherent culture. All forms of fascism, to my mind, weak or strong, are built on a totalizing notion of culture that is comparable to the erasure of difference. Whereas in radical pedagogy difference is seen as absolutely central, not only in terms of learning different discourses, but also in terms of what it means to address student perceptions and experiences in ways that put them inside of the curriculum rather than outside of it. We can take up the issue of cultural differences only by recognizing that educators and students have to be border crossers, to move into different zones of culture, and address relations of power, as part of the politics and pedagogy of enrichment, social justice, and democratic struggle.

LECH WITKOWSKI: In all practical pedagogical efforts and educational systems, the development of curriculum and the selection of certain theoretical or cultural contexts is labeled with the term "canon" . . .

HENRY A. GIROUX: Right . . .

LECH WITKOWSKI: Now, you perceive mass culture or popular culture as something which has to be linked with the canon in order to give education a role to play in developing, promoting, and increasing the everyday competencies and capacities needed for students to function in a postmodern world. In your more recent work you talk about "decentering the canon," you seem to distrust the canon as the way to organize educational programs. What would be the alternative strategy for developing curricula?

HENRY A. GIROUX: I think that what we have to do is to ask ourselves certain questions that precede the issue of canonicity: What are schools for, what purpose do they have? Who is served by such purposes? What role does knowledge and its relationship to power have in constituting particular versions of citizenship, authority, history, and justice? If in fact schools have as their central purpose the responsibility to educate people to govern, to live in the world, to understand how history shapes them and where they come from, then the notion of the canon must be addressed from at least two perspectives. First, the canon cannot be removed from the ideologies and practices it legitimates as part of a broader process of social and moral regulation. In other words, the canon must be seen as an ideological and political attempt to organize and reconstruct history, teaching, and learning in particular ways. This is not altogether bad unless the notion of the canon is elevated beyond the realm of history, criticism, and social engagement. In other words, canons are something we struggle over rather than simply submit to. Second, the concept of the canon must be rearticulated in terms of a multiplicity of canons. This means that the canon cannot be thought of as some reified form of knowledge handed down from the past that one simply passes on out of reverence. We have to ask ourselves: What's the relationship between knowledge and power? How do we organize knowledge and power in such a way as to provide the greatest possible conditions for people to be able to develop their diverse capacities and needs, enlarge the spheres of social justice to all aspects of human life, and actively promote the multiplication of diverse critical public cultures? That is, how can the question of the canon contribute to helping students and others become agents in shaping their future? If educators are going to develop a notion of the canon that is decentered and multiple, educators may need to be more attentive to addressing the curriculum as an ongoing critical dialogue over what knowledge contributes to educating students for positions of leadership and social responsibility in a vastly changing multicultural and multiracial world. To develop and enter into dialogue with the knowledge and social relations that constitute any canon means it has to be recognized as an ideological construct configured within particular relations of power. Canons emerge out of particular interests, social relations, and contexts. They are as much about policing knowledge as they are about creating borderlands of genuine inquiry. Moreover, canons are almost always on the side of the powerful. This makes it all the more imperative that canons be refigured in postdisciplinary terms as a borderland of knowledge and values that serves as a place of transit in which a wide variety of cultures and traditions can be critically analyzed and debated. There is another set of questions, ideological in nature, that I think we've both raised—and that is: how are canons used to secure particular forms of authority? Whose interest is served by that authority? How does that authority correlate with a project of democratic radical reform? Authority is the central issue! If we can't ask these questions, it seems to me that the notion of academic canons becomes ammunition for securing hierarchies of power that simply serve very privileged groups of people. A decentured curriculum must challenge any notion of canonicity.

LECH WITKOWSKI: Well, I have read your texts for a number of years now, and it always struck me that one of the most essential challenges you bring into pedagogy is the one linked with language, not only with a particular vocabulary but also an opening up of new theoretical perspectives, new ways of perceiving traditional terms. Let's talk about your basic categories, and in this way discuss the specificity of your language. It seems to me that there are a number of such categories. One of them is what you call in your texts "emancipatory authority."

HENRY A. GIROUX: Right . . .

LECH WITKOWSKI: Given the multiple perspectives from which one can take up this term, it seems to open itself up to a series of contradictions because on one side it promises resistance to a particular form of authority while at the same time there exist those traditional pedagogues using the concept of authority in rather oppressive ways. There are, for example, the so-called humanistic psychologists, and those pedagogues who romanticize an image of emancipation from authority while denying the possibility of agency. How would you defend your concept of "emancipatory authority," showing that it simultaneously avoids the danger of authoritarianism in the traditional sense and promotes the autonomy of individuals involved in emancipatory struggle?

HENRY A. GIROUX: The concept of "emancipatory authority" denotes a range of meanings and these need to be struggled over in terms of contexts and content. For instance, in the United States, and I can only speak from this context, the notion of authority is often equated with a definition of authoritarianism. And what we often find is that people on the Left who are progressive often believe that the only route to progressive pedagogical action lies in giving up authority. Of course, my argument is that to give up authority is to renounce the responsibility of politics, struggle, and commitment as educational projects. Students must be able to enter into discourses and into social relationships that would make problematic not only their own stake in authority but also the very notion of authority itself; that is, how it's used and what kinds of possibilities it contains. So it seems to me that there is a double movement here. First, to define the pedagogical as a political act necessitates that teachers assume responsibility for establishing conditions for students to be able to theorize, address critically their relationship to each other and the world, and negotiate the contradictory and antagonistic instances that position their everyday lives. But of course, such a view of authority must always be subject to debate, recognize its own partiality, and be open to change. Second, it seems to me that the question of authority is always central in defending the kinds of pedagogy I incorporate within my own classroom. This means, in part, developing an ethical discourse that references my rationale and use of classroom authority. In doing so, I situate myself not within a discourse in which my authority is taken for granted and therefore uncontestable but, in fact, is rendered visible as an ethical, political, and social construct. So it seems to me that authority both provides a basis for action that is problematic and speaks to a particular set of interests, but it also provides a rationale for me to be able to define myself as a transformative and engaged public intellectual. Authority, in this case, becomes both a necessity and an object of dispute.

LECH WITKOWSKI: OK. The other category I find essential to your work is that of "civic courage," where you emphasize the fact that schools very often silence people and teach them to accept their silent position in society, as opposed to promoting their ability to speak to their own interests and to speak for themselves—to have civic courage. And I see it as linked essentially with another aspect of your theory where you indicate the necessity for school to become part of a democratic "public sphere" . . .

HENRY A. GIROUX: Right . . .

LECH WITKOWSKI: How would you see the chance and how would you analyze the possibilities to insert into the daily practice of schools the promotion of civic courage with that necessary but hard-to-meet condition of making school part of the public sphere?

HENRY A. GIROUX: This is a very important question, one that I have been grappling with for some time. It is absolutely one of the most fundamental and central dimensions of my work. If there is a consistency in my writing over the last twenty years it is around this issue, and I want to make that qualification before I answer your question. It seems to me that, if we are going to talk about the issue of schooling from the perspective of critical pedagogy, a number of important concerns must be addressed. One starting point is to recognize that there is always the danger that the conservative agenda for education is premised on adapting students and other people to existing configurations of power. In this case, the language and pedagogy of adaptation is about a form of schooling not linked to civic courage but civic cowardice. I believe educators must guard against notions of schooling which abstract the concept of the public from the schooling process. This approach is especially evident in the United States in those reform movements in which the notion of the public and all of its attendant issues of rights, responsibilities, and obligations are pitted against issues of privatization, the logic of the market, and the overemphasis on individual competitiveness and achievement. In this perspective, learning is reduced to satisfying the highly individualized needs of what is euphemistically called excellence. In this formulation, the issue of equity is at odds with rather than necessary to pedagogical work. This is a barely disguised discourse which privileges the rich, whites, and males.

Conversely, I start with the assumption that schooling is an absolutely central public service in the life of a nation. Schools offer the opportunity for a nation to dedicate itself in a self-reflexive way to forms of education dedicated to responsible citizenship, while simultaneously speaking to the responsibilities of future generations struggling for democracy. The central issue driving these concerns is that democracy must be viewed as a site of practices where government by the people is defined as part of the ongoing struggle over what democracy means. Democracy is not simply inherited. At every moment democracy has to be struggled for. So the question becomes, how do we educate students to believe that schools are more than simply vehicles for social and economic mobility but in fact provide a noble service essential for expanding power, economic and political, so that various groups can participate in the shaping of the nation? How do we educate students to believe that, in fact, schools should be the first line of defense in taking up the issues of equity, justice, and freedom?

In addition, it seems to me that to talk about civic courage in the way I suggest is to argue that anyone who is critically educated must always realize that any act of struggle for democracy involves a risk. One cannot simply think in terms of being safe, quiet, secure, and comfortable. Critical education requires that both teachers and students become border crossers and in some fundamental way realize that there are consequences—consequences that may require one to pay a very dear price. After all, the fight over justice and the principles of democracy always involves taking risks. The foundation for freedom and critical learning matters, but if educators are not to take freedom for granted, they will have to learn how to take a chance; that is, they will have to learn how to practice what might be called a pedagogy of risk. But such a risk is not about furthering one's career, it is about expanding the sphere of power and popular control over the conditions of work, learning, and sustaining public life. Finally, when I talk about the public sphere I don't talk about it in the singular Habermasian sense: a unified public sphere. I talk about what it means to educate students to expand the possibilities for developing a variety of critical public cultures. As Nancy Fraser points out, there are two kinds of public cultures: strong and weak. A weak public culture offers the opportunity for massive deliberation and dialogue. People can make alliances in order to address issues central to the life of a democratic society. These are public spheres where people speak, become noisy, engage in vociferous dialogue, and open themselves to a variety of languages and views. A strong public sphere is where dialogue combines with the possibility for changing policy. It is not limited to the exchange of ideas, though such a process is crucial. In this sense, the notion of a diversified public sphere suggests forms of pedagogical practice in which students would learn how to take a position, debate, and struggle collectively to become the subjects of history.

LECH WITKOWSKI: It seems to me that one of the important aspects of your studies (work) in pedagogy is the fact that at the same time you are concerned with students—with what is happening to them, what kind of chance they have in educational institutions—you are very seriously concerned about what happens to teachers. And to a large extent the quality of citizenship promoted by schools in students depends on the leadership roles teachers assume as citizens and also as intellectuals. I am very attracted to your category of transformative intellectual, through which you redefine the principles and grounds for the (role and the space of) action for teachers.

HENRY A. GIROUX: Oh, yes!

LECH WITKOWSKI: Would you comment on this?

HENRY A. GIROUX: To talk about teachers in ways that both engage and empower them we have to address at least three things. One, educators have to rupture the division between thinking and implementation that so rigidly characterizes the organization of schools and curricula in the United States. Moreover, it is important that the legacy of this form of domination be understood historically, particularly in terms of its ties with scientific management, and the rise of behaviorism and eugenics. This division of labor has long been a part of an instrumentalist tradition defining teacher work, and suggesting that they don't have to exercise power through their ability to think, all they have to do is implement or carry out predetermined tasks defined by the state or others. This is a pedagogy of servility which subordinates the ability of teachers to the narrow imperative of carrying out other people's dreams and perspectives. So it seems to me that the notion of a transformative intellectual bridges the relationship between thinking and acting in a way that speaks to the possibility for teachers to exercise power productively in collaboration with others.

Secondly, we can't talk about teachers gaining some control over the production of knowledge unless we talk about the structural and historical conditions under which they have worked and struggled. If teachers are overworked, have too many students, are overloaded with too many preparations, it becomes clear that they are positioned, in Harry Braverman's term, to become deskilled. It becomes very, very difficult, in spite of what teachers know, ideologically and politically, for them to act under such conditions. So to talk about teachers as transformative intellectuals is also to talk about teachers having some control over the very conditions under which they work.

Thirdly, it seems to me, and this is very, very crucial, we cannot locate teachers simply in one space, i.e., in the classroom. Teachers are also cultural workers who need to engage other educators in a variety of sites in order to expand the meaning and places where pedagogy is undertaken. This affords teachers the opportunity to develop alliances, see the relevancies between their work and the pedagogical work of other cultural workers, and develop social movements that can mobilize against forms of learning that are oppressive and dominating. It is imperative in the post-modern world that educators position themselves in ways that link social commitment to public action, so that they can, in fact, exemplify for students what it means to be a public intellectual. A public intellectual engages the world in a way that addresses most seriously its most pressing problems. Thus the question of learning becomes linked to forms of activism that enhance the possibility for democratic life.

LECH WITKOWSKI: Yes, but here I understand that a crucial issue in pedagogy arises, namely, how to teach teachers to meet the challenges of democracy, equality, social justice, and to struggle for these in intellectual terms. Because this role which you are defining for teachers requires that teachers shoulder not only the responsibility for knowing the discourse of a particular discipline but also discourses that link it to other disciplines within a wider cultural context. What would be your basic suggestions concerning reformulation of ways to teach teachers to be intellectuals?

HENRY A. GIROUX: First of all you would completely have to redefine the very purpose of schooling. I mean, unless schooling can be situated within a different project, you can't redefine the role of teachers. If you define the role of schooling as something central to the construction of democratic public life, then it seems to me you immediately offer the rationale for educating teachers in a completely different way. I certainly cannot speak for Poland, but I can say with some truthfulness that in the United States teachers are often educated to be clerks, technicians of the state (though not without resistance, and in some cases they are not educated this way at all). Teachers often have no discourse for talking about public life. The language they generally learn is the language of methodologies, scientific management, professionalism. And it seems to me that what we need to do is to offer teachers a number of things. One, we need to offer them a different political language. They need to be able to situate themselves in a language of demystification so that they can recognize that all educational work is political work. Secondly, teachers need to be educated in a language of vision: a formative narrative of what it means to see themselves as agents of a kind of different future, one which opens up rather than shuts down the possibilities for social justice. Teachers need a discourse of critique and a language of possibility; they need to be able to, in some way, interrogate the nature of what they do, but they also need to see beyond the horizons of the possible. Third, it seems to me that teachers need to participate in educational programs that completely challenge the current structure. The current educational programs are bound by academic disciplines that are highly individualized, insular, and have very little relationship to public life and popular culture. That will have to change. One challenge facing critical educators is the need to restructure these disciplines and the institutional structures that support them. These disciplines are capable of producing a form of terrorism, that is, a form of epistemological and ethical violence. They separate the world in ways that are good for creating professionals but very bad for creating public intellectuals. And finally, of course, we have to find ways to get teachers actively involved in the process of public life, so that when they go into their classrooms they address issues that bear some relationship to the everyday lives of the students they teach. This is not about simply creating a motivational pedagogy, but is meant to make clear that students have a responsibility as well in addressing such issues.

LECH WITKOWSKI: Out of the variety of categories you develop in your texts recently, it seems to me that coming to the forefront of your analysis is the term of "border." As a matter of fact, you even try to reformulate the project you are doing as "border pedagogy." If I am not mistaken, at least one aspect of this border pedagogy is linked with the promotion of the idea of "crossing borders," of trying to avoid closure, of avoiding an inside where there would be no passage outside. For teachers and for teacher education this means, if I am not mistaken, that there should be an avoidance of closed disciplinary borders into which they are inserted as a background for playing their role. How would you develop other aspects of this border concept in your project of pedagogy?

HENRY A. GIROUX: I think that the concept of border suggests something very subversive and unsettling. It means moving into circles of uncertainty, it means crossing into different cultural spheres, it means recognizing the multiple nature of our own identities. It means understanding and challenging rather than assuming a kind of security within the confines of academic disciplines. Educators have to become more than intellectual tourists. We must move into other spheres where we take up the specificity of different contexts, geographies, different languages, of otherness, and recognize the otherness in ourselves. The term suggests practices that reject the reified language of management, intellectual tourism, and standardized approaches to education. And we also have to recognize the partiality of our own views.

What would all of this mean in practical terms for teachers? It means that we have to be able to explore other subject areas that we weren't trained in. We have to be able to forge new links academically. What would this mean for students? It means that we have to be able to both affirm and interrogate differences in the classroom and that such differences can be used to invoke possibilities for the emergence of new identities, new subjectivities, and new languages. We need to hybridize the concept of identity, curriculum, and schooling. We have to be more attentive to the language of travel, transit, differences, and hybridization. As educators, we have to realize that we cannot teach anything unless we understand what the categories of meaning are that students bring to the classroom. If we don't understand this, how are we to have a dialogue with students, how are we to engage both their strengths and their weaknesses? Moreover, it seems to me that we have to begin to refigure what it means to draw from different kinds of disciplinary structures. As educators, we have to cross over into the postdisciplinary borderlands of literary studies, media literacy, postcolonialism, critical anthropology, feminism, and political theory. Border pedagogy suggests that the foundationalism that has informed Western thought for so long has to be challenged so that as we move into new territories, we can create the conditions for engaging in new dialogues, while at the same time expanding the possibility for those dialogues. And it also suggests that we are all border intellectuals; we don't simply exist in what I call theoretically safe zones of identity. Our identities change; they are complex, in the sense that nobody is ever at home. The concept of homelessness means an ever-becoming present and an ever-becoming possibility in terms of who we are. Hope arises from being able to recognize that in a vastly shifting world we don't have to stand still and there is no need to stand still.

LECH WITKOWSKI: Your texts are now becoming more and more visible in Poland thanks to translations and we look forward to having more of your work available, but as I have to conclude our interview we should talk a little bit more about your teaching experience. Because while you are pedagogue and researcher you are also pedagogue and teacher. And I wonder, what would be your suggestions given your practice, experience, and theoretical position concerning the best methods of arranging interactions among students, and how would you comment on your personal relationships with students? Your language and your proposals for educational reform are sometimes too difficult to be understood by mature pedagogues, therefore I assume that there are also some students who on an intellectual or political basis challenge your authority as teacher. How do you respond to this difficulty?

HENRY A. GIROUX: There is an apparent contradiction that lies at the heart of teaching, a form of pedagogy that I'm always very self-conscious about, one that I try to avoid in my own teaching practices. The French sociologist Pierre Bourdieu is suggestive here with his concept of symbolic violence. I apply this concept in highlighting a central contradiction in pedagogy, that is, the contradiction between being theoretically or politically accurate and pedagogically wrong at the same time. Recognizing the importance of this contradiction helps me to attend to a number of important issues in my teaching. For example, I always try to create for my students a very safe space from which to talk, work, and engage the relationship between knowledge and power, on the one hand, and discourse and ethical responsibility on the other. I know that whenever students take up new languages, problems, knowledge, and then attempt to use them to engage their own views that their identities, to varying degrees, are always at stake. Always! I begin by criticizing the alleged objectivity of teacher talk by making clear my own politics and the language I use to speak from that position. This not only makes the partiality of my own position clear, it also invites them to enter into the discourse of the class so as to engage, challenge, or transform it as they see fit. I also provide my students with a variety of texts that theorize from a number of perspectives about important issues taken up in the class. At stake here is not merely teaching them the theories of others, but giving them the tools to theorize their own positions so that they may eventually assume responsibility for taking over the conditions for the production of knowledge within the class.

I don't subject my students to endless narratives or lectures on the virtues of the working class, or the virtues of a particular political position. My concept of the political does not suggest inserting students into a particular political doctrine as much as it reflects the need to understand how the operations of power and ideology work in schools and other sites and how, given that fact, one can never work pedagogically outside of the sphere of politics. Of course, I teach about the relationship between class, race, sexism, as well as issues concerning the state, the politics of representation, and other considerations, but I don't teach these issues as markers for a hip political correctness. On the contrary, I teach these issues because I believe they are crucial for students to understand those forces outside of education that both shape and are shaped by educational institutions. I also believe that it is imperative for students to do their own theorizing about how they might address such issues.

My students are constantly engaged in writing, talking, and reading a variety of texts. They don't just read texts on critical pedagogy. They also write and speak in my classes. My classes are always conducted in a seminar fashion. Films are viewed, books read, articles taken up, but any issue raised is always open for analysis. Moreover, I make sure that at least half of the class assignments are produced by the students in my class. I do make sure that every student writes position papers which the entire class then reads and discusses. Students are also given the opportunity to construct their own class projects and work collectively in doing so. In short, at the risk of great simplification, I try to do at least three things. One, I expand the notion of pedagogy, teacher work, and the ethics of responsibility and in doing so introduce them to alternative languages that broaden the notion of education beyond the sphere of the school. Second, I give students the opportunity to speak from their own experiences and to address different traditions, histories, and theoretical perspectives. And three, I make it clear that students must be responsible for what they say, so that the class becomes a laboratory for engaging the world in a way which allows one to raise questions without being punished. In my classes, I try to give students a sense of what it means to work collectively with differences that may be incommensurable, but at least share a sense of social justice, the importance of agency, and recognize how such differences intersect relationally across and within their boundaries and borders. Underlying this approach is a reworking of the notion of a democracy that builds upon rather than dismisses the views of others.

Of course, there is no guarantee that my students will emerge from my classes with their minds changed about anything. Or they may leave my classes rejecting every premise I put forth. This is not to admit to a form of pedagogical failure as much as to recognize that students have to make up their own minds. And that the most we can do as educators is to provide teachers with a sense of what it means to limit their role to being technicians or to take up what it means to be a public intellectual. My role pedagogically is to provide the conditions for them to be able to see beyond their own commonsense assumptions, and to be capable of interrogating the diverse positions they take up. These are modest but radical goals. And it seems to me that, by basing my work on these pedagogical principles, students do not come into my class thinking, "Oh no, in order to pass this course I have to come out being a critical pedagogue like Henry Giroux." Not at all! Hopefully, they will leave the course believing in a form of social responsibility that necessitates taking a position they can believe in and defend; that being in the world demands that they are accountable for what they do. That's it.

LECH WITKOWSKI: There is talk, not only in Poland, about the overwhelming crisis of pedagogy. Now, it seems to me that your way of doing pedagogy, of understanding the challenge pedagogy has to meet, offers a way out of this crisis. Are you optimistic in your efforts? Do you feel that in the face of postmodernity—which we won't discuss any more now—that the crisis of schooling can be met by the reformulation of pedagogy or that the obstacles are so strong that the chance for success via educational reform would be minor?

HENRY A. GIROUX: I'm a strategic optimist, in the sense that I believe that where there is struggle there is no success without hope. One always has to imagine the unimaginable. If I were living in West Berlin seven years ago, I would never have imagined that in my lifetime the Berlin Wall would no longer exist. History is open. That's what agency is about. I think that the notion of radical hope has to be at the core of any critical pedagogy. And when I say "radical hope" I mean the belief that human beings, though they struggle within historical limits and we can never underestimate those limits, it is always possible to imagine that what we do can matter, that it can make a meaningful difference. It can count. I am not suggesting that educational work should be viewed in a grossly utopian sense, that we should overestimate its strengths and limitations in changing identities and institutional structures. But I do believe that teachers and other cultural workers have an obligation to plant seeds of hope. It is not a matter of sloppy utopianism to believe that it is important for future generations to look back on the work we are doing as educators and to say that in our time we recognized the moral and political significance of deepening and expanding the possibilities for improving the quality of human life. That's my sense of hope.

LECH WITKOWSKI: I am very grateful that you've agreed to do this interview and I am sure that it will play its role in promoting radical educational reform among pedagogues committed to emancipation and social change in Poland and elsewhere.

HENRY A. GIROUX: I would like to say that I am extremely grateful for being here and that my correspondence with you over the last five years has been as enormously helpful to me as hopefully mine has been for you.

LECH WITKOWSKI: Thank you, very much.

HENRY A. GIROUX: Thank you.

Notes

1 Consuming Social Change: The United Colors of Benetton

1. A different version of this essay is forthcoming in a volume edited by Carol Becker and published by Routledge.
2. In spite of the recent campaign against postmodernism being waged by many on the Left, some theorists have refused to define postmodernism under a totalizing discourse. In this instance, postmodernism is engaged dialectically with respect to its strengths and weaknesses. For example, see Teresa Ebert, "The 'Difference' of Postmodern Feminism," *College English* 53, no. 8 (1991): 886–904; Judith Butler, "Contingent Foundations: Feminism and the Question of Postmodernism," in *Feminists Theorize the Political*, ed. Butler and Joan W. Scott (New York: Routledge, 1992), 3–21; and Stanley Aronowitz and Henry A. Giroux, *Postmodern Education* (Minneapolis: University of Minnesota Press, 1991).
3. For an example of the varied discourses informing a politics of consumerism, see Mica Nava, *Changing Cultures: Feminism, Youth, and Consumerism* (Newbury Park, Calif.: Sage, 1992); Mike Featherstone, ed., *Consumer Culture and Postmodernism* (Newbury Park, Calif.: Sage, 1991); W. F. Haug, *Critique of Commodity Aesthetics: Appearance, Sexuality, and Advertising in Capitalist Society* (Minneapolis: University of Minnesota Press, 1986); William Leiss, Stephen Kline, and Sut Jhally, eds., *Social Communication in Advertising* (London: Methuen, 1986); Sut Jhally, *The Codes of Advertising* (New York: Routledge, 1990); Martin Davidson, *The Consumerist Manifesto* (New York: Routledge, 1992); and Stuart Ewen, *All Consuming Images* (New York: Basic Books, 1988).
4. David Bailey and Stuart Hall, "The Vertigo of Displacement," *Ten.8* 2, no. 3 (1992): 15.
5. Andrew Payne and Tom Taylor, "Introduction: The Violence of the Public," *Public* 6 (1992), 10.
6. More recent work on the relationship between the discourse of the public and the related issues of politics, violence, difference, and democracy can be found in Nancy Fraser, "Rethinking the Public Sphere," *Social Text* 25–26 (1990): 56–80; Henry A. Giroux,

Schooling and the Struggle for Public Life (Minneapolis: University of Minnesota Press, 1988); Henry A. Giroux, *Border Crossings: Cultural Workers and the Politics of Education* (New York: Routledge, 1992); W. J. T. Mitchell, ed., *Art and the Public Sphere* (Chicago: University of Chicago Press, 1992); and Rita Felski, *Beyond Feminist Aesthetics* (Cambridge, Mass.: Harvard University Press, 1989). See also *Public* 6 (1992), a special issue on the public sphere and the issue of violence.

7. Sharon Waxman, "Benetton Laid Bare," *Miami Herald*, February 8, 1993, C15.

8. Benetton, Advertising Campaign Copy, Spring–Summer 1992, 5.

9. Michael Stevens, "Change the World, Buy a Sweater," *Chicago Tribune*, December 11, 1992, 33.

10.. Les Back and Vibeke Quaade, "Dream Utopias, Nightmare Realities: Imaging Race and Culture within the World of Benetton Advertising," *Third Text* 22 (Spring 1993): 69.

11. Benetton, Spring-Summer 1992, 4. It is important to note that Benetton's appeal to racial harmony does in some instances address questions of affect and desire which mobilize forms of identification that support Benetton's notion of difference. I am not supporting a reductionistic attempt to suggest that there can only be one reading of these ads, nor am I supporting the notion that these ads do not construct desires, identification, and affective investments that are the outcome of Benetton's own campaign history.

12. Carol Squires, "Violence at Benetton," *Artforum* 30 (May 1992): 18–19.

13. On the issue of promotional culture, see Andrew Warnick, *Promotional Culture* (Newbury Park, Calif.: Sage, 1991).

14. Noreen O'Leary, "Benetton's True Colors," *Adweek*, August 24, 1992, 28.

15. Benetton is not only publishing, with Ginko Press, a book entitled *United Colors of Benetton*, which "vividly displays the Benetton corporate philosophy," it is also publishing a book in 1994 entitled *What's the Relationship between AIDS and Selling a Sweater?* which chronicles various responses to the controversial Benetton ads. Both books appropriate the controversy over Benetton's ads to spread the company's name and to generate profits. It seems that nothing is capable of existing outside of Benetton's high–powered commercialism and drive for profits. Spike Lee is one of the most high-profile celebrities to endorse Benetton's campaign. See the interview with Spike Lee, which was sponsored as an advertisement in *Rolling Stone* on November 12, 1992.

16. Ingrid Sischy, "Advertising Taboos: Talking to Luciano Benetton and Oliviero Toscani," *Interview*, April 1992, 69.

17. Peter Fressola quoted in Squires, "Violence at Benetton," 18.

18. Benetton, Spring-Summer 1992, 2.

19. Warnick, *Promotional Culture*, 181.

20. Susan Willis, "Disney World: Public Use/Private State," *South Atlantic Quarterly* 92, no. 1 (Winter 1983): 133.

21. Raymond Loewy quoted in Ewen, *All Consuming Images*, 247.

22. Benetton, Advertising Campaign Copy, Fall-Winter 1992, 2.

23. Oliviero Toscani quoted in Sischy, "Advertising Taboos," 69.

24. Stuart Hall, "The Meaning of New Times," in *New Times: The Changing Face of Politics in the 1990s*, ed. Hall and Martin Jacques (London: Verso, 1990), 116–33.

25. Stuart Hall, "Brave New World," *Socialist Review* 91, no. 1 (1991): 57–58.

26. Clare Ansberry, "Workers Are Forced to Take More and More Jobs with Fewer Benefits," *Wall Street Journal*, March 11, 1993, 1.

27. "Interview with Luciano Benetton," *Colors* 3 (Fall–Winter 1992–93): 2.

28. For a succinct analysis of the relationship between post–Fordism and capitalism, see David Harvey, "Flexibility: Threat or Opportunity," *Socialist Review* 91, no. 1 (1991): 65–75.

29. Back and Quaade, "Dream Utopias," 77.

30. Luciano Benetton and Oliviero Toscani quoted in Sischy, "Advertising Taboos," 69.

31. Ewen, *All Consuming Images*, 248.

32. Abigail Solomon-Godeau, *Photography at the Dock* (Minneapolis: University of Minnesota Press, 1991), 145.

33. Roland Barthes, *The Eiffel Tower*, trans. Richard Howard (New York: Hill and Wang, 1979), 72.

34. Roland Barthes, *Mythologies*, trans. Annette Lavers (New York: Noonday Press, 1972), 143.

35. Douglas Crimp, "Portraits of People with Aids," in *Cultural Studies*, ed Lawrence Grossberg, Cary Nelson, and Paula Treichler (New York: Routledge, 1992), 118.

36. Dick Hebdige, "After the Masses," in *New Times: The Changing Face of Politics in the 1990s*, ed. Stuart Hall and Martin Jacques (London: Verso, 1990), 83.

37. Ewen, *All Consuming Images*, 264.

38. Tony Bennett, "Texts in History: The Determinations of Readings and Their Texts," in *Post-Structuralism and the Question of History*, ed. Derek Atridge, Geoff Bennington, and Robert Young (New York: Cambridge University Press, 1987), 72.

39. Racial representations and their effects on shaping cultural practices are analyzed in Sue K. Jewell, *From Mammy to Miss America and Beyond* (New York: Routledge, 1993); Sander L. Gilman, *Difference and Pathology: Stereotypes of Sexuality, Race, and Madness* (Ithaca: Cornell University Press, 1985); and Jan Pieterse, *White on Black: Images of Africa and Blacks in Western Popular Culture* (New Haven: Yale University Press, 1992).

40. This is not to suggest that both of these visual representations could not be seen differently. For instance, it is possible that the image of a black and white hand handcuffed together might be read as "we're all in this together." Different readings do take place, but at issue here is injecting the reading of such images into a historicity and a set of power relations that more narrowly define the limits of a sloppy relativism or the equally banal assumption that the range of reading choices is infinite.

41. Hal Foster, *Recordings: Art Spectacle, Cultural Politics* (Seattle: Bay Press, 1988), 6–7.

42. On the dialectics of consumerism, see Featherstone, *Consumer Culture and Postmodernism*, and Nava, *Changing Cultures*.

43. Hebdige, "After the Masses," 89.

44. Bill Moyers, Transcript of "The Public Mind," WNET Public Affairs Television, 1989, 14.

45. David Bennet and Terry Collits, "The Postcolonial Critic: Homi Bhabha Interviewed," *Arena* 96 (Spring 1991): 47–48.

2 Politics and Innocence in the Wonderful World of Disney

1. Roger I. Simon, "Forms of Insurgency in the Production of Popular Memories: The Columbus Quincentenary and the Pedagogy of Counter–Commemoration," *Cultural Studies* 7, no. 1 (1993): 77.
2. David Bailey and Stuart Hall, "The Vertigo of Displacement," *Ten.8* 2, no. 3 (1992): 19.
3. This issue is taken up in Henry A. Giroux, *Border Crossings: Cultural Workers and the Politics of Education* (New York: Routledge, 1992); Stanley Aronowitz, *Roll Over Beethoven: The Return of Cultural Strife* (Hanover, N.H.: University Press of New England, 1993); Gina Dent, ed., *Black Popular Culture* (Seattle: Bay Press, 1992); Paul Gilroy, *"There Ain't No Black in the Union Jack": The Cultural Politics of Race and Nation* (Chicago: University of Chicago Press, 1991); Trinh T. Minh–ha, *When the Moon Waxes Red* (New York: Routledge, 1991); bell hooks, *Black Looks: Race and Representation* (Boston: South End Press, 1992); Lawrence Grossberg, *We Gotta Get Out of This Place: Popular Conservatism and Postmodern Culture* (New York: Routledge, 1992); and Lawrence Grossberg, Cary Nelson, and Paula Treichler, eds., *Cultural Studies* (New York: Routledge, 1992).
4. Stuart Hall, "What Is This 'Black' in Popular Culture?" in Dent, *Black Popular Culture*, 24.
5. Edward Said, *Culture and Imperialism* (New York: Alfred A. Knopf, 1993), 323.
6. For a critique of theoretical positions that argue that the "real" issues in left politics are undermined by discourses concerning identity, representations, agency, and culture, see Judith Butler, "Contingent Foundations: Feminism and the Question of Postmodernism," in *Feminists Theorize the Political*, ed. Butler and Joan W. Scott (New York: Routledge, 1992), 3–21, and Michele Barrett, "Words and Things: Materialism and Method in Contemporary Feminist Analysis," in *Destabilizing Theory*, ed. Barrett and Anne Phillips (Stanford: Stanford University Press, 1992), 201–17.
7. Kobena Mercer, "Back to My Routes: A Postscript on the 80s," *Ten.8* 2, no. 3 (Winter 1992): 36.
8. Toni Morrison, *Playing in the Dark: Whiteness and the Literary Imagination* (Cambridge, Mass.: Harvard University Press, 1992), 49–50.
9. Jon Weiner, "Murdered Ink," *Nation*, May 31, 1993, 743.
10. On the issue of memory and politics, I am indebted to these writers: Simon, "Forms of Insurgency"; Harvey Kaye, *The Powers of the Past* (Minneapolis: University of Minnesota Press, 1991); Walter Adamson, *Marx and the Disillusionment of Marxism* (Berkeley: University of California Press, 1984); Richard Terdiman, *Discourse/Counter-Discourse* (Ithaca: Cornell University Press, 1985); Yose Hayim Yerushalmi, *Zakhor: Jewish History and Jewish Memory* (New York: Schocken Books, 1989); and James E. Young, *Writing and Rewriting the Holocaust: Narrative and the Consequences of Interpretation* (Bloomington: Indiana University Press, 1990).
11. Roger I. Simon, "For a Pedagogy of Possibility," *Critical Pedagogy Networker* 1, no. 1 (1988): 2.
12. Hall, "What Is This 'Black' in Popular Culture?" 30.
13. James Clifford, "On Collecting Art and Culture," in *Out There: Marginalization and Contemporary Cultures*, ed. Russell Ferguson, Martha Gever, Trinh T. Minh-ha, and Cornel West (Cambridge, Mass.: MIT Press, 1990), 164.
14. Hall, "What Is This 'Black' in Popular Culture?" 26.

15. Adamson, *Marx and the Disillusionment of Marxism*, 238.

16. See Jane Kuenz, "It's a Small World after All: Disney and the Pleasures of Identification," *South Atlantic Quarterly* 92, no. 1 (Winter 1993): 63–88, and Susan Willis, "Disney World: Public Use/Private State," *South Atlantic Quarterly* 92, no. 1 (Winter 1993): 119–37.

17. A. Dorfman and A. Mattelart, *How to Read Donald Duck: Imperialist Ideology in the Disney Comic* (New York: International General Editions, 1975).

18. Herbert Mitgang, "Disney Link to the F.B.I. and Hoover Is Disclosed," *New York Times*, May 6, 1993, B1.

19. Ibid., B4.

20. For example, see Weiner's comments on the Disney Company's involvement in preventing Marc Eliot's book *Walt Disney: Hollywood's Dark Prince* from being published by Bantam in 1991.

21. The ways in which the pedagogy of innocence is used in Disney's Touchstone films are too numerous to take up in this essay. But the way in which Disney erases serious historical, political, social, and economic issues by appealing to sentimental posturing, personal anguish, comic irony, and the virtues of a generous patriarchy can be seen in the rampant sexism and the ruthless attack on single, working–class mothers in *Stella* (1990); the right–wing nativism of *Green Card* (1990); the celebration of consumerism in *Scenes from a Mall* (1991); the refusal to deal with the capitalist principles in organized crime in *Billy Bathgate* (1991); the superficial humanist appeal to the virtues of medical research in *Medicine Man* (1992); and the "comic" and historically banal portrayal of working-class youth in *Newsies* (1992).

22. Theodor Adorno, *Minima Moralia: Reflections from a Damaged Life*, trans. E. F. N. Jephcott (London: New Left Books, 1974), 55.

23. Hollywood blockbusters such as *Rolling Thunder* (1977), *Coming Home* (1978), *The Deer Hunter* (1978), *First Blood* (1982), and *Born on the Fourth of July* (1990) focused on the plight of returning veterans, their personal reactions to the war, and their readjustment to a society that appeared to reject them. In these films, the war was brought home while subverting any substantive political and moral commentary on the war itself. In these films, the legacy of the Vietnam conflict is either displaced through a focus on the subjective experiences of veterans or, as in the case of the Rambo films, viewed as an expression of individual corruption and political ineptness on the part of U.S. government officials

    In the 1980s, films such as *Platoon* (1986), *Gardens of Stone* (1987), *Full Metal Jacket* (1987), and *Hamburger Hill* (1987) initiated another round of mythologizing. Reduced to the existential struggles and narratives of actual combat troops, the Vietnam War was rewritten as a coming-of-age tale. The war in these scenarios is viewed as a dehumanizing and apocryphal affair, but it is framed through a liberal and narrowly defined humanist focus on individual suffering

    At the height of the Reagan era, Hollywood rewrote the Vietnam War in the image of an unbridled and arrogant national machismo. Films such as *Uncommon Valor* (1983), *Missing in Action* (1984), *Missing in Action 2: The Beginning* (1985), *Rambo: First Blood Part 2* (1985), and *The Hanoi Hilton* (1987) used Vietnam as a backdrop to celebrate a tale of endless heroic rescues. Chemical warfare, forced settlements, and the burning of villages on the part of the United States military were written out of history as Hollywood invented wooden, macho men intent on saving the real victims of Vietnam, the MIAs, from the conveniently demonized Vietnamese. At stake in this version of popular memory was not the expurgation of collective guilt, but the construction of a vision of masculinity that resonated with the conservative image of national identity and patriotism that informed the Reagan years. A superb anthology on Hollywood films and the Vietnam War is Linda Dittmar and Gene Michard, eds., *From Hanoi to Hollywood: The Vietnam War in American Film* (New Brunswick, N.J.: Rutgers University Press, 1990). For two exceptional critiques of Vietnam War films, see John Pilger, "Vietnam, Another Hollywood Fairy Story," *Guardian*, 10 March 1990, 22–23, and J. Hoberman, "Vietnam: The Remake," in *Remaking History*, ed. Barbara Kruger and Phil Mariani (Seattle: Bay Press, 1989), 175–96

24. David Butler quoted in Seth Mydans, "Made in Thailand: New Films about Vietnam," *New York Times*, June 4, 1987, A19.
25. Barry Levinson's comments appear in Michael Reese, "Black Humor Goes to War," *Newsweek*, January 4, 1985, 50–51.
26. Jeffrey Katzenberg is quoted in John Culhane, "Robin Williams Belts Out Verbal Jazz in 'Vietnam,'" *New York Times*, December 20, 1986, 34.
27. Pilger, "Vietnam," 23.
28. For an interesting analysis of this issue, see the various essays in Robert Gooding–Williams, ed., *Reading Rodney King, Reading Urban Uprising* (New York: Routledge, 1993); see also Jan Pieterse, *White on Black: Images of Africa and Blacks in Western Popular Culture* (New Haven: Yale University Press, 1992), and Sander L. Gilman, *Difference and Pathology: Stereotypes of Sexuality, Race, and Madness* (Ithaca: Cornell University Press, 1985).
29. Judith Butler, "Endangered/Endangering: Schematic Racism and White Paranoia," in Gooding-Williams, *Reading Rodney King*, 15.
30. Morrison, *Playing in the Dark*, 82.
31. David Morley and Kevin Robins, "Spaces of Identity: Communications Technologies and the Reconfiguration of Europe," *Screen* 30, no. 4 (1989): 31.
32. Ibid.
33. See Stuart Hall, "Brave New World," *Socialist Review* 91, no. 1 (1991): 57–64.
34. Hilary Radner, "Pretty Is as Pretty Does: Free Enterprise and the Marriage Plot," in *Film Theory Goes to the Movies*, ed. Jim Collins, Hilary Radner, and Ava Preacher Collins (New York: Routledge, 1993), 67.
35. Suzanne Moore is right in arguing, in her article "Power Play" (*New Statesman and Society*, May 18, 1990, 47), that *Pretty Woman* is despicable precisely because the violence it perpetrates against women is disguised in the "innocence" of romance. She writes: "Yet, who will condemn *Pretty Woman*, which is full of the worst kind of lie where male economic dominance is twisted into pure romance? This is the long slow violence which turns the imbalance of power between the sexes from being part of the problem into being part of the solution. Which is about as close as I want to get to a definition of misogyny."
36. Radner, "Pretty Is as Pretty Does," 62.
37. Abigail Solomon–Godeau, *Photography at the Dock* (Minneapolis: University of Minnesota Press, 1991), xxii.
38. On the politics of pedagogy and representation, see Stanley Aronowitz and Henry A. Giroux, *Postmodern Education* (Minneapolis: University of Minnesota Press 1991), and David Trend, *Cultural Pedagogy: Art/Education/Politics* (New York: Bergin and Garvey, 1992).

39. See Simon, "Forms of Insurgency."
40. See Solomon-Godeau, *Photography at the Dock*.

3 Schools for Scandal: Whittling Away at Public Education

1. These examples are taken from Sheila Harty, *Hucksters in the Classroom* (Washington, D.C.: Center for the Study of Responsive Law, 1979), 18–20. See also Jean Brenkman, "Seeing Beyond the Interests of Industry," *Journal of Education* 162, no. 1: (1981)283–94. The classic statement on this issue is Vance Packard, *The Hidden Persuaders* (New York: McKay and Co., 1960). For more recent analyses of the shift away from simply the production of products toward the pedagogical concern with the relationship between people and products, see Judith Williamson, *Decoding Advertisements* (London: Marion Boyers, 1978); Stuart Ewen, *All Consuming Images* (New York: Basic Books, 1988); William Leiss, Stephen Kline, and Sut Jhally, *Social Communication in Advertising* (London: Metheun, 1989); Sut Jhally, *The Codes of Advertising* (New York: Routledge, 1990).
2. Susan Dillingham, "The Classroom as a Marketing Tool," *Insight*, September 24, 1990, 40.
3. One major player is Time-Warner, which owns 50 percent of Whittle Communications and is the world's largest magazine publisher. But the extent and scope of its capital and influence are illustrated in the following analysis from David Norlin, "Whittle and Education," *Z Magazine*, September 1992, 66:

   > Time-Warner [is] the world's largest magazine publisher, with a readership of around 120 million; it is Scott Foresman, Little-Brown, Time-Life Books and the Book-of-the-Month Club, making it one of the world's largest book dealers; it is the world's second largest cable operator, with 23 million subscribers to HBO and Cinemax; its total value is 18 billion, more than the combined gross domestic products of Jordan, Bolivia, Nicaragua, Albania, Laos, Liberia, and Mali; its largest shareholders are "a number of banks known for their interest only in bland popular entertainment." Profits are its most important product. It is, in short, one of the most fundamental controllers of information and ideas in the U.S. and the world.

4. Scott Plum quoted in Mark Walsh, "New Music Radio Channel—Including Advertising—Making Debut in Schools," *Education Week*, September 8, 1993, 15.
5. Janice Shamon, "Buying Low: Schools for Sale," *Z Magazine*, May 1992, 63.
6. Joseph Fenton quoted in Kathleen Deveny, "Consumer-Products Firms Hit the Books Trying to Teach Brand Loyalty in Schools," *Wall Street Journal*, June 11, 1992, B1, B6.
7. John S. Friedman, "Big Business Goes to School," *Nation*, February 17, 1992, 190.
8. Benno C. Schmidt, Jr., "Educational Innovation for Profit," *Wall Street Journal*, June 5, 1992, B1, B7.
9. Cyndee Miller, "Teachers Fight Channel One; Two Advertisers Drop Out," *Marketing News*, August 17, 1992, 10.
10. See Jonathan Kozol, "Whittle and the Privateers," *Nation*, September 21, 1992, 276–77.
11. It is now well known that "after his nomination as Secretary of Education, Alexander asked Whittle, Lavine Cooperman and others for their advice. . . . After his confirmation,

Alexander sold his home in Knoxville, Tennessee, for $977,550. He had paid $570,000 for it about a year before. The buyer was Gerald Hogan, a top executive of Whittle Communications. Hogan received a mortgage of $780,000 from the First Tennessee Bank, Alexander was on the board of the bank's holding company until he became Secretary of Education. Whittle is still on the board." Friedman, "Big Business Goes to School," 190.

12. Elaine Moseley, the principal of a corporate-financed high school in Chicago, quoted in Kozol, "Whittle and the Privateers," 277.

13. Jerome Johnston and Evelyn Brzezinski, "Taking the Measure of Channel One: The First Year," Institute for Social Research: The University of Michigan (1992), 1–4.

14. One student reported in *Education USA* that "time spent on Channel One . . . is pretty low key. It's seen as a way to wind down instead of getting us thinking. It's taken more lightly." See "High School Students Criticize Lack of Depth in School TV News; Learn More about Analyzing Media from Home than at School," *Education USA*, April 22, 1992, 65.

15. See Norlin, "Whittle and Education," 66.

16. Patrick M. Reilly, "Whittle Seeks Edison Funding of $750 Million," *Wall Street Journal*, May 5, 1993, B1, B14.

17. Jonathan Kozol relates the all too familiar story of Governor William Winter's attempt to get the legislature to pass a $60 million plan to upgrade public education in the state of Mississippi. Kozol writes, "The state's powerful oil corporations, facing a modest increase in their taxes to support the plan lobbied vigorously against it." Kozol, *Savage Inequalities* (New York: Crown Publishers, 1991), 132.

18. Editorial Comment, "Blame the Poor," *Progressive*, July 1992, 9.

19. For a superb, detailed analysis of these assaults, especially in the arts, see David Trend, *Cultural Pedagogy: Art/Education/Politics* (New York: Bergin and Garvey, 1992).

20. This is clear not only in the way in which the popular press has launched a reductionistic attack on multiculturalism, cultural difference, and radical social movements, but also in the mobilizing of conservative foundations and publishing houses to publish highly advertised books by leading neoconservatives, who have made prosperous careers attacking the alleged "new McCarthyism" on the Left. The examples are too numerous to cite, but Dinesh D'Souza's *Illiberal Education* (New York: Free Press, 1991) is a case in point.

21. Jonathan Rutherford, "A Place Called Home," in *Identity, Community, Culture, Difference*, ed. Rutherford (London: Lawrence and Wishart, 1990), 11.

22. Ibid.

23. "Interview with Homi Bhabha," in Rutherford, *Identity, Community, Culture, Difference*, 208.

24. See Paul Gilroy, *The Black Atlantic* (Cambridge: Harvard University Press, 1993), and Chandra Mohanty, "On Race and Voice: Challenges for Liberal Education in the 1990s," *Cultural Critique* 14 (Winter 1989–90): 179–208.

25. Kobena Mercer, "Welcome to the Jungle," in Rutherford, *Identity, Community, Culture, Difference*, 46.

26. Hazel Carby, "The Multicultural Wars," in *Black Popular Culture*, ed. Gina Dent (Seattle: Bay Press, 1992), 198.

27. Jeffrey Weeks, "The Value of Difference," in Rutherford, *Identity, Community, Culture, Difference*, 98.

28. Stuart Hall, "Ethnicity: Identity and Difference," *Radical America* 13, no. 4 (June 1991): 15–16.
29. Homi K. Bhabha, "The Third Space," in Rutherford, *Identity, Community, Culture, Difference*, 211.
30. Bhabha and Parekh, "Identities on Parade," 5.
31. Stuart Hall, "What Is This 'Black' in Popular Culture?" in Dent, *Black Popular Culture*, 23.
32. Kobena Mercer, "Back to My Routes: A Postscript on the 80s," *Ten.8* 2, no. 3 (Winter 1992): 38.
33. Hall, "What Is This 'Black' in Popular Culture?" 25.
34. Homi K. Bhabha, "A Good Judge of Character: Men, Metaphors, and the Common Culture," in *Raceing Justice, Engendering Power: Essays on Anita Hill, Clarence Thomas, and the Construction of Social Reality*, ed. Toni Morrison (New York: Pantheon, 1992), 238.
35. Lemuel Johnson, "Caliban's Orientalism, Caliban's Occidentalism: (de)Generating Utopias," a talk delivered at the Minority Discourse Conference, Irvine, California, June 5, 1992.
36. R. Radhakrishnan, "Canonicity and Theory: Toward a Poststructuralist Pedagogy," in *Theory/Pedagogy/Politics: Texts for Change*, ed. Donald Morton and Mas'ud Zavarzadeh (Urbana: University of Illinois Press, 1991), 122.
37. The attempt to redefine the concept of the relationship between critical pedagogy and cultural work is also taken up in Henry A. Giroux, *Border Crossings: Cultural Workers and the Politics of Education* (New York: Routledge, 1992), and Roger I. Simon, *Teaching against the Grain: A Pedagogy of Possibility* (Westport, Conn.: Bergin and Garvey, 1992).
38. This notion of pedagogy comes from Simon, *Teaching against the Grain*.
39. Hazel Carby, "The Multicultural Wars," in Gina Dent, ed. *Black Popular Culture* (Seattle: Bay Press, 1992), p. 194.

4 White Utopias and Nightmare Realities: Film and the New Cultural Racism

1. See Henry A. Giroux, *Border Crossings: Cultural Workers and the Politics of Education* (New York: Routledge, 1992).
2. Tony Bennett, "Putting Policy into Cultural Studies," in *Cultural Studies*, ed. Lawrence Grossberg, Cary Nelson, and Paula Treichler (New York: Routledge, 1992), 23–34.
3. Rita Felski, "Feminism, Postmodernism, and the Critique of Modernity," *Cultural Critique* 13 (Fall 1989): 36.
4. See Henry A. Giroux, *Schooling and the Struggle for Public Life* (Minneapolis: University of Minnesota Press, 1988).
5. Stuart Hall and David Held, "Citizens and Citizenship," in *New Times: The Changing Face of Politics in the 1990s* (London: Verso, 1990).
6. Ibid., 176.
7. Ellen Willis, "Multiple Identities," *Tikkun* 6, no. 6: 58.
8. See Giroux, *Border Crossings*.
9. See Jonathan Kozol, *Savage Inequalities* (New York: Crown Publishers, 1991).

10. Samuel Lipman, "Redefining Culture and Democracy," *New Criterion* 8, no. 4: 15–16.

11. Pat Buchanan quoted in Charles Krauthammer, "The Real Buchanan Is Surfacing," *Cincinnati Enquirer*, March 3, 1990, A4.

12. Frank Kermode, "Whose History Is Bunk?" *New York Times Book Review*, February 23, 1992, 33.

13. Renato Rosaldo, *Culture and Truth* (Boston: Beacon, 1989), ix.

14. This is not to suggest that questions of identity are not addressed in a progressive way by left cultural critics. On the contrary, writers such as Diana Fuss, in *Essentially Speaking: Feminism, Narrative, and Difference* (New York: Routledge, 1989); Judith Butler, in *Gender Trouble: Gender and the Subversion of Identity* (New York: Routledge, 1990); bell hooks, in *Yearnings* (Boston: South End Press, 1990); Jonathan Rutherford, in *Identity, Community, Culture, Difference*, ed. Rutherford (London: Lawrence and Wishart, 1990); Michele Wallace, in *Invisibility Blues: From Pop to Theory* (London: Verso, 1990); Lawrence Grossberg, in *We Gotta Get Out of This Place: Popular Conservatism and Postmodern Culture* (New York: Routledge, 1992); Stanley Aronowitz, in *The Politics of Identity* (New York: Routledge, 1992); Emily Hicks, in *Border Writing: The Multidimensional Text* (Minneapolis: University of Minnesota Press, 1991), and too many others to name here are attempting to rethink a politics of identity within a broader conception of cultural difference. But in doing so, many of these critics have failed to address how the construction of identity politics works as part of a broader pedagogical discourse to shape popular commonsense conceptions of identity, culture, and difference. What is often at stake in this work is exploring the intersection of and relationship between different identities, ethnicities, and political experiences within a particular field of domination. What is generally ignored is how these identities are taken up and engaged within particular histories, locations, and zones of everyday life as both a pedagogical and political issue.

15. Ilene Philipson, "What's the Big I.D.? The Politics of the Authentic Self," *Tikkun* 6, no. 6: 51–55.

16. Stuart Alan Clarke, "Fear of a Black Planet," *Socialist Review* 21, nos. 3–4 (1991): 37.

17. Ibid., 46.

18. For a brilliant historical and contemporary analysis of the political correctness movement, see Stanley Aronowitz, *Roll Over Beethoven: The Return of Cultural Strife* (Hanover, N.H.: University Press of New England, 1993). Specific examples of this work can be found in Paul Berman, ed., *Debating P.C.: The Controversy over Political Correctness on College Campuses* (New York: Laurel, 1992).

19. Howard Winant, "Postmodern Racial Politics in the U.S.," *Socialist Review* 20, no. 1 (1990): 125.

20. See Sander L. Gilman, *Difference and Pathology: Stereotypes of Sexuality, Race, and Madness* (Ithaca: Cornell University Press, 1985).

21. Theo Goldberg, ed., *Anatomy of Racism* (Minneapolis: University of Minnesota Press, 1990).

22. I take this distinction from Paul Smith, *Clint Eastwood: A Cultural Production* (Minneapolis: University of Minnesota Press, 1993).

23. Stuart Hall, "New Ethnicities," in *ICA Document 7* (London: ICA, 1988), 28.

24. See Paul Gilroy, *"There Ain't No Black in the Union Jack": The Cultural Politics of Race and Nation* (Chicago: University of Chicago Press, 1991); Winant, "Postmodern Racial

Politics"; Alain Policar, "Racism and Its Mirror Image," *Telos* 83 (Spring 1990): 99–108; Pierre-André Taguieff, "The New Cultural Racism in France," *Telos* 83 (Spring 1990): 109–22; and Clarke, "Fear of a Black Planet."

25. See Cornel West, "The New Cultural Politics of Difference," *October* 53 (Summer 1990): 93–109.

26. Hicks, *Border Writing*.

27. Hall, "New Ethnicities," 28.

28. Ibid.

29. See Robert Young, *White Mythologies* (London: Routledge, 1990); Richard Dyer, "White," *Screen* 29, no. 4 (1988): 44–64; and hooks, *Yearnings*.

30. See Nancy Fraser, "The Uses and Abuses of French Discourse Theories for Feminist Politics," in *Theory, Culture, and Society* 9 (1992): 51–71.

31. Winant, "Postmodern Racial Politics," 126.

32. Harold Johnson, "The Fire This Time," *National Review* 44, no. 10 (1992): 17.

33. Winant, "Postmodern Racial Politics," 132. One example can be found in the comments of the liberal historian C. Vann Woodward, in "Equal but Separate," *New Republic*, July 15 and 22, 1991, 43: "The cult of ethnicity and its zealots have put at stake the American tradition of a shared commitment to common ideals and its reputation for assimilation, for making a 'nation' of nations."

34. Clarke, "Fear of a Black Planet," 47.

35.. This issue is taken up in Dyer, "White"; hooks, *Yearnings*; and Young, *White Mythologies*.

36. One of the most important analyses of Los Angeles in cultural and political terms can be found in Mike Davis, *City of Quartz* (London: Verso, 1990). Of course, in light of the 1992 uprising, L.A. signifies more than postmodern hybridity; it also, I believe, sends a "wake-up call" to the rest of America. The message seems clear: the economic, political, and social conditions that have come to characterize the inner cities in the last decade cannot be allowed to endure. L.A. signifies the call for new leadership, new alliances, and the need for massive social, economic, and cultural reforms. But L.A. also makes visible the real legacy of the Reagan/Bush era, one which was aptly characterized by Ralph Nader when asked how he would grade Bush's first term: "I'd give him an F. All the trends that began under Reagan have accelerated under Bush: precipitous economic decline, staggering deficits, a lopsided balance of trade, growing unemployment, declining quality of life, rising personal-income taxes, failing banks, reeling real estate, unaffordable medical costs, fourth-rate schools, rampant street crime, unchecked corporate crime, an ignorant energy policy and abuses of the public trust by a government increasingly unaccountable for its actions—except to big business." Nader quoted in Deirdre Donahue, "Nader Rates, Berates Bush in *Playboy*," *USA Today*, May 8, 1992, 10.

37.. Phil Mariani and Jonathan Crary, eds., *Discourses: Conversations in Postmodern Art and Culture* (Cambridge, Mass.: MIT Press, 1990), 97.

38. Michael Dyson, "Growing Up under Fire: *Boyz N the Hood* and the Agony of the Black Man in America," *Tikkun* 6, no. 5 (November–December 1991): 75.

39. Joan Copjec, "The Unvermögender Other: Hysteria and Democracy in America," *New Formations* 14 (Summer 1991): 30.

40. Dyer, "White," 46.

41. See David Lloyd, "Race under Representation," *Oxford Literary Review* 13, nos. 1–2 (1991): 62–94.

42. Sharon Welch, *A Feminist Ethic of Risk* (Minneapolis: Fortress Press, 1989).

43. The ideological significance of this portrayal and its relationship to the new racism is captured by Paul Gilroy's discussion, in *"There Ain't No Black in the Union Jack"* (109–10), of the link often made between black youth and criminality:

> I am suggesting that the view of the blacks as innately criminal, or at least more criminal than the white neighbors whose deprivation they share, which became "common sense" during the early 1970s, is crucial to the development of new definitions of the black problem and new types of racial language and reasoning. As culture displaced anxiety about the volume of black settlement, crime came to occupy the place which sexuality, miscegenation and disease had held as the central themes and images in the earlier discourses of "race." Crime, in the form of both street disorder and robbery was gradually identified as an *expression of black culture* which in turn was defined as a cycle in which the negative effects of "black matriarchy" and family pathology wrought destructive changes on the inner city by literally breeding deviancy out of deprivation and discrimination.

44. Edward Said quoted in Mariani and Crary, *Discourses*, 96.

45. See Roger I. Simon, *Teaching against the Grain: A Pedagogy of Possibility* (Westport, Conn.: Bergin and Garvey, 1992).

46. See Henry A. Giroux and Peter McLaren, "Media Hegemony: Towards a Critical Pedagogy of Representation," in *Media Knowledge: Readings in Popular Culture, Pedagogy, and Critical Citizenship*, ed. James Schwoch, Mimi White, and Susan Reilly (Albany: SUNY Press, 1992), xv–xxxiv.

47. Chandra Talpade Mohanty, "On Race and Voice: Challenges for Liberal Education in the 1990s," *Cultural Critique* 14 (1989–90): 184.

48. See Herbert Schiller, *Information and the Crisis Economy* (New York: Oxford University Press, 1986) and *Culture Inc.: The Corporate Takeover of Public Expression* (New York: Oxford University Press, 1989); and Cynthia Schneider and Brian Wallis, eds., *Global Television* (Cambridge, Mass.: MIT Press, 1989).

49. Trinh T. Minh-ha, "Documentary Is/Not a Name," *October* 52 (1990): 85.

50. Hall, "New Ethnicities," 27.

51. Joan Borsa, "Freda Kahlo: Marginalization and the Critical Female Subject," *Third Text* 12 (Autumn 1990): 31.

52. Richard Kearney, *Poetics of Imagining: From Husserl to Lyotard* (New York: Harper Collins, 1991), 215–16.

53. Stuart Hall, "Cultural Identity and Diaspora," in *Identity, Community, Culture, Difference*, ed. Jonathan Rutherford (London: Lawrence and Wishart, 1990); 225.

54. Hall, "New Ethnicities," 28.

55. See Grossberg, *We Gotta Get Out of This Place*.

56. Anne Balsamo, "Feminism and Cultural Studies," *Journal of the Midwest Language Association* 24, no. 1 (1991): 56.

57. Biddy Martin and Chandra Talpade Mohanty, "Feminist Politics: What's Home Got to Do with It?" in *Feminist Studies/Critical Studies*, ed. Teresa de Lauretis (Bloomington: Indiana University Press, 1986), 193.

58. Bob H. Suzuki, "Unity with Diversity: Easier Said Than Done," *Liberal Education* 77, no. 1 (1991): 34.

59. See Hall, "Cultural Identity and Diaspora."

5 Pedagogy and the Critical Practice of Photography

1. Photography is not our primary concern, either as a technology or as an academic discipline. So why then do we address photographic practices with such interest? Our theoretical concern is the destabilization of "photography" as a particular institutionalization of photographic practices. As educators and cultural workers, we believe that Solomon-Godeau's sustained historical critique, in *Photography at the Dock* (Minneapolis: University of Minnesota Press, 1991), of the production and use of "art photography," and to a lesser extent the concept of "documentary practice," provides an important theoretical service for analyzing photography as a pedagogical practice. Employing the examples of postmodern and feminist representations as key reference points, Solomon-Godeau raises crucial questions about the complicity of photography in the reproduction of oppressive historical formations in addition to considering the possibilities of photographic practice intervening to disrupt this reproduction. Within this agenda, Solomon-Godeau articulates an incisive, passionate critical stance from which she addresses the professional community whose identities and commitments are formed within a concern for the practice and study of photography. As educators, we critically engage *Photography at the Dock* not to assess the adequacy of its arguments for this community, but to enter into dialogue with Solomon-Godeau's essays so that insights from her writing might inform our own pedagogical projects.

2. The notion of the photograph as an "event" is adapted and extrapolated from Michel de Certeau's discussion of "events" as a structuring foundation for historiographic writing. See de Certeau, *The Writing of History* (New York: Columbia University Press, 1988).

3. Ibid., 2.

4. Solomon–Godeau, *Photography at the Dock*, xxiv.

5. As our discussion will indicate, this position includes considerations of what photographs do to the viewer. The "event" status of the image, in its demand for intelligibility, requires a viewer to discursively position him- or herself to respond to this demand. How such a positioning acts on the process of subject formation is, of course, a central question for cultural workers.

6. Equally important here is the work of curators, who both define a discursive frame for the viewing of images and set the terms of their circulation and engagement. For an exemplary discussion of the pedagogical implications of one such practice, see Andrea Liss, "An Uneasy Witness," a review of photographic exhibition 19.9.41 A Day in the Warsaw Ghetto: A Birthday Trip in Hell, in *Afterimage* 19, no. 5 (December 1991): 15–16.

7. Solomon–Godeau, *Photography at the Dock*, 134.

8. Ibid., 37.

9. In light of these concerns we find it theoretically and politically disturbing that Solomon-Godeau has presented us with a politics of representation and difference that fails to discuss race as a significant category and ignores the work of contemporary black photographers.

10. For example, the exhibition space of the gallery not only has a material specificity that affects how a photograph will be seen by whom, but it is discursively located within ideological structures that define what a gallery is and what objects displayed in a gallery are supposed to mean. For an extended discussion of such issues see Rosalind Krauss, "Photography's Discursive Spaces," in *The Contest of Meaning: Critical Histories of Photography,* ed. Richard Bolton (Cambridge, Mass.: MIT Press, 1989).
11. Solomon-Godeau, *Photography at the Dock*, 179.
12. Ibid., 237.
13. Richard Kearney, *The Wake of Imagination* (Minneapolis: University of Minnesota Press, 1988), 370.
14. Nancy Fraser, *Unruly Practices: Power, Discourses, and Gender in Contemporary Social Theory* (Minneapolis: University of Minnesota Press, 1989), 29.
15. Richard Kearney, *Poetics of Imagining: From Husserl to Lyotard* (New York: Harper Collins, 1991), 211.
16. Ibid., 220.
17. R. S. Khare, "The Other's Double—The Anthropologist's Bracketed Self: Notes on Cultural Representation," *Oxford Literary History* 23 (1992): 5.

6 The Turn Toward Theory

1. Of course, the key thinkers who have influenced literary theory are Jacques Derrida, Michel Foucault, and Jacques Lacan. While it would be impossible to list a comprehensive number of sources in this tradition, a highly partial compilation of the various types of work informing many of the traditions in literary theory can be found in Harold Bloom et al., *Deconstruction and Criticism* (New York: Seabury Press, 1979); Ralph Cohen, ed., *Future Literary Theory* (London: Routledge, 1989); Richard Harvey Brown, *Society as Text* (Chicago: University of Chicago Press, 1987); Joseph A. Butigieg, ed., *Criticism without Boundaries* (Notre Dame: University of Notre Dame Press, 1987); and Lawrence Grossberg, Cary Nelson, and Paula Treichler, eds., *Cultural Studies* (New York: Routledge, 1992). An excellent analysis of the changing nature of critical pedagogy over the last decade can be found in William Stanley, *Curriculum for Utopia* (Westport, Conn.: Bergin and Garvey, 1992). See also, Henry A. Giroux, *Border Crossings: Cultural Workers and the Politics of Education* (New York: Routledge, 1992).
2. An example of this work can be found in Darryl J. Gless and Barbara Herrnstein Smith, eds., *The Politics of Liberal Education* (Durham: Duke University Press, 1992).
3. For an analysis of what has been called the "canon wars," see Henry Louis Gates Jr., *Loose Canons: Notes on the Culture Wars* (New York: Oxford University Press, 1992).
4. For a representative Marxist critique, see Robert C. Holub, *Crossing Borders: Reception Theory, Poststructuralism, Deconstruction* (Madison: University of Wisconsin Press, 1992). For a highly orthodox and in my view extremely reductionistic critique, see David Harvey, *The Condition of Postmodernity* (New York: Basil Blackwell, 1989). For a recent analysis of the turn toward culture in feminist theory and its various criticisms, see Michele Barrett and Anne Phillips, eds., *Destabilizing Theory* (Stanford: Stanford University Press, 1992), especially Michele Barrett, "Words and Things: Materialism and Method in Contemporary Feminist Analysis," 201–17. One example of a feminist critique of poststructuralism

that constructs its arguments out of a binarism that privileges "political" battles over the struggle over representations can be found in Teresa Ebert, "Ludic Feminism, the Body, Performance, and Labor: Bringing Materialism Back into Feminist Cultural Studies," *Cultural Critique* 23 (Winter 1992–93): 5–50. Not only does Ebert grossly misrepresent those theorists she dismisses as not being materialist enough, she also fails to address the complexity of the relationship between representation, textuality, and politics.

5. Of course, there are a number of theorists who have attempted to politicize the discourse of poststructuralism. This is especially true of feminists. A representative example would include Teresa de Lauretis, *Technologies of Gender: Essays on Theory, Film, and Fiction* (Bloomington: Indiana University Press, 1987); Joan W. Scott, "Deconstructing Equality-versus-Difference; or, The Uses of Poststructuralist Theory for Feminism," *Feminist Studies* 14 (1988): 33–50; Linda Nicholson, ed., *Feminism/Postmodernism* (New York: Routledge, 1990); Gayatri Chakravorty Spivak, *In Other Worlds: Essays in Cultural Politics* (New York: Methuen, 1987).

6. For instance, see Shoshana Felman and Dori Lamb, *Testimony: Crisis of Witnessing in Literature, Psychoanalysis, and History* (New York: Routledge, 1992); Donald Morton and Mas'ud Zavarzadeh, eds., *Theory/Pedagogy/Politics: Texts for Change* (Urbana: University of Illinois Press, 1991); C. Mark Hurlbert and Michael Blitz, eds., *Composition and Resistance* (Portsmouth, N.H.: Boynton/Cook Publishers, 1991); Bruce Henricksen and Thais E. Morgan, *Reorientations: Critical Theories and Pedagogies* (Urbana: University of Illinois Press, 1990); Patricia Donahue and Ellen Quandahl, eds., *Reclaiming Pedagogy: The Rhetoric of the Classroom* (Carbondale: Southern Illinois University Press, 1989); Gregory Ulmer, *Applied Grammatology* (Baltimore: Johns Hopkins University Press, 1985); Cary Nelson, ed., *Theory in the Classroom* (Urbana: University of Illinois Press, 1986); and Barbara Johnson, ed., *The Pedagogical Imperative: Teaching as a Literary Genre* (New Haven: Yale University Press, 1983).

7. Maria-Regina Kecht, "The Challenge of Responsibility," in Kecht, ed., *Pedagogy Is Politics: Literary Theory and Critical Teaching* (Urbana: University of Illinois Press, 1992), 12.

8. Michele Barrett, "Words and Things," 203.

9. See Jacques Derrida, *Of Grammatology*, trans. G. Spivak (Baltimore: Johns Hopkins University Press, 1976).

10. For a brilliant analysis of this issue, see Stanley Aronowitz, *The Politics of Identity* (New York: Routledge, 1992).

11. *Strategies* Collective, "Building a New Left: An Interview with Ernesto Laclau," *Strategies* 1 (Fall 1988): 24.

12. Judith Butler, "Contingent Foundations: Feminism and the Question of Postmodernism," in *Feminists Theorize the Political*, ed. Butler and Joan Scott (New York: Routledge, 1992), 8.

13. *Strategies* Collective, "Building a New Left," 25–26.

14. See Kobena Mercer, "Back to My Routes: A Postscript on the 80s," *Ten.8* 2, no. 3 (Winter 1992): 32–39.

15. For example, the wealth of feminist work in film theory, photography, sexual politics, and so on is too well known to mention here. Two outstanding examples are Abigail Solomon-Godeau, *Photography at the Dock* (Minneapolis: University of Minnesota Press, 1991), and Judith Butler, *Gender Trouble: Feminism and the Subversion of Identity* (New York: Routledge, 1990).

16. For example, see the series of essays in Colin Lankshear and Peter McLaren, eds., *Critical Literacy: Politics, Praxis, and the Postmodern* (Albany: SUNY Press, 1993). See also William Pinar and William Reynolds, eds., *Understanding Curriculum as Phenomenological and Deconstructed Text* (New York: Teachers College Press, 1992), and Patti Lather, *Getting Smart* (New York: Routledge, 1991).

17. In this regard, see Nancy Fraser, "The Uses and Abuses of French Discourse Theories for Feminist Politics," *Theory, Culture, and Society* 9 (1992): 51–71. I think Paul Jay is correct in arguing that "we need to recognize . . . how deconstructive thinking is exercised, and to what ends is ultimately dictated by the politics of each critic who draws on it as a well as by something inherent in deconstruction itself." Paul Jay, "Bridging the Gap: The Position of Politics in Deconstruction," *Cultural Critique* 22 (Fall 1992): 71.

18. For an argument against a totalizing view of poststructuralism, see Butler, "Contingent Foundations," 3.

19. Ibid., 6.

20. The intersection between pedagogy and poststructuralism can be found in the pioneering work of Cleo Cherryholmes, *Power and Criticism: Poststructural Investigations in Education* (New York: Teachers College Press, 1988). Cherryholmes's work is important because he is one of the few who have critically appropriated this work as part of a project of critique and possibility. On the other hand, there are a number of educational theorists who employ poststructuralist insights as part of a discourse of critique employed within the most self-serving binarisms. A representative selection of theorists in literary studies who have taken up the poststructuralism/pedagogy intersection can be found in G. Douglas Atkins and Michael L. Johnson, eds., *Writing and Reading Differently: Deconstruction and the Teaching of Composition and Literature* (Lawrence: University of Kansas Press, 1985).

21. Some of the most important challenges have come from Roger I. Simon, *Teaching against the Grain: A Pedagogy of Possibility* (Westport, Conn.: Bergin and Garvey, 1992); James Schwoch, Mimi White, and Susan Reilly, eds., *Media Knowledge: Readings in Popular Culture, Pedagogy, and Critical Citizenship* (Albany: SUNY Press, 1992); and Giroux, *Border Crossings*.

22. David R. Shumway, "Integrating Theory in the Curriculum as Theorizing—a Postdisciplinary Practice," in Kecht, *Pedagogy Is Politics*, 101.

23. See Joseph Harris, "The Other Reader," *Journal of Advanced Composition* 12, no. 1 (Winter 1992): 27–37.

24. For example, Michael Apple argues against such poststructuralism and postmodernism on the grounds that they have been appropriated in the interest of becoming a new form of cultural capital for elite academics who want to further their careers. This may be true, though hardly endemic to the theoretical discourses in question, but it tells us nothing about how these theories actually work in specific contexts in either progressive or reactionary ways. Both poststructuralism and postmodernism are multiaccentual and have developed an undeniable force in modern educational and social theory. It might be more interesting for Apple and his cohorts to explain the conditions that support such discourses rather than attributing certain motives to the people who use them. See Michael Apple, *Official Knowledge: Democratic Education in a Conservative Age* (New York: Routledge, 1993).

25. Mas'ud Zavarzadeh, "Theory as Resistance," in Kecht, *Pedagogy Is Politics*, 35; see also Mas'ud Zavarzadeh and Donald Morton, "(Post)modern Critical Theory and the Articulations of Critical Pedagogies," *College Literature* 17, nos. 2–3 (1990): 51–63.

26. This theme is taken up in a number of essays in Morton and Zavarzadeh, *Theory/Pedagogy/Politics*.
27. Susan Horton, "Let's Get 'Literate': English Department Politics and a Proposal for a Ph.D. in Literacy," in Kecht, *Pedagogy Is Politics*, 135.
28. See Stanley Aronowitz and Henry A. Giroux, *Education under Siege*, 2d ed. (Westport, Conn.: Bergin and Garvey, 1994), and Peter McLaren, *Life in Schools* (New York: Longman, 1988).
29. Mas'ud Zavarzadeh, "Theory as Resistance," 41.
30. Joan W. Scott, "Experience," in Butler and Scott, *Feminists Theorize the Political*, 25–26.
31. Mas'ud Zavarzadeh, "Theory as Resistance," 13.
32. Ibid., 45.
33. Richard Ohmann, "Teaching Historically," in Kecht, *Pedagogy Is Politics*, 174.
34. Walter Benjamin, "Theses on the Philosophy of History," in Benjamin, *Illuminations*, ed. Hannah Arendt (New York: Schocken Books, 1969), 257.
35. Ohmann, "Teaching Historically," 187.
36. Ibid.
37. See, for instance, Henry A. Giroux, *Schooling and the Struggle for Public Life* (Minneapolis: University of Minnesota Press, 1988).
38. John Clifford, "A Burkean Critique of Composition Praxis," in Kecht, *Pedagogy Is Politics*, 227. See also Henry A. Giroux, "Disturbing the Peace: Writing and Pedagogy in the Cultural Studies Classroom," *College Literature* (in press).
39. I take up the problematic issue of the call for clarity in writing in Henry A. Giroux, *Living Dangerously* (New York: Peter Lang, 1993).
40. This position is explored in a number of essays in Patrick Shannon, ed., *Becoming Political: Readings and Writings in the Politics of Literacy Education* (Portsmouth, N.H.: Heinemann, 1992).
41. Butler, "Contingent Foundations," 13.
42. Nancy Fraser, *Unruly Practices: Power, Discourse, and Gender in Contemporary Social Theory* (Minneapolis: University of Minnesota Press, 1989), 113.
43. This is not meant to suggest that critical educators or cultural workers merely highlight the suffering or victimization of oppressed groups. This is certainly a crucial part of any pedagogical project, but there is also the need on the part of such educators to uncover the institutional and ideological dynamics of such suffering. Cornel West is instructive here in arguing that a concern with moral suffering must begin with the nihilism or crisis of hope that has come to pervade black communities. Hazel Carby adds an important note to this issue by arguing that the current concern with identity and difference must not be used as a code word for simply talking about race; moreover, the emphasis on differences cannot be reduced to an emphasis on the construction of identity but must be concerned with the historical and relational operations of power. See Cornel West, "Nihilism in Black America," in *Black Popular Culture*, ed. Gina Dent (Seattle: Bay Press, 1992), 37–47; Hazel V. Carby, "The Multicultural Wars," in Dent, *Black Popular Culture*, 187–99.
44. See Ulmer, *Applied Grammatology*; Donahue and Quandahl, *Reclaiming Pedagogy*; Henricksen and Morgan, *Reorientations*; Susan L. Gabriel and Isaiah Smithson, eds., *Gender in the Classroom* (Urbana: University of Illinois Press, 1990); Mas'ud Zavarzadeh and

Donald Morton, "Theory Pedagogy Politics: The Crisis of 'the Subject' in the Humanities," in Morton and Zavarzadeh, *Theory/Pedagogy/Politics*, 1–32.

45. David Shumway, "Integrating Theory in the Curriculum," 94.

7 Does Anybody Write in the Cultural Studies Classroom?

1. One of the most important critiques of cultural studies around this issue of purpose and meaning has been made by Meaghan Morris, "Banality in Cultural Studies," *Discourse* 10, no. 2 (1988): 3–29.
2. This issue is taken up in Sarah Franklin, Celia Lury, and Jackie Stacey, "Feminism and Cultural Studies: Pasts, Presents, Futures," in *Off-Centre: Feminism and Cultural Studies*, ed. Franklin, Lury, and Stacey (London: Harper Collins, 1991), 1–19; John Clarke, *New Times and Old Enemies: Essays on Cultural Studies and America* (London: Harper Collins, 1991), especially chapter 2; Benita Parry, "The Contradictions of Cultural Studies," *Transitions* 53 (1991): 37–45; and Stuart Hall, "Cultural Studies and Its Theoretical Legacies," in Lawrence Grossberg, Cary Nelson, and Paula Treichler, eds., *Cultural Studies* (New York: Routledge, 1992), 277–86.
3. See, for example, Cary Nelson, "Always Already Cultural Studies: Two Conferences and a Manifesto," *Journal of the Midwest Modern Language Association* 24, no. 1 (Spring 1991): 24–38; Cary Nelson, Paula A. Treichler, and Lawrence Grossberg, "Cultural Studies: An Introduction," in Grossberg, Nelson, and Treichler, *Cultural Studies*, 1–22; and Tony Bennett, "Putting Policy into Cultural Studies," in Grossberg, Nelson, and Treichler, *Cultural Studies*, 23–34.
4. See Nelson, "Always Already Cultural Studies," 32.
5. Stuart Hall, "What Is This 'Black' in Popular Culture?" in *Black Popular Culture*, ed. Gina Dent (Seattle: Bay Press, 1992), 22.
6. Some of the most forceful expressions of this position can be found in Lawrence Grossberg, *We Gotta Get Out of This Place: Popular Conservatism and Postmodern Culture* (New York: Routledge, 1992); Hall, "Cultural Studies and Its Theoretical Legacies"; and Lawrence Grossberg, "The Formation of Cultural Studies: An American in Birmingham," *Strategies* 2 (1989): 114–49.
7. See, for instance, a variety of writers in Grossberg, Nelson, and Treichler, *Cultural Studies*.
8. Lawrence Grossberg, *We Gotta Get Out of This Place*, 18.
9. Ibid., 18–19.
10. For a representative sample of this type of critique, see any of the major theoretical sources of cultural studies, especially the Center for Contemporary Cultural Studies in Birmingham, England. Some examples of this approach are Stuart Hall, "Cultural Studies: Two Paradigms," *Media, Culture, and Society* 2 (1980): 57–72; Stuart Hall, "Cultural Studies and the Center: Some Problematics and Problems," in Hall et al., eds., *Culture, Media, Language: Working Paper in Cultural Studies* (London: Hutchinson, 1980); Richard Johnson, "What Is Cultural Studies Anyway?" *Social Text* 6, no. 1 (1987): 38–40; and Morris, "Banality in Cultural Studies."
11. See Stanley Aronowitz, *Roll Over Beethoven: The Return of Cultural Strife* (Hanover, N.H.: University Press of New England, 1993). For an analysis of the relationship between

pedagogy and cultural studies, see writers such as Chandra Talpade Mohanty, bell hooks, and others in Henry A. Giroux and Peter McLaren, eds., *Between Borders: Politics and Pedagogy in Cultural Studies* (New York: Routledge, 1994). See also a few articles in Grossberg, Nelson, and Treichler, *Cultural Studies*. Also, see various issues of *College Literature* under the editorship of Kostas Myrsiades. It is quite revealing to look into some of the latest books on cultural studies and see no serious engagement with pedagogy as a site of theoretical and practical struggle. For example, see Patrick Brantlinger, *Crusoe's Footprints: Cultural Studies in Britain and America* (New York: Routledge, 1990); Graeme Turner, *British Cultural Studies* (London: Unwin Hyman, 1990); John Clarke, *New Times and Old Enemies* (London: Harper Collins, 1991); and Franklin, Lury, and Stacey, *Off-Centre*. In David Punter, ed., *Introduction to Contemporary Cultural Studies* (New York: Longman, 1986), there is one chapter on identifying racism in textbooks. It is worth noting that in a recent review analysis of Grossberg, Nelson, and Treichler, *Cultural Studies*, Fredric Jameson completely ignores the issue of pedagogy. See Fredric Jameson, "On 'Cultural Studies,'" *Social Text* 34 (1992): 17–52.

12. While there are too many sources to cite here, see R. W. Connell, D. J. Ashenden, S. Kessler, and G. W. Dowsett, *Making the Difference* (Boston: Allen and Unwin, 1982); Julian Henriques, Wendy Hollway, Cathy Urwin, Couze Venn, and Valerie Walkerdine, *Changing the Subject* (London: Methuen, 1984); James T. Sears, *Growing Up Gay in the South: Race, Gender, and Journeys of the Spirit* (New York: Harrington Park Press, 1991); Michelle Fine, *Framing Dropouts* (Albany: SUNY Press, 1991); Roger I. Simon, *Teaching against the Grain* (Westport, Conn.: Bergin and Garvey, 1992); and James Donald, *Sentimental Education* (London: Verso, 1992).

13. For instance, while theorists such as Jane Tompkins, Gerald Graff, Gregory Ulmer, and others address pedagogical issues, they do it solely within the referenced terrain of literary studies. Moreover, even those theorists in literary studies who insist on the political nature of pedagogy generally ignore, with few exceptions, the work that has gone on in the field for twenty years. See, for example, Shoshana Felman and Dori Lamb, *Testimony: Crisis of Witnessing in Literature, Psychoanalysis, and History* (New York: Routledge, 1992); Bruce Henricksen and Thais E. Morgan, *Reorientations: Critical Theories and Pedagogies* (Urbana: University of Illinois Press, 1990); Patricia Donahue and Ellen Quandahl, eds., *Reclaiming Pedagogy: The Rhetoric of the Classroom* (Carbondale: Southern Illinois University Press, 1989); Gregory Ulmer, *Applied Grammatology* (Baltimore: Johns Hopkins University Press, 1985); and Barbara Johnson, ed., *The Pedagogical Imperative: Teaching as a Literary Genre* (New Haven: Yale University Press, 1983).

14. An incident revealing this disparagement occurred when Gary Olson, editor of the *Journal of Advanced Composition*, interviewed Jacques Derrida. He asked Derrida, in the context of a discussion about pedagogy and teaching, if he knew of the work of Paulo Freire. Derrida responded, "This is the first time I've heard his name." Gary Olson, "Jacques Derrida on Rhetoric and Composition: A Conversation," in *(Inter)views: Cross-Disciplinary Perspectives on Rhetoric and Literacy*, ed. Olson and Irene Gale (Carbondale: Southern Illinois University Press, 1991), 133. It is hard to imagine that a figure of Freire's international stature would not be known to someone in literary studies who is one of the major proponents of deconstruction. So much for crossing boundaries. Clearly, Derrida does not read the radical literature in composition studies, because if he did he could not miss the numerous references to the work of Paulo Freire and other critical educators. See, for instance, C. Douglas Atkins and Michael L. Johnson, *Writing and Reading Differently: Deconstruction and the Teaching of Composition and Literature* (Lawrence: University of Kansas Press, 1985); Linda Brodkey, *Academic Writing as a Social*

Practice (Philadelphia: Temple University Press, 1987); and C. Mark Hurlbert and Michael Blitz, eds., *Composition and Resistance* (Portsmouth, N.H.: Boynton/Cook, 1991).

15. Raymond Williams, "Adult Education and Social Change," in *What I Came to Say* (London: Hutchinson–Radus, 1989), 157–66. See also Raymond Williams, "The Future of Cultural Studies," in Williams, *The Politics of Modernism* (London: Verso, 1989), 151–62.
16. Ibid., 158.
17. Simon, *Teaching against the Grain*, 15.
18. Lawrence Grossberg, "Bringin' It All Back Home—Pedagogy and Cultural Studies," in Giroux and McLaren, *Between Borders*, 15.
19. Simon, *Teaching against the Grain*, 46–47.
20. Judith Butler, "Contingent Foundations: Feminism and the Question of Postmodernism," in *Feminists Theorize the Political*, ed. Butler and Joan W. Scott (New York: Routledge, 1992), 13.
21. Both the two considerations and the quote come from Morris, "Banality in Cultural Studies," 20.
22. Cornel West, "The New Politics of Difference," *October* 53 (Summer 1990): 93–109; Diane Ravitich, "Multiculturalism: E Pluribus Plures," *American Scholar* (Summer 1990): 337–54.

8 Paulo Freire and the Rise of the Border Intellectual

1. An excellent analysis of this problem among Paulo Freire's followers can be found in Gail Stygall, "Teaching Freire in North America," *Journal of Teaching Writing* 1, no. 1 (1988): 113–25.
2. Robert Young, *White Mythologies: Writing History and the West* (New York: Routledge, 1990), 158. For a brilliant analysis of the ways in which radical and liberal theorists often ignore the history and legacy of imperialism, see Edward Said, *Culture and Imperialism* (N.Y.: Knopf, 1993).
3. Joan Borsa, "Towards a Politics of Location," *Canadian Women Studies* 1, no. 1 (Spring 1990): 36.
4. Ernesto Laclau quoted in *Strategies* Collective, "Building a New Left: An Interview with Ernesto Laclau," *Strategies* 1 (Fall 1988): 12.
5. *Strategies* Collective, "Building a New Left," 27.
6. My use of the terms "exile" and "homelessness" has been deeply influenced by the following essays: Carol Becker, "Imaginative Geography," School of the Art Institute of Chicago, unpublished paper, 1991; Abdul JanMohamed, "Worldliness-without-World, Homelessness–as–Home: Toward a Definition of Border Intellectual," in *Edward Said: A Critical Reader*, ed. Michael Sprinker (Cambridge, Mass.: Basil Blackwell, 1992), 96–120; Edward W. Said, "Reflections on Exile," in *Out There: Marginalization and Contemporary Cultures*, ed. Russell Ferguson, Martha Gever, Trinh T. Minh–ha, and Cornel West (New York: New Museum of Contemporary Art and MIT Press, 1990), 357–66; Biddy Martin and Chandra Talpade Mohanty, "Feminist Politics: What's Home Got to Do With It?" *Feminist Studies/Critical Studies*, ed Teresa de Lauretis (Bloomington: Indiana University Press, 1986), 191–212; and Caren Kaplan, "Deterritorializations: The Rewriting of Home

and Exile in Western Feminist Discourse," *Cultural Critique* 6 (Spring 1987): 187–98. See also selected essays in bell hooks, *Talking Back* (Boston: South End Press, 1989) and *Yearnings* (Boston: South End Press, 1990).

7. JanMohamed, "Worldiness-without-World," 116.
8. I have taken this term from JanMohamed, "Worldliness-without-World."
9. See the excellent criticism by Kathleen Weiler, "Freire and a Feminist Pedagogy of Difference," in *Politics of Liberation: Paths from Freire*, ed. Peter McLaren and Colin Lankshear (in press).
10. Benita Parry, "Problems in Current Theories of Colonial Discourse," *Oxford Literary Review* 9 (1987): 28.
11. See for example, Paulo Freire, *The Politics of Education* (New York: Bergin and Garvey, 1985); Paulo Freire and Donaldo Macedo, *Literacy: Reading the Word and the World* (New York: Bergin and Garvey, 1987); Paulo Freire and Ira Shor, *A Pedagogy for Liberation* (London: Macmillan, 1987); and Myles Horton and Paulo Freire, *We Make the Road by Walking: Conversations on Education and Social Change*, ed. Brenda Bell, John Gaventa, and John Peters (Philadelphia: Temple University Press, 1990).
12. Paulo Freire quoted in Freire and Antonio Faundez, *Learning to Question: A Pedagogy of Liberation* (New York: Continuum, 1989), 13.
13. Theodor Adorno quoted in Said, "Reflections on Exile," 365.
14. Martin and Mohanty, "Feminist Politics," 197.
15. Becker, "Imaginative Geography," 1.
16. JanMohamed, "Worldiness–without–World," 10.
17. Said, "Reflections on Exile," 365.
18. JanMohamed, "Worldiness–without–World," 3.
19. Edward W. Said, *Orientalism* (New York: Vantage Books, 1979).
20. Cornel West, "Decentering Europe: A Memorial Lecture for James Snead," *Critical Inquiry* 33, no. 1 (1991): 4.
21. Young, *White Mythologies*, viii.
22. For excellent discussions of these issues as they specifically relate to postcolonial theory, see Parry, "Problems in Current Theories of Colonial Discourse," 27–58; Abdul JanMohamed, *Manichean Aesthetics: The Politics of Literature in Colonial Africa* (Amherst: University of Massachusetts Press, 1983); Gayatri C. Spivak, *The Post-Colonial Critic: Interviews, Strategies, Dialogues*, ed. Sarah Harasym (New York: Routledge, 1990); Young, *White Mythologies*; and Homi K. Bhabha, ed. *Nation and Narration* (New York: Routledge, 1990). The ways in which binary oppositions can trap a particular author into the most essentialist arguments can be seen in a recent work by Patti Lather. What is so unusual about this text is that its call for openness, partiality, and multiple perspectives is badly undermined by the binarisms structured around a simple, gendered relation of truth to illusion. See Lather, *Getting Smart* (New York: Routledge, 1991).
23. Spivak, *The Post–Colonial Critic*, 42.
24. This position is explored in two articles by Helen Tiffin: "Post-Colonialism, Post–Modernism, and the Rehabilitation of Post–Colonial History," *Journal of Commonwealth Literature* 23, no. 1 (1988): 169–81, and "Post–Colonial Literatures and Counter-Discourse," *Kunapipi* 9, no. 1 (1987): 17–34.
25. Young, *White Mythologies*, 119.

26.. Linda Hutcheon, "Circling the Downspout of Empire," in *Past the Last Post*, ed. Ian Adam and Helen Tiffin (Calgary, Canada: University of Calgary Press, 1990), 176.

27. Judith Butler, "Contingent Foundations: Feminism and the Question of Postmodernism." in *Feminists Theorize the Political*, ed. Butler and Joan W. Scott (New York: Routledge, 1992), 12–13.

28. I explore this issue in Henry A. Giroux, *Border Crossings: Cultural Workers and the Politics of Education* (New York: Routledge, 1992).

9 Traveling Pedagogies

1. This interview was recorded on a videocassette at the Institute of Pedagogy, University of Poznan, Poland, on March 16, 1992, while Henry A. Giroux was paying a visit to the Center for Education and Cultural Studies, Nicolas Copernicus University of Torun, hosted by Lech Witkowski within the research project sponsored by KBN grant no. 1–1171–91–02.

Index